HEARTBREAKERS

HEARTBREAKERS

Women and Violence
in Contemporary Culture and Literature

JOSEPHINE G. HENDIN

First published 2004 by
PALGRAVE MACMILLAN™
175 Fifth Avenue, New York, N.Y. 10010 and
Houndmills, Basingstoke, Hampshire, England RG21 6XS.
Companies and representatives throughout the world.

PALGRAVE MACMILLAN is the global academic imprint of the
Palgrave Macmillan division of St. Martin's Press, LLC and of Palgrave
Macmillan Ltd. Macmillan® is a registered trademark in the United
States, United Kingdom and other countries. Palgrave is a registered
trademark in the European Union and other countries.

ISBN 0–312–23700–6 hardcover

Library of Congress Cataloging-in-Publication Data
Hendin, Josephine.
Heartbreakers : women and violence in contemporary culture and
literature / by Josephine G. Hendin.
    p.   cm.
    Includes bibliographical references and index.
    ISBN 0–312–23700–6 (cloth)
    1. Violence in women.   2. Women in popular culture.   3. Violence
in popular culture.   4. Women in mass media.   5. Violence in mass
media.   6. Women in literature.   7. Violence in literature.   I. Title.

HQ1233.H46   2004
364.3'74—dc21

                                                            2003054855

A catalogue record for this book is available from the British Library.

Design by Letra Libre, Inc.

First edition: January 2004
10 9 8 7 6 5 4 3 2 1

Printed in the United States of America.

CONTENTS

ACKNOWLEDGEMENTS

Michael Flamini, editorial director of Palgrave Macmillan and, blessedly, my editor, lent his lively intelligence to shepherding this book. Georges Borchardt and DeAnna Heindel made valuable suggestions for the project and oversaw it with grace, wit, and unfailing courtesy.

I am grateful to the Abraham and Rebecca Stein Faculty Fund of the English Department of New York University for its generous support of this book. Lahney Preston and Scott Michael Cleary provided enterprising and capable research assistance in the preparation of the manuscript and I appreciate their help. My colleague, Marilyn Gaull, provided dynamic encouragement for undertaking this project. Lucy Rosenthal read the manuscript as it evolved and encouraged its growth. My husband, Herbert Hendin, provided the sustained engagement, loving humor, and support that made my work possible.

I thank the writers who brought so much inventive energy to the subject of violence by women and made dark experiences so illuminating to explore.

CHAPTER 1

THE HEARTBREAKER EFFECT

AN EXQUISITELY BUILT BLONDE RIDES A MAN HARD AS SHE TIES HIS WRISTS to the headboard of their bed. When he reaches orgasm, she stabs him with an ice pick again and again. She climaxes as we see her breasts spattered with his spurting blood even as the camera avoids her face. *Basic Instinct* begins with these shocking images and goes on to enshrine the violence of woman as an erotic thrill. Michael Douglas, as a sexually obsessed detective who pursues Sharon Stone as chief suspect, is both excited and chilled by her cold intelligence, her ice pick, and her powerful allure. Both characters have an edgy, urban chic that presents violence as a stylish game in which all the players are conspirators against trust. The mixture catapulted Sharon Stone into a reigning *fin de siècle* sex symbol. *Basic Instinct*'s success at the box office was only a slick example of a new fascination with violent women, the men who are drawn to them, and the culture that surrounds them. In fiction, film, and media, violent women are new icons who dramatize in extreme ways transformations in intimacy, social life, and public attitudes.

Reversing primal expectations of love, the violence of women toward lovers, husbands, and children brings home the shock of the new. Conflicts over women's roles, depicted in the encounter with surprising, intimate violence, render the controversy over modernity as no abstraction but as the direct experience of the anxiety and excitement of change. Across fiction, film, and media news, the emergence of violent women dramatizes a repudiation of the ways of thinking about women that have marked the past three decades. Portrayals of violent women, I believe, constitute an attack on the fashionable discourses—political, sociological, and aesthetic—used to define, justify, and explain the nature and position of women. Violent women in fiction and poetry constitute an attack on postmodern representation theory, that discourse that claimed to capture them in all their modernity.

Violence by women is a communication sent like a letter bomb to repudiate ideologies of the left or right, to disavow the either/or of liberationist or traditionalist views. Its explosive methods use appropriation and revision to script a woman's life in innovative ways. The literature of violent women provides no simple polemic but rather expresses a gathering of energies and arguments that, taken together, seize control of the subject of female aggression. Its communications may exploit the rhetoric of female victimization for new effects. It may draw on media culture that has made violent crimes a pathway to celebrity, or it may invoke premodern myths of female power for new purposes. It insists on telling female stories in singular ways. In fiction and poetry, violence serves to explode stereotypes, rewriting conventional female scripts from the dark side.

The proliferation of violent female figures in media accounts and films suggests the collision between our cultural uneasiness about the transformation of women's roles and the imaginative richness provoked by change. Depictions of brutal actions may not provide any programmatic challenge to cultural assumptions, but their effect is revolutionary in undermining settled attitudes. Emerging in films, in news stories of sensational crimes, and in media spectacles, violent women arouse not only fascination but also extreme and often contradictory reactions. They are used as justification by men for the violence *against* women. They are cited on the post-Marxist left as evidence of exploitation by capitalist-controlled media using women as eye candy to promote consumption. Their violence is invoked by the right as evidence of feminist excess. Others praise them as fighters against the victimization of women, or condemn them as signs of cultural anarchy. The tension, desire, rage, and curiosity they evoke reveal our encounter with the violence of women as trauma. Media accounts of crime provide a measure of the social controversies surrounding violence; the responses of art go further into the psychological and moral issues involved. The originality of the violent women in fiction in explaining their actions underscores the failure of fashionable discourses of representation to encompass the meanings that violence by women can hold.

This book brings together films, media accounts of actual crime, and serious fiction in which violence by women plays an important role. I hope to convey through the imaginative richness of fiction and the social controversies surrounding actual crimes the role of the violent woman as attacker of discourses that have sought to explain the female role. I believe this process will pinpoint those changes in intimacy, self-conception, and behavior surrounding the violence of women that are, in less extreme form, widespread in the culture but otherwise difficult to formulate. Violence is a measure of social stress, a barometer of the pressures on individuals in our culture who do not succumb to them as well as on those who do. The violent women discussed in this book highlight and dramatize the pressures on women who are not violent and on a culture still absorbing their changing roles. Media accounts of actual crimes, sensational acts in film, and the imaginative construction of violence in fiction together provide a social and imaginative panorama.

How actual violence by women is described in the media not only reveals specific acts but highlights the fears, anxieties, and hopes that are dramatized by women whose acts challenge all our past notions of female vulnerability. Riveted by spectacular crimes, the media have made violence a major occasion for communal discourse and a fast track to celebrity. Our public culture has used the criminal investigation or trial to talk about morality through its violation. Tales of violence—told by reporters, perpetrators, detectives, and defendants—convey the moral complexity of what passes in forms of speech that use language as a double agent, both embodying and seeking to transcend violence itself. Prosecution and defense attorneys weave ethical and psychological explorations out of murder, commanding the talk-show pulpits in our new 24/7 church, CNN. Crimetalk is our form of social and moral inquiry.

Our public discourse is dominated by media that have broken the wall between reality and spin, entertainment violence and actual murder, depicting violent women in extreme stereotypes in which they are magnets for ideological and sexual warfare. They may be demonized, glamorized, or trivialized along the path to celebrity status as warriors in dramas of ideological conflict. Are they victimized creatures manipulated by men, troublemakers who must be eliminated before infecting their sisters, or reformed sinners turned penitent do-gooders? Infotainment crime offers a mixture of ideological differences and sexual warfare.

Social and sexual strife converged in the media accounts of the crime and fate of Karla Faye Tucker. Out for a thrill one night, she broke into the house of Jerry Dean. She found him sleeping, straddled him, and, when he began to resist, reached for an ax that was lying next to his futon. Riding him and slashing his chest and throat eleven times with the ax, she had an orgasm. "I popped a nut," she confided to her sister, who turned her in to the police (Pearson 182).

The commentaries surrounding Tucker's crime, incarceration, and punishment reflected the charged atmosphere of sexual politics surrounding the violent crimes of women. A diminutive woman with engaging good looks, Tucker was sentenced to death and described with an anger that suggested she had become a target for the fear that she was one of a new breed of unnatural women who must be stopped. A particularly savage death-penalty debate surged around her appeals. Her radiant smile and earnest claims of remorse seemed to inflame those who claimed women had an equal right to die, those against death sentences altogether, and those who could not reconcile her physical delicacy, religious conversion in prison, and prison ministry with her crime. She was, depending on the speaker, a fallen angel, risen once again; a Jezebel who had dishonored womanhood; or a cold-blooded, unnatural killer.

Supported by both Pope John Paul II and Pat Robertson because of her rebirth in Christ and her desire to spend her life continuing her prison ministry, Tucker's appeals of her sentence and accounts of her redemption and past crime combined extremes of both Christian exaltation and erotic violence. When Tucker's appeals were exhausted in 1998, she became the first woman executed in Texas in one hundred years. Her execution was itself a media event steeped in an extraordinary mixture of forgiveness and raging vindictiveness: The *New York Post* coverage was headlined, "Karla's Last

Words: 'I Love You All.'" The *Chicago Tribune* article said: "Outside more than 1,000 onlookers and protesters gathered on all sides of the capital punishment issue sang gospel songs, yelled football game chants, said prayers and played a video of Tucker" (Brownstein 104–5). The *Houston Chronicle* described her as "the pickax murderer who charmed television audiences worldwide with her coquettish smile and talk of Jesus" (Brownstein 105). The competing narratives surrounding her case continued beyond her death.

As martyr, Tucker was mourned as a reformed sinner who could have turned others from the path of violence had she been permitted to continue her ministry in a life sentence. But Tucker still drew the venom of those who had mocked her hope for a commutation of the death sentence to one of life without parole. Then governor of Texas, George W. Bush, ridiculed her appeal of her death sentence in a *Talk* magazine interview in September 1999 by mimicking a female voice saying, "Please don't kill me." In news accounts and chat rooms, at the time of her execution, others joined him in cheering the executioner and mocking Tucker's physical delicacy or declaring she had gotten the equal rights women said they wanted.

Infotainment news had made of Tucker not only a killer celebrity, but also a focal point. The competing narratives about her crime, transformation, and punishment illustrated the use of a bizarre and unusual case as the focus of public anxiety. Tucker's erotic enjoyment of her murder was as shocking as the murder itself. Women have generally expressed their wildness through their sexuality, but the combination of ax murder and orgasm epitomized for many the dark side of women's empowerment.

Violence by women often turns the public sphere into a battlefield on which competing commentaries meet like media driven armies in sexual warfare. The unusual and bizarre case of Lorena Bobbitt, on trial in 1994 for severing her husband's penis with a kitchen knife, aroused sharp political fervor. Her crime, celebrated or condemned as a feminist protest against the selfishness of a man concerned during sex only with his own orgasm, was treated like a political protest for a cause. One had to be against, for, or thoughtful about her crime. It became the subject of nearly two thousand news stories including one called "Sharia Feminism," in *The American Spectator* (December 1993), the meditative "Feminism Confronts Bobbittry" by

Barbara Ehrenreich in *Time* (January 24, 1994) and a *Newsweek* story displaying the photograph of a popular button that declared "Lorena Bobbitt for Surgeon General" (January 24, 1994).

The politics of intimacy were writ large even in the headlines that saw the crime and its aftermath as a sexual comedy and trivialized the violence of what had happened. The odyssey of the severed penis became news—Lorena Bobbitt had thrown it from her car while fleeing the scene, men searching the surrounding fields recovered it, and surgeons reattached it to its owner, John Wayne Bobbitt. That restoration made it easy not to take Lorena's act seriously. T-shirts signed by John Wayne Bobbitt and offered for sale at the trial of his wife for severing his penis announced "Love Hurts." News stories about the case had such titles as "Hanging by a Thread," and the couple inspired endless quips on *The Tonight Show* with Jay Leno ("Both will have a hard time getting a date"). Even as Lorena Bobbitt faded into fragility and tears on the witness stand, she seemed not to mind being treated as a feminist joke. An actual crime had become a comic entertainment in which word games sustained a lighthearted look at sexual rage. With John Wayne Bobbitt assuring the world that his reattached part worked well, trivialization of a woman's sexual rage made it all a comedy of bad manners.

Tormented intimacy produced far sharper sexual warfare in the rage recorded in media accounts of women who murdered husbands or lovers. When the profoundly battered Francine Hughes went on trial for killing her husband, her long suffering as his wife aroused in many onlookers as little sympathy as her past cries for help had elicited support. On the night she killed him, she had called the police, asking for protection from her husband who was beating her. The police came but only left her at home with him. That night she set fire to their bed while he slept. Her act provoked rage even among those who had witnessed her husband's abuse and knew how deeply she had suffered. Ann Jones reports a neighbor saying, "she should sit in prison the rest of her life. . . . If she gets out of this," he told reporters, "there'll be lot of dead guys lying around." Another man feared acquittal would mean "an open season on men" (Jones 289–90). The *Washington Post* headlined a story: "Vigilante Justice Back in Women's

Movement." *Time* called the retaliation of battered women "A Killing Excuse." In *Newsweek*'s "Wives Who Batter Back," all that was lamented was the rise of what it called "frontier justice." The ineffectual efforts made on behalf of women who had sought help and protection through legal means were not criticized (Jones 290).

Karla Faye Tucker, Lorena Bobbitt, and Francine Hughes performed very different acts of violence, but each became a magnet for rage or ridicule. Each disrupted established convictions about the natural capacity of women for brutal acts. The narratives woven around each woman's violence by the media are far less subtle and complex than the narratives one encounters in fiction or poetry. The media and the defense attorneys sought to incorporate the events into familiar tales—of redemption for Tucker, of female hysteria for Bobbitt, of a victim's right to self-defense for Hughes. What such acts actually meant to the women performing them or how those meanings evolved before and after the event are almost never explored.

Despite the media coverage of sensational acts, violence by women has not received much serious study. The anxiety aroused by the violence of women is only one of the reasons for not probing further. Admittedly, more violence is committed by men than women, and domestic violence against women remains a terrifying problem. A more pervasive justification for ignoring violence by women is that taking it seriously has been seen as a betrayal of those in need of help, or a reactionary effort to roll back the successes of empowerment and support the patriarchy. Ironically, those who should grant the ability of women to speak and act for themselves and try to understand their actions in the context of their actual lives have been among the least willing to address the violence of women, even as a symptom of social disruption. In the nineteen seventies, that unwillingness led to attacks on criminologist Freda Adler in *Sisters in Crime* and sociologist Rita James Simon in *Women and Crime* as simply promoting an argument against the liberation of women (Brownstein 97–98). To promote that liberation, it has seemed to many to be important to insist that women are silenced victims.

The need to explore what violent acts mean to those who commit them and how such acts express the lives of women or their interaction with others is becoming more accentuated as the rates of violence increase. Statistics indicate a trend of increasing actual criminal violence by women and a narrowing of the gap between female and male violence. The Uniform Crime Reports of the Federal Bureau of Investigation, for example, indicate that "from 1987 to 1996, the number of reports of women arrested for a violent crime increased by 53 percent, compared to an increase of 23 percent for men. From 1992 to 1996, the number of reports of women arrested for a violent crime increased by 23 percent, while declining by almost 5 percent for men" (Brownstein 99). Rates of victimization for men and women are also equalizing. A Bureau of Justice Statistics report on "Female Victims of Violent Crime" concluded that from 1973 to 1994 "violent victimization rates of women and men converged" (Brownstein 102). Because the actual number of women arrested for violent crime is lower than the number of men arrested, such changes have been ignored.

The politics of sex have militated against developing political, social, psychological, and critical discourses that will address the violence of women as meaningful. Established structures of power, thought, and language that have been used in the past to describe women are not suited to a serious exploration of violence by women. Prejudice against exploring the subject is widespread and unites otherwise opposed ideologies, each of which is invested in ignoring it. Traditionalists and some feminists are odd bedfellows in regarding women as beyond violence. Adam Smith ruled them out of the combative free market into a domesticity in which they served as moral capital only their husbands could spend. Custodians of the lesser virtues, women were idealized by Smith as moral educators in "those gentler exertions of self-command . . . chastity, industry and frugality" (Smith, VI, iii, 13). Subordinate to men, they were freed from the public sphere by their restriction to the private domain of the family where their "civilizing" effect was felt. Currently, utopian views also occur on the left and among liberationists. For example, the otherwise hardheaded sociologists Turpin and Kurtz argue that the way to end all forms of violence—political and economic as well as domestic—is to inculcate men everywhere in the world with female values such as nonviolence and cooperation, end male dominance in every culture on earth, and, by doing so, usher in a world based on female ideals of harmony (222–23).

Denial of the significance of violence by women received unwitting support from the findings of those "difference feminists" epitomized by Carol Gilligan whose 1982 book, *In a Different Voice,* argued persuasively that the socialization of women for cooperation is distinct from the acculturation of men, who are raised to be competitive and combative. Less measured affirmations of the moral superiority of women, based on their socialization for nonviolence and disavowal that they can and do commit violence, have proliferated. Intemperate forms of denial, obviously influenced by postmodern representation theory, insist that women who commit violence do so as men. For example, Naomi Segal claims that women never commit violence. She offers a rather opaque definition of violent women as really "men": "If violence must be against sentient material, it is ultimately performed in the secret name of a greater slavery . . . and for this reason I suggest that violence is always by men (is, rather, an act in the masculine position), by young men. . . . and against women (for the material is the maternal, and every figure of slavery is feminised)" (Segal 142). In such a climate anyone who sees the violence of women as meaningful in their lives as women can be accused of denying their moral and social superiority as victims and abandoning the prospect of a virtual heaven on earth. Fear that discussing violence by women is politically bad for women is widespread and has inflamed denials that violence by women exists at all or is meaningful if does exist.

Recent sociological contributions to violence studies have adopted a new rhetoric but not a substantially new way of looking at the role of violent women and have continued the silence surrounding the subject. Studies have recognized the importance of establishing relationships between personal acts of violence and social issues, and have even revived that mantra of the seventies, *the personal is political,* but the definition of *political* and *personal* applied is both traditional and limited. The most innovative recent approach in violence studies offers the ambitious conceptualization of violence as "a 'web' because the causes of violence, from interpersonal to global, are connected, as are the consequences" (Turpin and Kurtz 12). In doing so, web theorists affirm that "human rights violations in the private and public spheres are interrelated" and can explain issues of social oppression that affect people of different nations, races, religious groups, or classes and unify all areas of violence studies on a worldwide level (Eisler 163).

Perhaps concerned that acknowledging violence by women might serve only to dismiss global or institutionalized sources of violence, web theorists are not innovative in their identification of the meaning or motives for violence but instead focus on traditional, universal contributing factors such as poverty and political oppression. Accordingly, women everywhere are seen only as victims, the have-leasts among the have-nots of the world. They join poor men in being oppressed by male ruling elites whose seamless dominance shapes the economic, military, and political structures of nations into what Turpin and Kurtz describe as "a world in which half of the population lives on the verge of starvation, while a small percentage lives in unprecedented wealth" (222). Much of the recent social commentary on violence remains comparably ambitious in its aspirations for justice but limited by a conceptualization of the problem in purely dialectical terms. That model is usually applied to all cultures without regard for the position of women as other than victims of ruling elites.

Violence is most frequently described as deriving from an economics of greed in which issues of gender matter less than self-interest. Charles Derber begins a provocative discussion with the violent rape and vicious beating in 1992 of a young woman jogging in Central Park, presumed perpetrated by a group of young men who were "wilding" for fun, confessed to the crime, and were convicted. Derber draws analogies between the attack and the rapacity of nonviolent but ruthless capitalism. He traces the prevalence of violence in our own culture to the adoption by elites and the underclass of the spirit of an anomic, ruthless, and unbridled free market capitalism and the pursuit of "the American Dream." Criminal and legal forms of dominance, Derber argues, are flip sides of the pursuit of economic self-interest, intensified by "the Reagan revolution" (12). In Derber's view, the wilder is not socially alienated, but instead the product of oversocialization and "overconformity to a society whose norms and values are socially dangerous" (16). How this interpretation will be affected by the confession in 2002 of a serial rapist incarcerated for murder that he alone was responsible for the crime, an admission corroborated by DNA evidence, remains to be seen.

The language used by cultural critics to describe violence has been shaped and, I believe, overly narrowed by a reliance on translating the dialectic between wealth and poverty into social narratives that either defend violence by the poor as legitimate resistance or attack the violent poor by scripting tales of the elites' right to promote law and order to keep the underclass subdued. For example, Robert Elias believes violence is described in ways that castigate the perpetrator and justify and preserve entrenched power (121–22). More subtly, Philip Smith notes, "responses to violence can be substantially explained through social narratives. Members of civil society and civil institutions—in particular, the mass media—use narratives to interpret particular acts of violence, thus diffusing social norms about appropriate or inappropriate uses of violence" (92). What drives "social narratives" in his view are usually the needs of elites to control a rebellious and discontented underclass. While most such views originate on the ideological left, the conservative right joins them in lack of interest in individual motivation and in ignoring women as other than part—often the better part—of an underclass.

Although media accounts of violence inevitably provided vivid accounts of individual lives, little effort has been made to define the effect of such stories on norms or ideals of behavior or on the use of violence by women as an indicator of cultural changes that affect personal behavior or indicate increasing stress. Even psychiatrist James Gilligan, writing in "Violence: Reflections on a National Epidemic," does not stress the need to explore the meaning of violence to individuals or the ways in which they perceive their own acts. He sees "structural violence" as something apart from the behavior of the individual, as a continuous process of exposure to economic deprivation, because the "deadliest form of violence is poverty." The individual does not, so to speak, even own his or her own violent act. According to Gilligan, we should not "apply moral categories" to those who commit violence because doing so will use moral judgment to maintain political and economic oppression: "American violence is the result of our collective 'moral choice' to maintain those social policies that in turn maintain our uniquely high level of violence; and I call that choice a moral choice because it is very explicitly rationalized, justified and legitimized on moral grounds, in moral terms" (23). He continues: "Any approach to a theory of violence needs to begin with a look at the structural violence in this country" (191–92).

Violent women in the media, film, and, most of all, in fiction and poetry constitute an attack on the depersonalization of structural, programmatic ideologies, whether revolutionary or conservative. Even the most radical political ideologies that idealize violence against any and all oppressors are rejected. In practice, such ideologies have often only submerged women further and justified violence against them by the frustrations men feel in poverty, a fact rarely noted by their supporters. For example, Frantz Fanon is often praised by his supporters as the architect of the modern ideology of terrorism as a means of restoring humanity and creating solidarity among the oppressed. Fanon advocated extreme violence against the French as colonizers of Algeria. Fanon's many sympathizers usually ignore that the "humanity" they claim he restored did not, for Fanon, include women, even those Algerian women who risked their lives in actions against the French. Sheila Rowbotham provides an informed analysis of Fanon's support for the domination of women. Fanon claimed: "Acceptance of their men as masters prevented Algerian men from really bowing to their colonizers. The Algerian man remained sure of his manhood because he controlled his own women so completely" (qtd. in Rowbotham 239). When the terrorists claimed credit for expelling the French, they "liberated" themselves but ended the promise, as Rowbotham has shown, of freedom for women, leaving them worse off than before by reversing laws passed by the French that had guaranteed minimal rights to women.

Violent women in fiction, media, and the news constitute an attack on the political discourses that have most aroused and frustrated women's hopes for autonomy. The truth claims of film, fiction, and poetry differ from the claims of ideological propaganda. What role can imaginative writing and even popular art play?

The power of fiction, poetry, and, in some cases, film holds the promise of revealing the depth of meanings violent action contains for the individual and her vision of our social world. The power and psychological complexity of imaginative art simply exceed the ability of the approaches that have dominated academic discussions over the past two decades to address such individualistic and complex meanings. I see violent women in fiction and poetry as, in effect, waging an assault on those theories of representation that ignore them as women.

Violence by women in fiction constitutes an attack on the critical theory that has guided much academic discourse about the position of women in literary art, relegating them to anonymity and silence by definition. Forming a prevalent style of conception and analysis, such approaches have built a prison out of language. Violent women find that prison a staging ground for a break-out. Their narrative strategies succeed in dismantling the structures of language, psychology, and misogyny that have held them captive. But first, a description of the jail.

AGAINST POSTMODERN REPRESENTATION THEORY: WOMEN IMPRISONED BY METAPHOR

The dominant theoretic approaches to gender, sexuality, and representation in academic life over the past thirty years have derived from Jacques Lacan's rewriting of Freud in line with French poststructural linguistics, and Jean Baudrillard's post-Marxist analysis of society as dominated by late capitalism operating through the media to impose its agenda. Whether embraced as an accurate description of contemporary "unreality" said to be fostered by a media that serves capitalism, or rejected as a hysterical attack on the West, capitalism, and common sense, that psychosocial mixture has for the past several decades constituted the theoretic framework for discussion of sex, literature, and representation. Although it has enabled fresh recognition of the power of language and incorporated abstract concepts of the feminine in its formulations, it has also grossly distorted both and failed to address behavioral change. Although embraced and perhaps intended as a liberating discourse meant to free the discussion of sex from biological determinism and to focus on the linguistic and cultural origins of self-concepts, it has only imposed another form of tyranny on women, locking them conceptually in a jail of narrow definition.

Although a full analysis of this school is beyond the scope of this book and its influence has waned, the following discussion suggests and illustrates its limitations in approaching the subject of violent women. These limitations include its lack of interest in addressing individual differences or the specific circumstances of women, its inability to come to grips with the subject of affect and emotion, its rigid affirmations of stereotypical female passivity while claiming to address modernity and change, its opaque mixture of abstraction and misogyny, and its vexed relation to feminism. In brief, the violent woman who has emerged in film, media, and fiction as an icon of change has been ignored by the very postmodern theorists whose work claimed to define the new, the modern, the different.

Without discussing the full reach or merit of all that may be derived from their views, I would like to illustrate what I mean by summarizing Jacques Lacan's most influential definitions of male and female, Jean Baudrillard's post-Marxist applications of Lacanian theory to a social world he sees as ruled by a capitalist-dominated media, and Slavoj Žižek's particular take on the view of women as the "unrepresentable." All involve a general depersonalization of women; a use of the concept of the "feminine" as a wedge against women, evident in an oscillation between abstractions rarely grounded in any empirical evidence; and misogyny, apparently grounded in personal animus.

In his most "liberating" declaration, Lacan announced: "Woman does not exist. Nothing can be said about women." Lacan replaces Freud's Oedipal drama, with its fight between father and son for possession of the mother as the path to selfhood, with linguistic stages. In that paradigm, the ego is only a linguistic construction. Male and female are only linguistic sites in a geography that consigns the female to marginality while according the male position greater, but not complete, access to the center of power and authority, conceived of as the symbolic center, the symbolic "phallus" or "Name of the Father."

Although Lacan's emphasis on linguistic paths to selfhood seems to sever absolute connections between biology and gender and to replace "nature" with "nurture," conceived of as socialization by mastering language, his formulation of language itself constructs a prison out of metaphors distinctly, to use Hélène Cixous's word, "phallogocentric." The world of language in which we become "speaking subjects" and can engage in the mediations that constitute what Lacan sees as active participation in public life is defined by him through the metaphor of "the phallus, the "Name of the Father" or "Law of the Father" or simply the "Law" or the "code." French postmodern representation theory adopts these categories. It declares that the feminine position is without the phallic agency to represent itself. In effect, it denies the biological basis of sex and rigidly affirms it through metaphor. Consigned to a pre-verbal stage known as the "Real," women remain without agency through their lack of access to the symbolic code, the "phallus." Unable to represent themselves, they are always objects represented by the phallic symbolic code and therefore always defined by men.

While often invoked as the "new" new, Lacan's psychology is very much another master narrative about "patriarchy." Advocates of its theoretic validity invariably become trapped in the retrogressive implications of their own formulations. As Craig Owens puts it in it his insightful commentary, "excluded from representation by its very structure, [women] return within it as a figure for—a representation of—the unrepresentable—(Nature, Truth, the Sublime, etc.)" (59). Because the law of the signifier, the symbolic realm of mediation leading to autonomy and authority, is male, women are seen only as beings without meaningful agency, stuck in a structureless chaos of images and desires. As true subjects or individuals with agency, women are ruled out of representation: "women have been rendered an absence within the dominant culture" (59).

What results is an odd combination: the desexualization of women along with the assertion of a universal linguistic category of subordination defined as "feminine." That includes all of those who are denied agency in representation—the poor, minorities, gays, the disabled and others, all of whom are in the category of the "feminine" and presumably cannot speak for themselves. As Owens remarks, "in order to speak, to represent herself, a woman assumes a masculine position; perhaps this is why femininity is frequently associated . . . with false representation, with simulation. . . . [Lacanian analyst Marie] Montrelay . . . identifies women as the 'ruin of representation'" (59).

Owens recognizes the Lacanian model as an impasse between a feminist critique of patriarchy that demands self-representation for women and a postmodern view of such representation as ruled out by the theoretic model itself. Moreover, "patriarchy" is equated with the triumph of a capitalist-dominated media that produces representations of women to further its goals and denies women a self-initiated voice. In theory, representation must be rejected as having any relation to experience because it is only the unreal, manufactured product of a capitalism that controls reality for its own purposes and needs—usually described as promoting consumption—through media images. Such circular logic creates a closed system in which all representations of women reflect both male need and the total dominance of an apparently "phallic" capitalism.

As Craig Owens writes, "the 'enunciative apparatus' of visual representation—its poles of emission and reception—admit only one vision—that of the constitutive male subject—or rather, they posit the subject of representation as absolutely centered, unitary, masculine" (58). This is because its images are presumably tightly controlled by a triumphal global capitalism whose "organs of domination—the media, museums, publishing houses—"dictate what is seen, relegating us to a life of consuming the images and narratives they select. In doing so, capitalism excludes, co-opts, or destroys opposition and crushes the feminine "Other." In this economy, the only political mission of art is to expose this process of domination by revealing "the structure of power" that "authorizes certain representations, while blocking, prohibiting or invalidating other representations denied legitimacy" (Owens 59).

Those who are denied representation by the media that serve capitalism are in the feminine position. Thus Lacan's linguistic conception of being correlates with the post-Marxist politics of oppression in which women along with other downtrodden groups are denied a potent voice and kept furthest from the center of power as "the Other." Jean Baudrillard is the most celebrated and notorious voice of the political implications of this logic. How his political argument is challenged by the literature of the political violence of women is discussed in chapter 4.

Both men (in the feminine position) and women are presumed victims in the analytic and paranoid versions of capitalist dominance provided by practitioners of postmodern representation theory. But the failure of its crucial concept of the "feminine" as a collective description of oppression is evident when its followers seek to apply their concept of the feminine to those interactions between men and women that constitute public and private experience. For example, Slavoj Žižek attempts to provide a Lacanian answer to the simple question: How are the desires of men and women different from each other? His answer reveals an almost complete inability to distinguish definitions of the desire of men and women as linguistic positions from clichéd and naïve stereotypes:

> How, then, does 'desire is the desire of 'the Other' different in the case of men and women? [sic] The masculine version is, to put it simply, that of competition/envy. 'I want it because you want it, in so far as you want it'— that is to say, what confers the value of desirability on an object is that it is already desired by another. The aim here is the ultimate destruction of the Other, which, of course, then renders the object worthless—therein lies the paradox of the male dialectic of desire. The feminine version, on the contrary, is that of 'I desire through the Other,' in both senses of 'let the Other do it' (possess and enjoy the object, etc.) for me' (let my husband my son . . . succeed for me), as well as 'I desire only what he desires, I want only to fulfill his desire.' (*Plague of Fantasies* 118)

Žižek simply confuses and then equates the feminine as a linguistic position with the experience of being female as he understands it. No thought is given to the dynamics of that experience or the psychology of any woman, or her relationship to any specific "Other" or any other contingent circumstance that might contradict his assertions that the lives of women are only vicarious.

Although Žižek understands the banality of this position, he cannot improve on it. He returns to a definition of the female only to restate his confusion of the subject as a linguistic position with what he claims is the experience of women in a way that again reveals the misogyny that distorts his thinking. He begins with a statement invoking Lacan's formulation of "the void of the subject" and writes, "What, however, if this cliché nevertheless points toward the feminine status of the subject? What if the original subjective gesture, the gesture constitutive of subjectivity is not that of autonomously 'doing something' but rather, that of the primordial substitution, of withdrawing and letting another do it for me, in my place?" Žižek's evidence for this is drawn from another mass of clichés rich in contempt for women in situations in ordinary life: "Women, much more than men, are able to enjoy by proxy, to find deep satisfaction in the awareness that their beloved partner enjoys success or has attained his or her goal." He tries to develop this into a universal principle he calls "interpassivity": "Interpassivity complicates the standard opposition of man versus woman as active versus passive: sexual difference is inscribed into the very core of the relationship of substitution—woman can remain passive *while being active through her other, man can be active while suffering through his other*" (*Plague of Fantasies* 119).

This provides a vision of the linguistic subject based on the confusion of the feminine linguistic position with female masochism and self-erasure and with an affirmation that male discovery of his own feminine "other" is through "suffering." Not surprisingly, Žižek does not offer examples of very many men applying for the opportunity for feminine suffering.

Women have bodies seen as "castrated" because of the absence of the penis, as Freud had it, but they bear a burden added by Lacan: they lack the direct access to the "phallus"—the symbolic order of language conceptualized in its image. In this literalized, fetishized vision of language, women who act cannot do so as women but by definition are male or in the male position. Insofar as women are victims, vessels of circulating images and desires, "impure" and unmediated by language, and lack access to capitalism's command of signs and symbols of control, they avoid the predatory imperialism of the phallic symbolic code. However, their inability to actively choose suffering presumably minimizes their ability even at that. The best "women" are, according to Jean Baudrillard, biological men.

The budding misogyny nourished by this paradigm blossoms into full bloom in Baudrillard's commentaries. There is, for starters, his faith that he and perhaps even other men are better at being "feminine" than women, presumably because they advocate vicarious, passive female existence. Baudrillard asks what "will turn me into a woman. That will come about by espousing here and now—passionately—the position of femininity itself.

Now for feminists this is unpardonable. For this position is more feminine, with all the supreme femininity it implies, than that of women will ever be" (*Cool Memories 1980–1985*, 7).

Nor can this kind of assertion be passed off as simply solidarity with the silenced "Other," because Baudrillard continually levels personal animus against women who appear to be claiming even simple forms of equality that do not require any speech at all, much less mastery of the symbolic code. The sight of women enjoying a male stripshow inspires Baudrillard to write: "What is obscene . . . is the egalitarian demand for the right to pleasure" (*Cool Memories 1980–1985*, 50).

Baudrillard's comments outdo Žižek's in their frank self-exposure of misogyny as his theoretic model breaks down under what can charitably be described as adolescent bravado and naïveté in describing the burden of choice men bear in exercising agency: "All situations where you have to make a choice come down to this: do you prefer a woman with a very ordinary body but an attractive face, or one whose body is attractive, but whose face is nothing special? The problem is a false one. It is always preferable to be in a situation where there is no choice to be made either because the woman is perfect or because she is the only one available" (*Cool Memories 1980–1985*, 98).

The loving generosity of women inspires only greater contempt: "She can jettison her existence, her plans and her passions at a single stroke. She is only committed to reality through a secret electoral pact, by which she will stand down if she is losing. She never assumes responsibility for her existence, which allows her to wipe out at a stroke and to slide, like a good hysteric, towards another life. A strange life, spun out entirely towards a goal of transaction. Let a man ask her to give it up, to sacrifice the whole of it, and it all ceases to exist" (*Cool Memories 1980–1985*, 58).

Lacan himself, invited to a conference on female sexuality, observed in his "Guiding Remarks for a Congress on Feminine Sexuality," "what is unquestionably involved here is a conceptual foregrounding of the sexuality of woman, which brings to our attention a remarkable oversight" (qtd. in Owens 78 n. 8).

That is not really an oversight at all. It seems to me a direct expression of the utter lack of interest in who women really are, how they live in their complexity, the narratives they weave around their actions, and how they see themselves. By simply denying them the capacity to achieve agency or any self to speak for, women are ruled out of concern. How much easier it is to linger in the fantasy of utter female abjection and to enable those misogynistic fantasies of assault and control supplied by Baudrillard: "Better than those women who climax are those who give the impression of climaxing, but maintain a sort of distance and virginity beneath the presence of pleasure, for they oblige us with the offer of rape" (*Cool Memories 1980–1985,* 6).

Ironically, Baudrillard's voice erupts from a dark well of misogyny in which woman is in the passive, immobilized position of the abstract linguistic category of the feminine and a real target, fit for simultaneous attack by both "phallic code" and penis. Baudrillard's remarkable admissions point the way to a critique of his own views. They may even illustrate the kind of ironic failure Foucault had in mind when he complained of the "unintended hegemonic consequences of the liberating discourse." They are surely a predilection elevated to the status of an ideology, not a persuasive analytic description.

REINFORCING ABJECTION: THE FEMINISM THAT ISN'T

What is generally referred to as French feminism is equally under attack by the American literature of violent women. The followers of Lacan include a number of distinguished women intellectuals who deny agency and self-representation to women as women. Julia Kristeva finds ever more ingenious reasons to accuse women who achieve assertive or powerful positions in the world or who are self-affirming as selling out the "feminine position" and aping not simply the male position but the brutality she believes it constitutes. The "symbolic contract" that keeps women stuck in a morass of unstructured images and emotions she sees as equivalent to "the social contract." That contract, as she describes it and condemns virtually all alternatives, appears to be immutable regardless of how oppressive it might be. By definition, protest, reform, and change are impossible. Kristeva argues that to exercise power is only to enter the violence of the sociosymbolic contract that is defined as "the symbolic order of language" and the "speaking subject" (the phallus, the Law of the Father). For women to achieve power in the real world involves not only "immersion in the terror of the 'symbolic contract' but also 'a kind of inverted sexism'" and participation in the murder and terrorism of the phallic code. Women are caught between "The Terror Of Power Or The Power of Terrorism" ("Women's Time" 477–80).

Kristeva's rather dismal view of the capacities of women and her horror of women as authority figures flower in her contempt for them as authors. She fails to address the command of the formal structures of language and narrative required by the practice of writing. In a world seen as all text, filled by people who are defined as linguistic categories, should not the instantiation of language in the particular structures of novels, poems, or short stories occupy a distinctive place? Kristeva does not reconcile formal requirements or narrative control with her definition of the sociosymbolic contract or of the feminine position as an all-defining linguistic category. Instead she appears to despise both individual expression in general and the capacities of the self altogether. She sees imaginative writing by women as "a reiteration of a more or less euphoric or depressed romanticism and always an explosion of an ego lacking narcissistic gratification" ("Women's Time" 478). This comment is far from any realistic assessment of the structural, thematic or formal properties of the fiction and poetry discussed in the chapters that follow, but it expresses Kristeva's investment in the abjection of women and the "feminine" position.

In Kristeva's no-exit world of female passivity, any effort at change, reform, or improvement through feminism, political effort, or even individual success is a violation of what one might call Kristeva's penal code, which defines feminists as inevitably fakes, criminals, or terrorists because they operate in the masculine, phallic position as false beings: "It must be pointed out, however, that since the dawn of feminism, and certainly before, the political activity of exceptional women, and thus in a certain sense of liberated women, has taken the form of murder, conspiracy, and crime" (Women's Time 481).

The "crime" may be violating Kristeva's law of female abjection by entering the public world rigidly defined as male, brutal, and inevitably tyrannical.

By that logic, any form of resistance to abjection can be construed as a violent repudiation of the sociosymbolic contract and an act of terrorism. For Kristeva, no way exists to achieve verbal agency or to enter the symbolic code as a woman. Doing so makes one a killer male. She does recognize the effort as a "phantasmic necessity on the part of speaking beings to provide themselves with a *representation* (animal, female, male, parental, etc.) in place of what constitutes them as such" ("Women's Time" 483).

It is not clear what opportunities this list of alternative possibilities contains, but it seems to include some future promise for women who depict themselves as animals. Kristeva predicts a retreat from "anthropomorphism" as if the "problem" of woman were not in any way resolvable in human terms (484).

American portrayals of violent women constitute an attack not simply on the antifeminist, antihuman bias of French representation theory but also on its claims on the discourses of "modernity" it uses to justify its claims to addressing change. A major appeal of the French school and its offspring in academic discussions has been its claim to address the set of changes associated with "modernity." However, it defines modernity in terms of what it sees as a collapse of the West's "grand *récits*," those explanatory narratives of enlightenment humanism that celebrated rationalism, experience, individualism, and the like. A full exposition or appraisal of these views, sometimes referred to as "postmodernism" as well as "modernity," is beyond the scope of this discussion, but brief mention of its relevance to the discussion of their connection to modernity, women, and change is useful.

In her defense of the antifeminist elements in the Lacanian school and its offspring, Alice A. Jardine claims its success in coming to grips with "modernity" may require the sacrifice of feminism along with other forms of humanism. Her analysis in *Gynesis* is premised on a condemnation and, I think, trivialization of American feminism for its failure to engage with those French theoreticians she describes as tackling the problems of modernity.

What's "new"? To answer that question, Jardine adopts a conception of modernity, rooted in her assent to an extremist ideological argument against the West, a quarrel that led Baudrillard to claim: "AIDS in Africa,

THE HEARTBREAKER EFFECT   23

drugs South America, terrorism Islam, debt the Third World [*sic*]. Economic crashes and electronic viruses are, more or less, the West's only success" (*Cool Memories 1980–1985,* 70). Jardine is more temperate in her remarks, but shares a definition of modernity as the rejection of "parts or all of the conceptual apparatuses inherited from nineteenth century Europe. This includes, necessarily, those that are based in movements of human liberation—including of course, feminism. Why this rejection? The major reason has been cautiously and painstakingly laid out in texts written over the past twenty-five years: our ways of understanding in the West have been and continue to be complicitous with our way of oppression. These writers have laid bare the vicious circles of intellectual imperialism and of liberal and humanist ideology" (*Gynesis* 24).

Even if one were to accept such outrageous statements as an accurate description of the full impact of the West, one would have to question the dubious assumption that all ideologies not based on western modes of understanding are without "vicious circles of intellectual imperialism" of their own. As Jacques Derrida has pointed out, the "logical structures" used to critique the processes of western thought are no different from the rationalism they condemn. Jardine celebrates the feminine linguistic position as an alternative to rationalism, as a liberating space of "nonknowledge" coded as *"feminine."* She coins the word *"gynesis"* to call for "the putting into discourse of 'woman' as that *process* diagnosed in France as intrinsic to the condition of modernity . . . [producing] an object [that] is neither a person nor a thing, but a horizon . . . [tending toward] a reading effect" (*Gynesis* 25). This "reading effect" would presumably be free of the imperialism attributed to binary logic in particular and western thought in general. It would involve the direct encounter with the presymbolic and to use Deleuze's word, the "chaosmos" that is, presumably, unrepresentable (*Gynesis* 137).

Defining modernity as the destruction of the "imperialism" of logic and humanism involves a feat of linguistic aggression in its own right. For Jardine it involves doing away with male and female as anything but effects of language. Like Žižek and Kristeva, she is hard put to define how this works in practice. She sees "effects of language" in terms of dismembered body parts. One might, Jardine suggests, "self-consciously throw both sexes, and their sexual organs, into a metonymic confusion of gender. . . . Both 'men's' and 'women's' bodies become truly cut up, fragmented bodies: penises, anuses, breasts, vaginas are cut from the images of their representations in order . . . to imagine a new kind of body" (*Gynesis* 139).

All this sounds somewhat primitive for a theory Jardine defines as the essence of "modernity," much less an improvement on rationalism. It imprisons the figuration of human beings in a charnel house of body parts. This conception of modernity in terms of static fragments, the "void of the subject," or as unreal, dismembered bodies paves the way for Baudrillard's vision of modernity as an endgame in which there is no possibility for resistance or reconstruction of either the feminine or phallic or any living language. There are two main reasons: by definition the alternative is "unrepresentable," and all difference is consumed anyway in the process of media representation. In *Forget Foucault,* Baudrillard writes:

"In fact the revolution has already taken place. Neither the bourgeois revolution nor the communist revolution: just the revolution. . . . power is only there to hide the fact that it no longer exists" (50–51). While most think that the media control the masses, Baudrillard affirms that masses "envelop and absorb the media—or at least there is no priority of one over the other. The mass and the media are one single process. Consumers consume consumption!" (*Silent Majorities* 44–45).

Speech as a communication is silenced in this process. Baudrillard sees the only truly "subversive speech" as "graffiti" because it doesn't "oppose one code to another" but "simply smashes the code" (*Political Economy* 184). A language of resistance never develops because TV is "a social control" in that it establishes the *"certainty that people are no longer speaking to each other"* (*Silent Majorities* 21–22). The result is not new meaning but the recognition that there is no meaning and no possibility for conveying interaction other than repudiation of the effort to mean anything. Baudrillard moves toward absolute meaninglessness, indifference, and the death of death as well as life. He is so absolute in his faith in unreality that he rules out even nihilism and death: "it would be beautiful to be a nihilist, if there were still a radicality—as it would be beautiful to be a terrorist, if death, including that of the terrorist, still had meaning. . . . Death no longer has a stage, neither phantasmatic nor political on which to represent itself, to play itself out, either a ceremonial or a violent one. . . . We are in the era of events without consequences (and of theories without consequences). . . . there is no more hope for meaning" (*Simulacra & Simulation* 164).

The codification of the concept of the feminine in current representation theory entraps women in a depersonalized well of abjection to which there is no personal, linguistic, or political solution. It conceals a retrogressive and reactionary politics masked by assertions of solidarity with oppressed "others" and even praise for the struggle against "the West" as the locus of a tyrannical desire for control while aping the totalitarian energies it purports to condemn. It denies the importance of language it claims constitutes identity by affirming not only universal meaninglessness but even the loss of a meaningful difference between being dead and alive. That is a difference violent women know. They hurl acts of calculated violence and the practice of writing itself against abstraction, using both to contest facile talk of "unreality." Far from lacking agency in speech or mastery of language, the violent women of fiction are masters of logic games and invention, using narrative skill to express their own take on violent action and its meanings. They not only exploit their lives as women and overt acts of violence to affirm the immediacy of their agency, but also use their verbal skill to break out of the prison house of linguistic theories of the "feminine." They hurl a powerful, experiential art against all that denies their expressive strength.

THE HEARTBREAKER AS A CULTURAL FORCE

Violent women in literature return the empirical energies of realism, the reach of emotions, and the narrative richness and meaning of language to center stage. Violence by women in the chapters that follow restores much that has been ruled out by recent approaches to representation and by narrow, ideological views of women that prevail on both the left and right. The high value this literature places on experience, on depicting even extreme action in the context of a woman's life and view of herself as a woman, illustrates the power of literary realism as experiential art. Driven by empirical energies, the literature of violent women provides anatomies of intimacy and public life as women experience them. Violence provides dramatic crises that become the occasion for more complex and subtle narratives that extend far beyond what rigid sexual categories have allowed. The meditative, verbally inventive woman who commits violence emerges as a figure for modernity, as an embodiment of striking change.

The chapters that follow explore violence expressed by women in intimate sexual and family relationships, acts of child murder, political terrorism, and in violent games played as entertainment. Each chapter emphasizes major meanings and motivations for the violence of women: all share a common expressive and communicative power. To read these messages requires going beyond conventional structural and economic explanations for contemporary unrest.

The need for a new vocabulary to describe extreme transformations in general has been noted in passing but has never been pursued as a way of understanding the violence of women. Writing in 1972, Irving Howe described a current "crisis of civilization" that "has to do not so much with the workings of the economy or the rightness of social arrangements," which can be corrected by reforms in social policy (14). It involves changes in values and practices that are "atmospheric and behavioral, encompassing and insidious" (22). It derives from many factors ranging from mass culture to the "partial breakdown of the transmission agencies—received patterns of culture, family structure, and education—through which values, norms and ideals are handed down from generation to generation" (23). Howe claimed a crisis of civilization "works itself out in ways we don't readily understand and sometimes, far from working itself out, it continues to fester. A social crisis raises difficulties, a crisis of civilization dilemmas. A social crisis is expressed mainly through public struggle, a crisis of civilization mainly through incoherence of behavior" (14).

What is striking about Howe's formulation is his use of an important distinction between "social" crisis and what he called a "crisis of civilization" flowing from an "incoherence of behavior." Both affect the public sphere, but the former is more readily described in conventional economic and social terms and correctable through policy. Howe recognizes that the latter is outside of both. The former lends itself to quantitative and structural study, while the latter requires a qualitative approach. I believe the imaginative depth of the literary narratives discussed in the chapters that follow provides qualitative portraits of the meanings and motives for violence experienced and expressed by individuals and is a step towards a qualitative approach to the meaning of violence by women. What Howe called "incoherence" I see in this context as transformations in character and behavior that are actually coherent and meaningful if differently explored. They are in part those changes now being projected in dramatic and exaggerated form in the imaginative renderings and sensational coverage of violent women.

Violent women embody a new kind of crisis that seems to overrun traditional political categories and to call into question the stability of our bedrock relations with each other—within the family, in intimacy, and in our conception of citizenship. Meaningful narratives of violence by women offer a key to what I would characterize not as a "crisis of civilization" but as disruptive, qualitative changes in our culture. Violence by women in accounts of actual crimes, films, and serious literature discloses the ways in which the actions of individual characters intersect with culture and, taken together, weave changes in social, family, and sexual life into a coherent story of change. It is an overarching, communicative violence that forges narratives that are strikingly different from those of male violence. These differences are inscribed even in traditional American master narratives of male conquest and native narratives of female retaliation.

ON HOME GROUND: AMERICAN MYTHS AND THE WAR BETWEEN THE SEXES

Although the focus of this book is on contemporary literature and culture, some qualitative differences between the violence of men and of women are evident in core myths of American violence. The violence of men has been seen in terms of the master narratives of American history and culture: the conquest of the frontier and celebration of power that surface in both popular and mythic forms of the western in which cowboys and Indians wage their struggle for land. But there is a counternarrative of female violence that underscores how comparably embedded its mythic stature is in American culture and how differently it must be addressed. While the master narrative of historical conquest lends itself to political and social analysis in its explorations of the competition for land, power, and wealth, the counternarrative of female violence lends itself to more subtle forms of exploration of its meanings and motivations.

The most persuasive work on the master narratives of violence in American culture and literature has been rooted in tales of conquest modeled on the Indian wars. It follows a repetitive paradigm over time: the most powerful men subdue serial opponents in conflicts ranging from the Puritan wars against the Indians, to the struggles of the rural poor and urban labor against moneyed elites. Richard Slotkin's impressive studies, *Regeneration through Violence: The Mythology of the American Frontier 1600–1860, Fatal Environment: The Myth of the Frontier in the Age of Industrialization 1800–1890,* and *Gunfighter Nation: The Myth of the Frontier in Twentieth Century America,* locate all violence in the myth of the frontier. Slotkin sees the conquest of the land and the Indians who lived upon it as a unifying drama that serves as the model of all social violence from the Indian wars of the seventeenth century to the labor unrest of the nineteenth century and contemporary gun culture. The drive for serial conquests is aligned with the historical conquest of the land or the struggle for economic or physical power over others.

Slotkin's use of myth brings the idea of self-transcendence to violence and unifies the representation of the violence of men. He sees as the defining mythic act an Indian practice in which the victorious warrior consumes the heart and appropriates the courageous force of his vanquished but heroic foe. By doing so, he prevents his foe from rising again, acquires his power, and strengthens himself. Complete domination "through a sanctified and regenerative act of violence" uses that ritual to achieve the "harmony" of incorporation and control. The concept of "sanctification" and "regeneration" through violence brings the sacred and the self-inflating together in a historic practice and highlights the role of violence in a way that sanctions male domination. The relationship of women to this practice is not Slotkin's concern.

Although the violence of men correlates with a mythic narrative of conquest and domination Slotkin applies to the sweep of American history, the violence of women tracks that tale of conquest like a dark shadow. It provides alternative myths of violence that are different in origin and expression and require new and more subtle appraisals of power and meaning. I believe it invokes those narratives, discussed in detail in chapter 6, that speak directly to the spiritual, intellectual, and psychological traditions of our culture. The origins of mythic female violence are grounded in the power of women to mobilize core mythologies associated with birth, sex, and care. It is a violence that both arouses and violates visions of woman as mother, lover, and comforter. It outrages primal associations of women with forgiveness and nurture. Where male myth sanctifies the bloodshed of men, celebrating conquest, mythic female violence is steeped in ambivalence, complexity, and nuance. A Native American myth highlights the differences in an originary American tale of female violence.

Mourning Dove, an Okanogan Indian from the northwest, transcribed a striking myth surrounding the connection between birth, sexuality, and violence. In *Coyote Stories,* she recorded the tale of incest between Brother and Sister that produces an infant son. Sister seems to be the ultimate sufferer: she is abandoned by her brother and parents and cast out of the tribe with her child. Brother hunts her down and kills their child, whom he sees only as the mark of his "crime." But Sister carries her baby's body until she reaches a river, breaks it into pieces, and casts them all over the river and the countryside, telling the pieces, "You are to follow your father until he dies with sickness. In the future, people will have sickness and not always live in happiness" (1539).

This myth of a woman whose actions bring disease into the world captures the far darker, all-pervasive, diffuse dimensions of female aggression. It contrasts sharply with the male warrior who consumes the heart of his vanquished opponent in a final completion of conquest and infusion of personal strength. Sister's violence is rooted in the symbolic associations of woman with the sources of both life and death. She combines the themes of sexuality, fecundity, and anxiety over unseen and unexpected destruction. Sister is outraged in all the family connections and experiences figured in the three violations she endures: as sister (by incest), as daughter (by abandonment), and as mother (by the murder of her child). In striking back, Sister, in effect, reenacts the fertile sexuality that produced the baby's life but turns her creative power into a virulent form—the pieces of her dead baby serve as "seeds" she casts to earth to sow a future of suffering and death. She reveals the complexity and depth of female retaliation: far-reaching, indirect, and insidious, her vengeance is wreaked on the human race as well as on the man who wronged her. Unlike the conqueror who incorporates the power of his victim, Sister gains nothing but the knowledge of her massive future destructiveness.

The Native American myth of Sister also implies the killer narcissism of Brother who regards his child as nothing more than the product of his actions, a being he can control by eliminating it as if it were only an unwanted extension of himself, a waste product. He tells himself he can end his troubles by one act of murder. Sister proves him wrong. The fact that a brother and sister produce the baby of death adds still another dimension—it is a symbolic acknowledgment that male and female can each display a killing self-absorption and an affirmation that violence springs from a common origin but yields divergent expressions.

Sister's use of the dead baby to sow endless trouble gives to the baby's body a separate and terrible future as an infection in all living bodies. Maternal and paternal roles are condensed in this myth as Sister combines them in "sowing" the seeds of infection in nature. Her aggression is all the more sweeping because she seems to have been so outwardly compliant and submissive to Brother while directing her destruction at the world at large. Sister does not attempt to kill Brother directly. Instead she unleashes a force that will engulf all of humankind. She sends the message, "if you cannot accept the life I create, I will create death instead!" Sister creates a superhuman violence that haunts associations to the violence of women, and links it to a force in nature. It is an infection in life itself. Her baby's "future" is biological terrorism. Once unleashed, there is no stopping its power to kill.

MEDEA AND THE SHOCK OF THE NEW

The unanticipated, all-consuming, relentless quality of female aggression defines its mythic stature. It signifies the fear that the violence of woman violates both nature and society and reveals terrible and frightening change.

Sister and Medea are sisters in the mythic association of violence with the sudden exposure to the new, the strange, and the association of violence with mysteries of birth, death, and power. Both employ spells and curses. Medea adds to that a calculated and ruthless intelligence and the ability to manipulate men and affect kingdoms as well as nature through language.

Standing at the wellsprings of western literature, the legend of Medea introduced female aggression on a superhuman scale once considered the province of goddesses alone. First emerging in the "Voyage of the Argonauts," her tale captured for the pre-Hellenic world a conception of the new and marvelous that could be represented in the figure of a beautiful woman who could wield power over nature and destabilize the social and moral order.

The Medea of myth is a priestess of Hecate, Goddess of the dark underworld, and a royal princess of Colchis. Medea can wreck the order of both society and nature. Her passion destabilizes kingdoms. For love of Jason, an adventurer in search of the Golden Fleece and glory, she betrays her father, the king who has vowed to keep the Golden Fleece under his protection. Medea's knowledge of witchcraft and magic spells confer on Jason superhuman victories and masculine power in war, enabling him to perform extraordinary feats—to overcome soldiers that grow from the soil, a fire-breathing dragon, and every obstacle. After enabling Jason to obtain the Golden Fleece, Medea even kills her own brother to ensure that she and Jason can escape her father's pursuing army. After she has fled with Jason to Corinth, borne him two sons, and even resurrected his father from the dead to please him, she learns Jason is leaving her to marry the princess of Corinth, who will one day make him king.

Medea's rage at Jason overturns both society and nature in another way. She destroys another kingdom by killing the king and the princess of Corinth, violates human nature by killing the children she had with Jason, curses him with the prediction that he will die a wanderer, and flouts the laws of nature by flying through the air to escape. Bereft of his sons and his prospects as a future king, Jason fumes as he sees her escaping through the air on a chariot drawn by flying dragons. And she is not yet finished. Medea lands in Athens, marries the king, and exults in her new authority as queen. Her future seems to be pure and uninhibited power.

The myth suggests several qualities that help constitute the heartbreaker effect. The tale illustrates both the fascination and revulsion aroused by the use of a violent woman to convey the marvelous, the unexpected, and the unknown. It combines physical beauty, power, and violence in seductive form but suggests that the power of Medea comes not from her beauty but from her intelligence and command of language expressed in the potent spells she casts. These can reverse death, confer power, and include curses that define the future for her hapless victims. Her intelligence is manipulative—she is able to deceive and outwit her father, Jason, and the princess of Corinth, whose vanity and naïveté Medea is sure will draw her to the gift of poisoned clothing Medea uses to kill her. The myth suggests a destabilizing and frightening combination of sexuality, violence, and domestic upheaval that upsets all traditional notions of male dominance. Each of these factors merits additional comment.

The Medea myth underscores a model of male-female connections that combines both the erotic and the familial, bringing violence home in terms of the dependency of men. Medea is not only the source of Jason's heroic success but also the first representation of a mother-lover to a child-man. She is at once the all-powerful mother who nourishes and satisfies his fantasies of greatness and all his sexual desires. She is also a projection of the first seemingly all-powerful and malevolent being, the omnipotent, evil mother who undermines, starves, and destroys, leaving Jason in impotent rage. The politics of their relationship have larger psychological importance in underscoring a destructive intimacy between two egotists so malignant as to disrupt both public and private life. Her refusal to obey her father and Jason, or to sacrifice herself for her children, expresses her rejection of the conventional female role. Medea emerges as a primary figure of overwhelming emotional, sexual, and political chaos. She embodies the overthrow of all that secures stability.

Mother love is the bedrock assumption about the nature of woman and the stability of the family. In the immense scale of her ruthlessness, Medea's violence seems to overturn and change the very conception of human nature. That overturning contributes to the heartbreaker effect. The glue that secures human nature is protective mother love. By killing her children,

Medea not only hurts Jason but also destroys the vulnerable side of herself and all that remains of her past capacity for love. The association of love with weakness looms large in the literature of child murder and the fantasies surrounding it. Destroying the impulse to love is widely seen by violent women in contemporary portrayals of real and literary child murders as necessary for every kind of empowerment.

Overturned expectations of womanhood are enshrined in the literature of violent women who can be seen as Medea's spiritual daughters. Exceptional will, knowledge, and intelligence are the hallmarks of witches and those who conjure violent spirits. All these make Lady Macbeth one of Medea's spiritual heirs. Lady Macbeth violates virtually every female norm: of hospitality and affection by killing her guest, the fatherly King Duncan; of the subordination of wife to husband in her accusations that Macbeth is too timid to do the job; and in her cries to the spirits: "unsex me here, / . . . Come to my woman's breasts, / And take my milk for gall, you murd'ring ministers, / Wherever in your sightless substances / You wait on nature's mischief" (*Macbeth* I,V, 40, 48–51). Shakespeare, however, splits the female will to violence from the female capacity to tolerate, accept, and control it. He divides the lady from the witch, conferring on the latter an unalloyed violence untroubled by guilt. It is three sisterly witches who, in their closeness, their terrible, bubbling brew, and, most of all, their fluent use of equivocal language, propel Macbeth toward violence. The three sister-witches complete a vision in the play of female violence enacted through the remorseless manipulation of men and speech.

Mastery of language is an attribute of the violent women of legend or myth. They are frequently represented as witches whose language skills include the ability to overturn all the laws of nature with curses, magic spells, and incantations. The verbal craft of black magic invariably accompanies violations of human nature by unconventional behavior that terrorizes fathers, lovers, husbands, and children. Medea's spells are the origin of Jason's power to trump her father, the protector of the Golden Fleece. Her knowledge overturns the superiority in strength nature confers upon men. Medea supplies an ancestral female model of defiance of all expectations—for resignation to male authority, for acceptance of male abandonment, for love for her children above all self-interest. In Euripides's tragedy, *Medea,* Jason claims she is not human at all, not a woman but a "lionness fiercer than . . . Scylla in nature . . . cursed witch! child murderess!" (755–56). Jason's vision that violence in women is itself a corruption of human nature presages a refusal on the part of men to accept female violence as human, an attitude consistent with the hellish witches, darkness, and apparitions that fill *Macbeth.* Sister, although at first only a helpless victim of incest and ostracism, knows and utters a curse that brings disease and death to human experience. Sorcery and black magic haunt the imagination of female violence because they symbolize fear of woman's powers of speech, powers that use intelligent manipulation to overcome physical weakness.

Male fear, suspicion, and desire are an important contribution of the Medea legend to the heartbreaker effect. That mixture was carried directly into the American imagination of the mythic violence of women. They loom large in Nathaniel Hawthorne's retelling of the story of Jason and Medea for American children in *Tanglewood Tales* (1851). His version is virtually a warning that the woman who is willing and able to give even a powerful man everything he has ever wanted is not offering a free lunch: "Gazing at Medea, [Jason] beheld a wonderful intelligence in her face. She was one of those persons whose eyes are full of mystery, so that, while looking into them, you seem to see a very great way, as into a deep well, yet can never be certain whether you see into the farthest depths, or whether there be not something else hidden at the bottom. If Jason had been capable of fearing anything, he would have been afraid of making this young princess his enemy; for, beautiful as she now looked, she might, the very next instant, become as terrible as the dragon that kept watch over the Golden Fleece" (407). Writing with a *frisson* of fear, Hawthorne suggests Medea's danger lies in the gleaming intelligence that animates her beauty and her passion. As she looks at Jason, Hawthorne describes her disturbing gaze: "Her black eyes shone upon him with such a keen intelligence, that he felt as if there were a serpent peeping out of them" (417).

The troubled desire and dependency of men, along with their fear of the destructive potential of female intelligence, are brought to crisis by the violence of women. The narratives men weave around powerful women often highlight their inability to judge women or to encompass the degree of their own dependency. Hawthorne's Medea even warns Jason: "Do not you see you are lost, without me as your good angel?" (420). He cannot see that. Medea symbolizes male hopes for an all-powerful, all-giving mother-wife who will use her strength only in the service of her needy man and will do so unconditionally. It never occurs to Jason that Medea's devotion might be affected by anything he does. Like Brother, who believes Sister will accept his need to repair his reputation as justification for murdering their infant, Jason discovers he was wrong. Narratives of violent women in contemporary American writing provide complex and often finely nuanced portraits of what goes wrong between men and women.

Great facility with language highlights the covert violence of manipulation. The use of language as a weapon and intelligence as a tool for coercion exploits the gap between the outward appearance of women and their hidden destructive power. These are still connected with metaphors of sorcery in the contemporary imagination of the witch-hunt. Arthur Miller's *The Crucible*, was set in Puritan New England during the Salem witch trials and used a young woman's exploitation of sorcery as a metaphor for the destructive power of a society's enthrallment by the "spell" of McCarthyism. Political terror in *The Crucible* originates with Abigail, the woman who, charged by the court with sorcery, uses a ruthless intelligence to manipulate the prejudices of the judge and court to accuse others of witchcraft. Her shrewd use of language inflames the court to execute nineteen people. The deadliest force of women is their power of persuasive and seductive speech.

Violence binds women in contemporary writing to mythic figures of the past. A democratization of violence casts today's killers who become celebrities through their crimes as modern legends in the media but also propels them beyond myth into the center of current social turmoil. Karla Faye Tuckers or Lorena Bobbitts become focal points for cultural arguments. Far more verbal depth is available in the fiction and poetry of violence in which apparently "ordinary" women demonstrate the complexity of meanings and motives violence holds for them. Seduction, manipulation, and murder in the pages that follow are practiced by "ordinary" women who are not witches weaving spells, but who can nevertheless lay claim to great verbal inventiveness and power.

The narratives women weave around violent action reveal their relation to the social world and their inner drives and expose their mastery of the processes of meaning and language. What earlier times conceived of as magic spells emerges as a communicative violence that exploits deceptive speech and images. Modern violence by women is an adventure in language.

COMMUNICATIVE VIOLENCE: DESTRUCTIVE EGOTISM AS A SPEAKING STYLE

The expressive power that characterizes violence narratives often serves the cause of justifying the act and depicting the motives of the woman who commits it. Destructive egotism has some relation to the "malignant narcissism" seen in pathological behavior and defined in a clinical, psychiatric context by Otto Kernberg (257). Communicative violence that reveals destructive egotism can be seen as a process of narration that operates according to a subjective logic of seizure, appropriation, complication, and the portrayal of one or more alternative truths with social as well as personal meaning.

Mourning Dove's narrative illustrates the combination of destructive egotism, spin, and communicative violence. Sister is the legendary cause of disease in the world. However, her story stresses not her vindictive egotism but her provocation to violence by the overwhelming violation of life she has suffered, appropriating for her the role of victim. Her grandiosity complicates a tale of retaliatory violence by unleashing disease against all of humankind, not just those who have wronged her. The sweeping damage she wreaks on all humanity is presented as a legitimate response to the inhumanity of her mistreatment. The curse she casts places her in the line of "witches" and spell-casters of myth. However, the creation of a justifying narrative for bringing disease to humankind involves a mastery of deceptive speech. The narrative appropriates the language of victimization, subjectivity, and oppression to present biological terrorism against all future generations as only an act of retributive justice.

Political and social analyst David E. Apter, whose work will be discussed further in chapter 4, has attempted to develop a discourse theory of violence that directly addresses the role of justifying narratives and the relationship between speech, interpretation, and social action surrounding actual terrorism. Of the relationship between actual and verbal violence, he writes: "People do not commit political violence without discourse. They need to talk themselves into it. . . . On public platforms [discourse] becomes inflammatory . . . results in texts . . . is interpretive . . . [and] engages the intelligences in ways out of the ordinary. It takes people out of themselves" (2).

Communicative violence is not limited to acts of terror but is evident in the calculated narratives surrounding violence in general and in the ways in which violent women tell their own stories. In the real world their narratives may be distinguished by outrageously deceptive and concealing speech ranging from lies of omission that mask the intentions surrounding their violence to lies of commission designed to complicate the meaning of the deed when it is revealed. Criminal violence reported in the news offers examples of this type of speech by multiple murderers who, in effect, twist language by reversing the connection between description, intention, and action. They are masters of doublespeak. Their claims of certainty that the world is hostile and deserving of the destruction they wreak are comparable to the destructive egotism of Sister in avenging the wrong done to her on all of humankind. Grandiosity may surface in their vision of themselves as agents of retributive justice.

Communicative violence surrounding murder can be both outrageous and meaningful. The language women who commit violent, random murders use to describe their motives often exploits rosy stereotypes of women, projecting their claims of love, virtue, or self-protection, even as they acknowledge killing. For example, Leslie Van Houton, the Charles Manson family member who saw herself as helping along a revolution that would bring Manson control of the United States, commented after joining in the Tate-LaBianca murders, "you really have to love someone to kill them." She saw no contradiction between writing in her victim's blood and claiming she was celebrating life and love. Goodstein and Glaberson describe how Lisa Duy carried a semiautomatic rifle into the KSL radio station in Salt Lake

City. She was primed to kill to protect her privacy from the radio station she believed was broadcasting information about her sex life. She opened fire and later explained, "it was like going to a beautiful island and I was spreading flowers at them, shooting at them" (*New York Times,* April 11, 2000, A24).

Having stabbed her psychologist and having tried to strangle her mother, Sylvia Seegrist said that murder was her way of being sociable and of demonstrating her social conscience. After carefully dressing in green army fatigues, Seegrist took a semiautomatic rifle, went to a shopping mall near Philadelphia, and opened fire. She "continued spraying bullets as she ran through the mall, killing three people and injuring seven, all strangers. Among the dead was a 2-year-old boy." From the cell in which she served a life sentence, she explained "that her killings were a form of public service" (*New York Times,* April 10, 2000, A14).

These actual "rampage killers" may reflect in dramatic and extreme form some of the uses of violence in blasting expectations of female dependency, love, and resignation to both perceived wrongs and their own neediness. For example, some of these women reserved their greatest fury for those who aroused their dependency. Seegrist had attempted to kill both the mother who cared about her and the psychologist who tried to help her. Getting caught seems to have mattered less than the passion to damage and humiliate those she needed. What appears to be as self-destructive as it was brutal to others is to Seegrist a way of establishing her invulnerability, her complete rejection of a need or desire for help or understanding, or even any despair at her own unremitting rage. She replaced her dependency on others with an elated act of violence. Her attempts to murder her mother and her doctor failed, but her random murders separated her from them for life.

Conventional wisdom holds that women use speech to express their emotions. But changes in the use of women's speech to express feeling are underscored by the explanations provided by women who were rampage killers. The mad logic evident in the actions and explanations of Van Houton, Duy, or Seegrist discloses an intellectual and cognitive continuity divorced from any connection between the deed and the emotion they feel. Their explanations are artfully structured and carefully split the two, enforcing a discontinuity between understanding and feeling. These killers know what they have done but refuse to recognize the deaths of others as important. This counterpoint between understanding, explanation, and emotion is sustained by the extraordinary grandiosity in which they remain guilt-free, seeing their actions only from their own point of view. They feel they do not have to take anyone else—neither those who have cared for them nor the strangers they killed—into account.

Splitting speech from action enables a manipulation of point of view that is at work in both media and literary representations of violence that are not presented as pathology. The destructive egotism displayed by the rampage killers expresses in an extreme form a radical personalization of issues found in many representations of less extreme violence by women. Evident in depictions of the dislocation between the act of murder and protestations of love for the victims, or in claims of altruistic killings for "social betterment" or the welfare of the victim, their destructive egotism also reflects a use of misleading and hypocritical speech to mask a complete transformation of their vision of human connection. The killers' grandiose refusal to acknowledge the value of any life but their own or any competing point of view is part of a larger and more sweeping identification with aggression and a denial of their own vulnerability. Perceiving the world as simply hostile, they seize as valuable weapons literal aggression and verbal structures of control. They dramatize currents at work in contemporary media and entertainment that stress cool, stylish violence. Their imaginative justifications for what they have done may constitute an attack on previous conceptions of female speech.

Women have been seen as the have-nots of structured language, doomed to communicate authentically only through emotions. That view is one of the casualties of these rampage killers. Van Houton, Seegrist, and Duy aggressively exploited entrenched verbal clichés about women by affirming themselves as loving friends, benefactors, and modest flower girls spreading bullets like petals. They seized control of female stereotypes to expose them. In contrast, in that major theoretical formulation of woman's abjection, Julia Kristeva's *Powers of Horror,* control of female stereotypes and the coherent order of language created by patriarchal culture are considered "male" while women are said to practice a language of the inexpressible, of feeling, and suffering in what appears to be a doomed effort at subversion of the linguistic source of "male" power conceptualized as the phallic symbolic code. If women become skilled in that code, they are by definition conceived of as male, false betrayers of the feminine position. Kristeva's introduction of psychology to the drama is based on her persuasion that the power of a male ruling elite's syntax extends to the very formation of self, forcing the exclusion of the "female," non-rational, emotive self from a power-oriented, grammatically "rational," male-dominated culture. She sees implication, intonation—all the evocative, alogical properties of language—in a political context as both feminine and always "other," always subordinate to "phallic" symbolic structures. But the use of language by violent women in both actual and imaginative representations transcends neat dialectics of class and sex and displays an inventive architecture and psychology of its own.

Rampage killers may all be mad, but it would be mistake to dismiss them as irrelevantly so. Their mad logic exploits stereotypical female norms, counterpoints feeling and action, provides rationalizations, and confers a cold illusion of control over the universe of aggression they inhabit. Grandiosity as a complex verbal style involves a use of speech and storytelling to consolidate power and pleasure. By splitting cause from effect, by compartmentalizing the results of their action and their own motivation, they achieve a control and mastery of its terms. They can cut away death from the pleasure of committing violence, which appears to remain guilt-free, wrapped in protestations of love.

Inner psychology and personal language are pitched as a siren's song, a seductive, personal lyric at odds with the events described. Women who are rampage killers provide extreme examples of women who seem not to experience any intrapsychic conflict and whose descriptions of what they do and their actions sharply conflict with each other. They have made a successful separation of intellectual awareness that they have killed from any emotional or affective awareness that others have died because of them. Splitting the pleasure of violence from an emotional response to death, seeing violence only from their own point of view as perpetrators, they dramatize a more complex process at work in fictional women who master the manipulation of stories to tell about their violence. By controlling the script, they secure their grandiosity, their power to claim all is what they say it is, and conquer any need to accept help or feel guilt.

Interactions with those who may not be the direct objects of violence are affected by the destructive egotism that shapes a vision of the world as a rapacious and hostile place that warrants aggression. From that perspective, no relationship is positive, and any display of weakness may provoke attack. Because of this, it is as necessary to destroy anything vulnerable or compassionate in oneself to protect against being attacked as it is to attack others. Efforts by others to thwart this process—to help or to relieve anger—are perceived as duplicitous ploys designed to weaken resolve. The helper can never be more than a competitor who must be humiliated, defeated, or killed.

Only omnipotent power enables feelings of freedom from fear, pain, and dread and the experience of elation. In this inversion of human connection, only aggression is a reliable way to relate to others. The stories told about aggression and the adoption of misleading, contemptuous, or hypocritical styles of communication help erase comparisons between right and wrong, good and bad, licit and illicit. This is a verbal style designed to negate both moral distinctions and the importance placed on love, warmth, and care by using language games to relieve the chaos of feelings and relationships. But the effects of such a style may be almost as sweeping as the damage wreaked by a rampage killer.

The media arena for public discourse is rife with manipulated communications, logic twisting, and language manipulation. Language distortion appears most strikingly in popular analyses of crime. As the media increasingly devote discussions of crime to the spin offered by prosecution and defense and focus primarily on strategies for conviction or acquittal, the strategic use of the narrative of violent action becomes more important than the actions that occasion the need for a strategy in the first place. Cynical and hypocritical modes of communication flourish in a public sphere in which violence narratives proliferate. The rhetorical strategies of the prosecutor and defense that have become grist for the media mill contribute to establishing competitive aggression as a speaking style. Communicative aggression has been virtually ignored by theorists of language largely because the role of style or language in shaping violence narratives is most often explored in terms of conformity to legal definitions of acceptable or unacceptable violence or limited conceptions of class antagonism.

Literary theorists of language who have sought to align speech and social trauma have not fully addressed the richness and diversity of the stories of violent women but have instead often remained committed to structuring narratives as an academic, Marxist dialectic. Raymond Williams, for example, explores class domination as a linguistic style, seeing little opposition between the laws of poetry and political dialectics. For him, the ruling class so encodes its power that standard grammar serves as an "inherent dominative mode," the ability of the ruling class to define what is linguistically "high" and "low" and to enact its speech as a standard of elitism. Mastery of language defines the possessors as upper class and consigns those without it to an underclass.

Contemporary reality has simply outstripped this narrowly focused conception of the meaning of language and its relationship to women. In a culture of spin, what counts most is a mastery of techniques for multiplying and controlling perspectives to *reshape* our sense of relationships and create a pliable "syntax" for a logic based on change. This was anticipated in one of the most talked-about essays of the early nineties, "Defining Deviancy Down," by Daniel Patrick Moynihan, which appeared in *The American Scholar.* Moynihan argued that as a culture we are dealing with unprecedented fragmentation of family and social life by redefining the resulting aberrations as normal. Violent women are the sharp edge of the crisis of redefinition Moynihan observed. They are and are represented as adept at using language as a tool for masking action as a problem in definition and redefinition and for normalizing their violence. The ongoing exploitation of "normalcy" is often a feature of the rebel against American norms.

Consider the language of self-definition surrounding Kathleen Soliah, a terrorist in the Symbionese Liberation Army of the seventies, who for more than twenty years lived successfully as Sara Jane Olson, a wealthy do-gooder and mom in St. Paul, Minnesota. Renaming herself was only one aspect of a sophisticated use of language to redefine herself and eventually to transform the response of others to her. As the *London Times* put it in a full-page story, "To her neighbors and family Sara Olson was the model suburban mum. Then the FBI arrested her. Has her secret past as a member of the revolutionary group that kidnapped Patty Hearst finally caught up with her?" (August 28, 1999).

Soliah-Olson has since been convicted of trying to blow up a Los Angeles police car in an attempt to kill two policemen in 1975 and of participation in a bank robbery in Carpenter, California that resulted in the death of a bank customer. She was, according to Patty Hearst, the heiress kidnapped by the Symbionese Liberation Army, one of her committed tormentors and brainwashers. In the *New York Times,* a gun-shop owner in St. Paul was quoted as putting Soliah-Olson "in the same category as Timmy McVeigh or the Unabomber" (January 30, 2000, A18). However, under arrest, Soliah insisted on being called Sara Jane Olson and redefined herself and her past by that renaming. She used an arch irony and verbal wit to force a moral equivalency between her past life as a terrorist and the name she took when she went underground and began her revision as a housewife and nurturer. Could the housewife redeem the bomb-maker?

Under indictment, Sara Jane Olson published a cookbook called *Serving Time: America's Most Wanted Recipes.* It was advertised as featuring such delicacies as "On the Lam Stew" and "Funeral Punch." Her photo on the cover shows her laughing and dancing a jig while holding handcuffs in one hand and a spatula in the other. Olson set up a website advertising her domestic talents and used her media skills to try to cook her indictment. Her conviction and harsh sentence suggest it was not her best recipe. From mansion to mean streets, the verbal skill of women in violent episodes dramatizes the hope for transformation through redefinition, the creation of an antiworld in which attempted murder is redefined through humor and irony. Telling stories that revise self-concepts around violent action often makes the drama of language as outrageous as the act it depicts.

Accounts of violence in which language-twisting plays a large role reflect an awareness that how we view violence has changed, that violence is seen by the larger society in new and different ways. Where once other people served as a check on aggression by reasserting norms of conduct, in our current, media-driven world, in which killing can confer instant celebrity and entertainment violence is widespread, no such check may appear. Instead the killer is the focus of attention, her relatives interviewed on Larry King, her crime featured on ABC's 20/20 or the subject of enthusiastic narratives of justification. Violence may even mark her emergence as star of those modern legends woven on infotainment news or late night talk shows.

SOUND AND LIGHT SHOW: VOICES AND IMAGES OF TRANSFORMATION

Violent women play a significant role in the media culture that uses mastery of persuasive language to represent violence as a positive change. Because women are considered non-violent, accounts of their violence often focus on their passages from passivity to action. The violence of women can offer a consuming experience, one that rivets attention, compressing everything into a spectacle that seems as much about the process of transformation as about violence itself.

Suited to visual media, the brutal actions of good-looking women are literally spectacles of transformation, charged collisions with stereotypical female gentleness. Some are as simple, troubling, and exhilarating as *Girl Fight,* a film about a female boxer that won the top prize for drama at the fall 2000 Sundance Film Festival. Although an account by Nancy Hass in the *New York Times* noted that "cheering on two women trying to knock each other senseless still troubles spectators," the film was only one of several about women boxers. *Shadow Boxers* was a documentary film about Lucia Rijker, who is considered a star of women's boxing; *On the Ropes,* featuring a professional boxer named Tyrene Manson, was nominated for an Oscar. Kate Sekules, an English journalist with a career as a professional boxer, Hass notes, published a memoir titled: "The Boxer's Heart: How I Learned to Love the Ring" (October 1, 2000 9:1). All the women boxers—amateurs and professionals—photographed for the *New York Times* story appear chic and conventionally feminine. A good-looking blonde who fought in the Golden Gloves (a competition that has included women boxers since 1995), Katya Bankowsky is both a competitive fighter and the director of *Shadow Boxers.* Asked why she boxed, she explained: "I fight because it stretches my idea of my self. Having grace and elegance bang up against violence and aggression is exhilarating" (*New York Times,* October 1, 2000 9:7).

In the media, visual images help define an identity violence that exploits beautiful women to embody changes encoded in the passage of women from vulnerability to violence. Violence is invariably described from the point of view of the aggressor and stylized to promote feelings of freedom or elation. Physical beauty and style join the use of language in popularizing extreme self-transformations by presenting violent aggression as part of a lusty pursuit of life, celebrity, and action.

In both the public discourse of the newspaper and media, violence can bring redemption from vulnerability, boredom, or ordinariness. Notable milestones in this process may have occurred in the emerging entertainments of the late sixties that began to stress cool violence and blur the line between politics, personality cults, and performance art. In films and actual political protests staged as theater for the television news, women played an interesting role. Both political activism and theater benefited from using attractive women who could use violence to embody self-transformation as a makeover and who could invoke oppression and revolt in equal measure. In 1967, a landmark film exploited the depression era to convey the unrest of the sixties counterculture through the shooter chic of Faye Dunaway as Bonnie Parker.

Bonnie and Clyde was a milestone in the emergence of graphic violence and a new icon—the poor girl as excited by shooting as she was adept at using language to achieve celebrity. Even before the release of *Bonnie and Clyde,* the ads for the film starring Faye Dunaway and Warren Beatty sparkled with the romance of a lethal mixture: good looks, armed robbery, and love in the 1930s as a revolt against the poverty the Establishment seemed to have visited on the nation with the crash of the stock market in 1929. Ads declared: "They're young . . . they're in love . . . and they kill people" (qtd. in Hoberman 125). Dunaway powerfully conveyed Bonnie's prior life as a bored small-town girl with nothing going for her and the sparkling apotheosis to stardom she achieves through handling a gun, robbing banks, and writing ballads. The covergirl for the March 4, 1968 issue of *Newsweek* as Bonnie, Dunaway was quoted in the lead story about her interpretation of the role of Bonnie Parker as "a girl with potential who is blocked" but who can kill, write the script, and seize the photo-ops that promote her own celebrity (Hoberman 133).

Politics served as metaphor for the violence that dispelled depression. Literally set in the Depression thirties, *Bonnie and Clyde* perceived the era through the lens of the prosperous sixties in which anger and depression were as much moods as economic facts and politics was theater in demonstrations geared to the six o'clock news. Appealing to both sixties political turbulence and counterculture attitudes, the scriptwriters, David Newman and Robert Benton, placed it among other "cultural artifacts that embodied 'the fun' of violence: *In Cold Blood,* the Broadway play *Marat/Sade,* the satire of Lyndon Johnson's leadership of the Vietnam War, *MacBird,* Andy Warhol's electric chair, and the music of the Rolling Stones. [All showed that] the rules of reaction have changed; it's not that old catharsis any longer, but that new kick" (qtd. in Hoberman 121).

The film was far more remarkable in presenting a woman who defined herself through scripting and situating her violence in a specific narrative. Bonnie wrote; she not only created a story of self-fashioning but also demonstrated that violence was the path to celebrity and chic. Dunaway as Bonnie established power and control through the imposition of a personal style, a combination of beauty, action, and language that became more striking as the film progressed.

Bonnie's path to celebrity through violence and self-invention is one of the passages described in the film. Dunaway's Bonnie, trapped in a shabby house and town, restlessly looking out of her window, sees Clyde trying to steal her family's car. She stops him from taking the car but flirts with him, joins him in an armed robbery, and drives off with him in a stolen car. Clyde tells her how to improve her hairstyle. Failing to perform sexually, Clyde shows her his gun and she caresses and strokes the barrel. Later, at a deserted farmhouse that has been repossessed by the bank, Clyde teaches her how to shoot. She is thrilled. The gun is not only a sexual object but also one that brings political status as a weapon against the Establishment—the bank that seized and now owns the property. When the evicted farmer and his family come back to the repossessed house for a last look,

Clyde gives them the gun to shoot up the place and strike back at the injustice of their loss. Bonnie and Clyde discover their identity and purpose as a renegade couple, announcing to the displaced family: "We are Bonnie and Clyde. We rob banks." Bonnie begins to write, record, and spin her version of their exploits in poetry, eventually publishing "The Ballad of Bonnie and Clyde" in a newspaper.

"You've made me somebody," Clyde says, reading the published poem in wonderment. She has outdone him by effectively weaving a Robin Hood narrative of heroism and generosity that spins their crime spree into an identity-forging violence that is bigger than both of them. Clyde has sex with her. Bonnie's shooting and writing are transformative: they inspire her creativity and fuel Clyde's sexual power. Poetry, pleasure, celebrity, and violence intertwine.

The elated, cool violence enshrined in *Bonnie and Clyde* made film history and combined the war against authority with fun-loving tricks and sadistic play. The sexiness of the pair helped break the wall between film and reality. Dunaway's Bonnie created shooter chic as both a physical and verbal style in the real world. Violence as a female style could be adopted by fashionistas as a "look." As Hoberman notes, "*Women's Wear Daily* announced 'the hot shade for spring' is 'the gun-barrel gray of Bonnie's pistol'" (133). The March 1968 issue of *Harper's Bazaar* showcased "The Gangster Game" (132). On January 12, 1968, the cover of *Life* heralded "Bonnie: Fashion's New Darling" (132). The role made Faye Dunaway a sex goddess whose apotheosis was the cover of *Newsweek* (March 4, 1968). Writing in *The New Yorker* in 2003, Louis Menand commented that in France, Brigitte Bardot, whose film *And God Created Woman* had made her a "kittenish sex goddess," sported Bonnie Parker clothes, and sang "The Ballad of Bonnie and Clyde" on French television (177). *Newsweek* called Faye Dunaway "the first American actress to electrify the world's moviegoers since Marilyn Monroe" (Hoberman 132).

The normalization of violence as chic went much further. Tom Wolfe coined the phrase "radical chic" to describe the support of fashionable New York for the Black Panthers and the extent to which the women of the Panthers were defining styles that later surfaced in *Vogue*. In his essay "Pornoviolence," he announced that violence is always "wrapped up, simply, with status" (184). But status seemed to him to be conferred by the ability to adopt violent causes with the skill of a socialite's choice of accessories. Establishment and counterculture seemed joined in a celebration of shooter chic as the style that could kill the curse of boredom.

Strategies for vivid communication transcended any cause with stirring calls to self-expression. While the Establishment celebrated Bonnie as outlaw, the counterculture loved the look of an adorable woman advocating violence. Todd Gitlin writes that at the 1968 Students for a Democratic Society convention, Weatherman Bernardine Dohrn "picked up a national following " and "fused the two premium female images of the moment: sex queen and streetfighter" (386). Gitlin puts her first among those "hip outlaws" who "made revolution look like fun" and likened the faction to joyride violence: "one of [the] signers of their manifesto, Gerald Long, had raved about *Bonnie and Clyde* for the *Guardian,* likening the 'consciousness-expanding' outlaws to Frantz Fanon" (386). A woman with a rifle became a New Left pinup. Hoberman points out that the *New Left Notes,* June 26, 1967, had featured a picture on the cover of a "a smiling, rifle-toting "New American Woman" (134).

Elites and the counterculture shared a fascination with "pornoviolence" as the ground was laid for good-looking women to become celebrities of the bomb. Bernadine Dohrn was photographed by fashion photographer Richard Avedon. Susan Stern would write of her time in the Weather Underground and her involvement in the 1968 protests in Chicago at the Democratic National Convention: "I felt *good.* I could feel my body supple and strong and slim, and ready to run miles, and my legs moving sure and swift under me. . . ." Celebrity came from being with the movement's elite cadre. Stern wrote, "I felt I was part of a vast network of intense, exciting and brilliant people" and only grew with Stern's involvement in the trial of the Seattle 7 (Stern 23, 27, 87).

Display was a form of self-invention as well. Stern painted "an eight-foot-tall nude woman with flowing green blond hair, and a burning American flag coming out of her cunt!" She explained that she "had painted what I wanted to be somewhere deep in my mind; tall and blond, nude and armed, consuming—or discharging—a burning America" (243). More than serving only as objects of desire for men, women were defining themselves through images that exploited sexual metaphors as gross as a devouring or running "cunt" to depict politicized sexual rage in female terms.

Images of violent women have lasted. The heiress Patty Hearst would be immortalized as a seventies icon holding a machine gun. The young woman kidnapped months earlier by the Symbionese Liberation Army had joined up and reappeared as Tanya the terrorist, caught by the surveillance camera filming their bank hold-up. In 2001 the picture accompanied the announcement that President Clinton had issued a pardon for her 1974 bank robbery for which she had served two years in jail (*Newsweek*, January 29, 2001). Even Bonnie's celebrity has lasted, underscoring the mixture of violence, femaleness, and narrative as a path to "immortality." In June 2000 the actual Bonnie Parker's manuscripts were auctioned on the Internet; Clyde's hat, replete with bullet holes, sold for $8,000. The film script's authors, Robert Benton and David Newman, writing in *Mademoiselle,* had declared their own romance with Bonnie as "a pretty girl who was both tough and vulnerable, who wrote poetry and shot policemen, who loved life and courted death" (qtd. in Hoberman 132). They predicted this mixture would have an ongoing appeal. They had declared that "if Bonnie and Clyde were here today, they would be hip. . . . Their style, their sexuality, their bravado, their delicacy, their cultivated arrogance, their narcissistic insecurity, their curious ambition have relevance to the way we live now" (Hoberman 131–32).

THE VIOLENCE OF WOMEN
AND THE WAY WE LIVE NOW

Unruly violence has posed a problem for those seeking a clear political dialectic that would unify all outbursts of violence. Richard Hofstadter, in his documentary history of violence in the United States, reviewed outbreaks of violence throughout American history and concluded that our violence, lacking a coherent political thrust, "has been too various, diffuse and spontaneous to be forged into a single, sustained inveterate hatred shared by entire social classes" (3). The violence of women, long ruled out as a historically significant phenomenon, has, I believe, enormous importance in illuminating apparently anarchic unruliness. It tracks the straightforward tale of American triumphalism like a shadow of darker possibilities.

The violence of women correlates with the psychological and intellectual narratives that bring openness, multiplicity, and unruliness to center stage and are as much a part of American heritage as the mythic narratives of the conquest of the frontier that have attempted to unify all American violence in terms of the triumphal power exerted by men. Beyond those historical myths of conquest lie the master intellectual narratives of American thought and possibility that tell a tale of openness and change. Multiplicity, subjectivity, and the power of individual choice to shape truth are all of vital importance in shaping visions of the violent actions of women.

The paradigms of American thought that structure the multiplicity and subjectivity of violent action and belief are crucial. Violence by women brings American intellectual narratives associated with pragmatism, cognition, and individualism together with inventive language stressing subjective truths and portraits of will in action. The unprogrammatic energies of violence by women exploit those American traditions of individualism, will, and subjective truth and are discussed in chapter 6. They do so from the dark side, exploiting their mechanisms and travestying their goals at the same time. The condensation of sexuality, aggression and inventive speech by violent women in films, newscasts, literature, and popular culture is a dark tribute to a surviving faith in the individual's power to create and convey meaning.

The violence of women demonstrates a logic of radical personalization. By that I mean in part a method of communication that writes the narrative of politics or culture as a confession. This is a personalization that reflects not so much a recoil from social concerns as a refusal to perceive a difference between private and public issues. In narratives of the violence of women, the problem of personal and social agency is infused with the force and immediacy of a life or death choice. That immediacy produces far-reaching effects.

In the variety and urgency of its drive for selfhood, openness to self-concepts, and insistence on felt experience, the American literature of violent women constitutes an assault by realism on postmodern unreality and nihilism. Its destructive egotism serves as a weapon against the depersonalization of the individual as an illusion of language found in French representation theory. In skillfully crafted narratives of self-invention, the literature of violent women rejects views of woman as incapable of agency and self-depiction. It explodes the post-Marxist fetishism of women as merely receptacles manufactured by capitalism, that French mega-phallus. Against the depersonalizations of gender, meaning, and politics, the fiction of violent women uses the dark side of women's lives to recall us to the power of experience, circumstance, and language. Through seizure, appropriation, and the exploitation of stereotypes, the literature of violence uses the basic experiences of women's lives to forge "revisionary" narratives of change.

Narratives of violent women enable both a critique of abstraction and a critique of the material condition of women at the same time. American narratives of violent women turn French theory against itself by hurling explicit accounts of violence against abstract denials that death exists, and by exploiting interpretative strategies to manipulate both the self-images of women and how others view them. Such narratives draw on American traditions of pragmatism and its vision of the power of will. By doing so, they seize a native intellectual tradition, discussed more fully in chapter 6, that emphasizes individual will, interpretation, action, and subjective truth. Violent women ground narrative in extreme experiences. They claim agency over the narratives they weave according to their subjective will even as their violence provides an unmistakable impact on others. In doing so they may offer the testimony of a troubled and cynical time to the surviving importance of our intellectual and aesthetic heritage.

Violence restores dramatic realism to a discussion exhausted by the sheer abstraction of academic theory, by refusal to acknowledge a woman's individualism, and by an insistence on Baudrillardian unreality. The dramatic situations found in the chapters that follow open up the narrative of violence to a view of aggression as a spectrum of mediations between traditions of the helplessness or virtue of women and contemporary insistence on redefining women's roles. Such mediations may emerge in the violent woman's progression of impulses from revulsion at violence, to inhibition over it, to its performance. All culminate in the narratives woven to explain what has happened. The patterns of violence that emerge reflect not only a persistence of core issues but also a great and inventive variety in the narratives used to describe them. All of them employ sophisticated speech and self-portrayals to manipulate not only the scenario of violence but also its meanings and reception by the surrounding society. Doing so enables a view of narrative violence as relational, as a means of exploring the impermanent and oscillating poles of women's experience of themselves and others in a time of change.

Such a relativistic, relational, and affective focus helps shape the question: How can revolutions in private life, in the defining self-concepts of womanhood, and in such elusive qualities as the texture of emotional life surface in imaginative narratives and public discourse?

The truism of the past that the sustaining values of culture operate through the family to transmit norms is turned inside out by violent women. The chapters that follow describe violent women whose actions suggest something new and different: models of how negative personal relations can interact with and determine larger cultural themes. Their actions use violence within the family to rivet the attentiveness of a society fascinated by trash TV and crimetalk that magnify dysfunction. Violence is now the building block of cultural attitudes evident in civil society in the infotainment news, in reality TV, and in mass-market films. Just as narratives of violent women exploit a past that includes American pragmatism's traditions of volition to support change, choice, and will, so serious fiction offers a more complex revelation of changes in the affect and texture of experience.

Violence as a spectrum of feeling and action that affects self-concepts and relations with others, and mobilizes reactions from the community at large is revealed in the narratives violent women weave around what they do. They are masters of a communicative violence that continuously reorients their relationships within the family and with the larger social world.

Although inventing, manipulating, and weaving styles of speech are all characteristic of narratives of violent women, their use of language serves purposes larger than scripting specific acts of real or fictional violence. The stories they tell help define areas of cultural confusion and doubt. Interest in such narratives increases as our security and confidence about ourselves and our culture are threatened.

All the patterns of violence described in this book share three major elements: the affective, communicative, and interrelational. Each of these requires a way of understanding the consciousness of the violent woman and the ways in which violence begins to color her feelings, communications, and relationships. Portrayals of violent women reflect an oscillation between passivity and empowerment, self-despair and grandiosity that keeps them spinning between extremes of self-affirmation and self-doubt played out through changes within relationships and in self-image. Emerson described the mood swings of the poet-writer torn between grandiose self-confidence and self-doubt in his remark in "Circles," "I am God in Nature, I am a weed by the wall" (286). He captured his alternations of glee at writing well and despair over his inability to do so by adding, "I am the vast ebb of a great flow." Conjoining wordcraft and being, narrative invention and self-construction, and balancing oscillations between grandiosity and self-doubt on violent action, may characterize the psychology of the violent women in many of the fictions discussed.

Defining the poles of inflated and deflated self-concepts and depicting the effort to achieve poise and balance within oscillations between those poles are primary uses of creative narratives about aggression. The violent woman represents her acts through a series of self-initiated descriptions that invariably exploit preexisting idealizations, sometimes affirming female altruism, gentleness, or kindness. Through such inventive narratives, she defines and controls relationships with others. In their variety, the violent women of fiction, film, and media provide a complex view of violence as a relationship that may encompass a broad spectrum of personal and political interactions. Their verbal inventions create and control a sweeping world view even as they forge new self-concepts. They can use self-initiated, interpretative narratives with skill. Far from being simply antirational, such narratives engage in calculated language twisting in their effort to undermine old stereotypes of subordination or self-denial, to reorient relationships, and to displace self-effacing, self-destructive images of vulnerability.

Many representations of violent women reveal a close connection between self-destructive and destructive fantasies. In fiction, characters reveal suicidal or masochistic fantasies that can be used comically or ironically as part of a narrative of beating out and gaining control of an antagonist who needs to perceive them as willing, passive sufferers. For example, in the entertainments explored in chapter 5, fictional women and actual participants in rock festivals are sisters in playing violence games. Ironic and in control, a woman may script sadomasochistic sexual play so as to use the prospect of her masochism as an instrument of control over her sexual partner who might delude himself that he is actually the sadist in charge. Once the bait is taken, he may discover he is not. In these situations, often comically described, the stereotypes of female masochism are explicitly used to critique female masochism and male misogyny.

Exultant deceptions are an important characteristic of relationships under reconstruction. These may involve lying or dishonesty as a dominant feature of the personal relationships described. Violent women may use narrative skill to mask motivations, feelings, and deeds to redefine the nature of obligation and trust. This association of freedom with violent "dishonesty" is often elaborated as a triumph over the credulity of others but in the process also expresses a surpassing need for stable truths.

Grandiosity and violence go intimately together. Death is the largest aggressor, the one who always wins. Death is embraced as an ally in the fiction of destructive intimacy discussed in chapter 2. So allied, the violent woman may see herself in a unique interaction with destructive power. She can control it or treat it as an erotic partner, invoking a long literary tradition of love as an overarching, annihilating passion.

Images of ruthless violence by passionate women have surprisingly broad, popular appeal. Pop culture eroticizes female violence by using gorgeous women as combat figures. The lovers-from-hell roles created by Glenn Close in *Fatal Attraction* or by Sharon Stone in *Basic Instinct* have been followed by Lara Croft, once a videogame-cartoon figure, who became flesh in the role created by Angelina Jolie in *Tomb Raider*. Carrie-Anne Moss in black leather in *Matrix* and *Matrix Reloaded,* now stars in a *Matrix* videogame. There is a proliferation of television serials such as

Alias, Witchblade, Black Scorpion, Buffy, the Vampire Slayer, Xena, Warrior Princess, and *Dark Angel* in which beautiful women are violent action heroines who may also have superhuman powers.

Current cultural ideals of beauty include cool lethality. For example, pinups of earlier wars were intensely female, depicted as available for sex but not combat. Curvaceous Jane Russell and Betty Grable were succeeded as sex queens by the vulnerably soft Marilyn Monroe. Sex goddesses of the past have been obsolesced as the soldier's ideal. In *Channels of Desire: Mass Images and the Shaping of American Consciousness,* Stuart Ewen and Elizabeth Ewen describe a shift toward women as embodiments of the culture of violence through an interesting change in desirable body image.

Desert Storm, the first war with Iraq, saw a new kind of pinup. According to Ewen and Ewen, she was a woman named Jacqueline Guilbord whose picture in an ad for Wrangler jeans was "pasted all over the war zone. She stood, slim and lanky, attired in weathered denim, leaning against a police car; hanging easily from her hand, a carbine. Today's pinup was tough fit, cool, and lethal. Soldiers wrote to her, claiming, 'your picture is a constant reminder of why we are here.' In a photograph, fierceness and desire, a union forged by the culture of violence, had become the stuff that dreams are made of" (234 n. 16). Women represent a new "ideal of extreme muscle definition and express a bodily rhetoric of power, intrinsic to the culture of violence" (234 n. 16). The unique colorations women's physical power brings to the emergence of women as "action heroes" are discussed in chapters 5 and 6.

Violent women are embodiments of modernity defined as alarming and exciting change. Their depiction in fiction and media holds an enlarging mirror up to transformations in intimacy, family life, and citizenship. I hope that by probing representations of the major expressions of violence by women in contemporary fiction, I can highlight areas of ordinary turmoil. Their violence cuts new paths through structures of power, language, thought, and action. They are at once exploited as symbols of fear and venerated as symbols of purpose. Their very presence is a double-edged sword carving out dilemmas of both power and submission. When Adam Smith called women the moral educators of his nation, he never had that in mind. But in the power of violent women in literature, media, and films to reveal some dangerous truths, perhaps, ironically, they still are.

Deadly intimacy, child murder, terrorism, and entertainment violence—each lays the groundwork for the formation of patterns of violence discussed in chapter 6. What emerges is a retaliatory violence that rebukes troubled intimacy, a performance violence related to the deformation of traditional roles, a destructive egotism that skewers both conventional radicalism and exploits positive American traditions of individualism, and an identity violence expressed in self-transforming violence games. Each pattern overlaps with the others, but all suggest changing visions of power, language, and psychology revealed in passages of women from vulnerability to violence. The portrait of women's lives that emerges may provide a qualitative panorama of our lives with each other and an idea of the emotional texture of our culture. In the dramatic intensity and depth of fiction, in the interaction of the concerns of fiction with the media that constitute our civil society, I hope to provide a clear sense of the texture of a troubled time, encountering profound changes even in areas of domestic and public life that once seemed settled and secure. The distance from literal bloodshed provided by fiction makes it possible to understand as narratives events that might be insupportable as fact. Most of all, the contemporary writers whose pages vividly convey that turmoil establish the continuing power, immediacy, and frequent brilliance of American literary art.

The violence of women in contemporary literature is Greek tragedy without gods. From deformations of intimacy to political and entertainment violence emerge traumas to family, love, citizenship, and joy. All present cultural change as personal crisis. All reflect alternative interpretations of structures of power, meaning, and language. Gilbert Murray commented even of the starker contrasts of Greek tragedy that its dramas presented "no villains, no monsters—no one who has not some real point of view for us to . . . consider." Violent women, fictive and real, are usually villains, but they too speak from the dramatic vortex of experience in which crises of culture and character become one.

CHAPTER 2

LOVE ON
THE KNIFE EDGE
AND LETHAL FAMILIES

LORENA BOBBITT TOOK A STEAK KNIFE, CUT OFF THE PENIS OF HER SLEEPING husband, twenty-six-year-old former marine, John Wayne Bobbitt, drove off with it, and threw it from her car window into an empty lot in Manassas, Virginia in 1993. The subject of about two thousand news stories and countless jokes on late-night talk shows, Lorena Bobbitt became the poster girl for the retaliatory violence of woman. "In the last few weeks, the avenging wife has become a new media model, [noted] Debra Haffner, executive director of the United States Sex Information and Education Council. [She's] part of this idea of women standing up for themselves and getting even, getting theirs. Lorena Bobbitt has created a lot of fear in men'" (Kaplan 54–55). The twenty-four-year-old manicurist found supporters in her native Ecuador, where "a feminist organization threatened to castrate 100 American men if Lorena did any time (Kaplan 55).

Why did she do it? Lorena had complained to the police: "He always [has an] orgasm," she said, "and he doesn't wait for me to have an orgasm. He's selfish. I don't think it's fair. So I pulled back the sheets and then I did it" (Adler 51). On trial, charged with "malicious wounding" and facing a possible maximum sentence of twenty years, she invoked battered wife syndrome and insanity defenses, and claimed not to remember the act (Smolowe 45).

Her sobbing testimony, carried on CNN and Court TV, included extensive and mostly verifiable accounts of Bobbitt's repeatedly beating, choking, and abusing her since their marriage in 1989 (*Washington Post*, January 15, 1994, A1). She testified that she cut off his penis because he had raped her just before. In a *Washington Post* story, one onlooker hailed the not guilty verdict as "a landmark decision. This country is in a state of denial about wife abuse. Maybe this will open people's eyes" (January 22, 1994, A9). Another commentator hoped: "Not only would men be less likely to insist that women belonged in the kitchen—but men would understand just how horrible sexual abuse was" (Kaplan 54). Leaving the courthouse, Lorena was greeted with cheers and chants from sympathizers who shouted: "Lo-re-na" (*Washington Post*, January 15, 1994, A1, A12). News accounts reported "a carnival atmosphere. Satellite trucks lined the road, radio deejays hooted and hawked wiener lunches [and] penis shaped candles." T-shirts that said "Love Hurts," autographed by John Bobbitt himself, sold for twenty-five dollars a piece (*Washington Post*, January 22 1994, A9).

The differences between his testimony and hers were equally bizarre. Charged with and acquitted of marital rape, John Wayne Bobbitt claimed he had never hit or abused Lorena or used the "Marine corps torture techniques" she claimed he knew (Kaplan 54). He described an entirely different marriage in which he had done everything possible to make her happy. Bobbitt had benefited from Lorena's remembering where she had thrown his penis. Found by a fireman, it was rushed to a 7–Eleven to be iced and was later surgically reattached in a nine-hour operation. The wife of one of the surgeons credited with reattaching the penis was harassed in a Virginia beauty parlor because of her husband's success. But standing before a huge phallus on the *Howard Stern Show* on New Year's, Bobbitt only smiled. He had pocketed $260,000 for his appearance and seemed amused. *No harm done,* his smirk seemed to say. *I'm still laughing.*

Nonstop media coverage of Lorena Bobbitt's act was almost never devoid of snickers and puns. In a *Newsweek* story titled "Hanging by a Thread," a subtitled box, "The Long and the Short," gave the length of the steak knife, the distance Lorena drove, penis in hand (1/2 mile), and the length of the trial (three days) (*Newsweek*, November 22, 1993). Pundits seemed obsessed with the story that many considered the mark of a significant change in male-female relations it was best to defuse by laughter. *Newsweek*'s featured "Lifestyle" section boasted a picture of a button declaring "Lorena Bobbitt for Surgeon General." In the surrounding text, no less a legal scholar than the highly respected Stephen Gillers of New York University punned: " A case like this alters our reality. We don't know what to make of that kind of disconnect" (Kaplan 52).

Pundits agreed there might be "powerful symbolism . . . in Lorena Bobbitt's act," but they were divided on its meaning (*Washington Post,* January 22, 1994, A9). When Lorena was found not guilty by reason of insanity and released from a mental hospital after a few days, the *Washington Post* reflected the controversy in "Women's Groups Hail a Verdict That Makes Some Grown Men Wail," which quoted Tom Williamson, president of the National Coalition of Free Men, a men's rights group with about two thousand members, condemning the verdict as "condoning taking the law into your hands and going to any lengths—even jungle savagery, mutilation and brutality" (January 22, 1994, A1). Stephanie Williams, head of a women's support group, said, "there are many Lorena Bobbitts. The only difference is that the others have done nothing to retaliate" (January 22, 1994, A9). Was this, as law professor Susan Estrich claimed, "every man's worst nightmare and many women's occasional fantasy" (Adler 50)?

The Bobbitt case became a cartoon, revealing in primary colors and starkly explicit action the war between the sexes. Cutting off a man's penis and throwing it away dramatized in its sheer outrageousness the rejection of passivity as a female style. Such repudiations take two extreme forms. On the one hand, grotesque or obscene acts are used to break taboos and violate expectations of female decorum; on the other, domestic scenes are subverted so that the kitchen and bedroom are used as sites for attacking men. The sexual power of men is attacked by destroying its symbols; or the entrapment of women in the home is subverted by exploiting the domesticity of women for violent purposes. Male authority and female violence are invariably positioned against each other.

Violence by women in intimate or family settings is always antipuritanical and transgressive. Most violence by women occurs within the home and between intimates. The conjunction of the grotesque and the family brings edgy violence home as a destabilizing force. In serious literature, the elemental roles of wife, sister, mistress, or daughter mobilize mythic and allegorical relationships. According to Peter Brooks, such primal roles lie at the heart of melodrama. But more than melodrama's emotional overkill is at stake. Serious literature elevates the importance of those core associations of women not to enlarge but to contract the emotional scale of violence by making extraordinary violence seem as commonplace as a steak knife. Freud saw what he called the uncanny as the invasion of unexpected and unpredictable horror into daily domestic routine. Harold Bloom interprets such breakthroughs as catalysts for the literary imagination of disaster he sees as the "catastrophe theory of creativity." In the contemporary literature of intimate violence by women, conventions of male power provide the starting point for creative female violence.

How can women characters, once relegated to suffering or bearing witness to violence, emerge as players and perpetrators? Theoretical constructions of the "feminine" and their substitution for the experience and agency of women, described in chapter 1, have little to contribute to understanding how women can see the twists and turns of intimacy. The violence of women in intimate relations provides a road map. It carves out a pathway to self-transformation that begins in a harsh vision of male attitudes, of exultant misogyny. The personalization of the larger social and economic facts of the subordination of women finds expression in the use of intimacy to calculate the distance women must travel to reach the center of control. In this personalization of social concerns, the bedroom and kitchen are crossroads where individual experience and cultural themes collide.

Intimate violence moves to the fore when formal, cultural definitions of intimacy are in doubt. In the real world, 80 percent of violent offenses by women occur in the home (Goldstein 77). Representations in imaginative fiction make that disruption meaningful, using crises of the bedroom and family to illustrate how cultural confusion can register in crises of character and behavior. What does it mean to be a wife, husband, daughter, or lover now? Even as our public culture continues to maintain orderly processes in the political world, family and divorce courts harbor battles over the definition of the family and its practices. Although incidents of wife battering may fill the police blotter and remain far more prevalent than violence by women, what shapes imaginative representations of both real and imaginary violence by women is not their victimization but their staging a turnabout. Violence by women that invokes payback for its justification disrupts more than its target and inspires male fear. Complex, harsh, and innovative, the literature of violent women in intimate situations erupts from troubled intimacy but uses it as the fuel for wider exchanges of power between husband and wife, father and daughter, brother and sister, women and their lovers.

The anti-romance of violence by women is about self-transformation as a journey whose beginning is crucial. Violence against men is often claimed to be retaliatory. It is frequently scripted as payback for male abuse. Narratives describing it frequently begin with a celebration of female innocence and attentiveness to the behavior of men. Violations of innocence establish the most fertile ground for plots of retaliatory violence. Was every woman once Persephone, the guileless young woman kidnapped by Hades, Lord of the Underworld? Violent women in intimacy exploit the belief that every woman is Persephone and every man can be the Prince of Darkness.

Modern accounts of woman's retaliatory violence can only be understood in the context of those male provocateurs who do women wrong. Male malice grounds the violence of women in a culture of misogyny. The patriarchal discourses of postmodern representation theory that hold women perpetually silenced and immobilized are simply ideological justifications for male brutality, reinforcing the misogyny of Baudrillard's comment on the uses of female innocence: "Better than those women who climax are those who give the impression of climaxing, but maintain a sort of distance and virginity beneath the presence of pleasure, for they oblige us with the offer of rape" (*Cool Memories 1980–1985*, 6).

American domestic antagonists are generally considered those husbands and wives who have fought historic battles in the sexual wars traditionally described in terms of the victories of men. In 1965, Norman Mailer's *An American Dream* celebrated a new hero: Rojak, who murders the powerful, rich, and assertive wife who is the "armature of his ego" and immediately afterward buggers her maid. The slaying of the "Great Bitch" was seen as the epitome of every man's desired revenge on a difficult and successful wife; buggering the maid as his fit reward. The personal was declared political in a novel said to affirm the enduring power of every male chauvinist's right and every feminist's inevitable comeuppance. Yet it's clear that the book was not only a kinky bit of male propaganda in the sexual polemics of the time but also the first interesting exposure of how intimacy and payback could turn theft into the real crime of passion.

Mailer's *An American Dream* was about the greed of an envious male. Rojak's power as killer and sodomizer is triggered by rage at his passive dependency on the woman who has seemed his "one accomplishment." Rojak cannot tolerate his own envy until he appropriates its object. Like the Indian warrior of legend who eats the heart of the brave killed in battle to incorporate his strength, Rojak appropriates his rich and powerful wife's life to aggrandize his own manhood. Your death makes me! is the message sent by Rojak's murder.

Combat is the metaphor for sexuality in novels that see the connection between intimacy and violence as both an unavoidable fact of man's nature and as destructive as a world war. The penis and the V–2 rocket terrorizing London in World War II are metaphors for each other in Thomas Pynchon's *Gravity's Rainbow*. Psychological Operations officer Tyrone Slothrop is the focus of a team of experts in London who are struggling to discover the cause of human aggression and notice that German V-2 rockets have fallen precisely on places where Slothrop has scored with women. A map he keeps of his sex sites and the team's maps of bombsites are identical. Does sex attract the bomb, or do intuitions of destruction inflame desire? Does intimacy provoke death or death intimacy? The sex war and world war appear interchangeable.

Sexual rage is the eroticized edge of the legacy of the Vietnam War as well. Burnouts from that war live under the pressure of a broad perversion of trust and hope disclosed in Robert Stone's *A Flag for Sunrise*. An embittered anthropologist, Holliwell, who worked for the C. I. A. in Vietnam, is aroused by the very sight of a young nun engaged in a struggle for the rights of the poor and oppressed in a Central American country, modeled on Nicaragua, on the edge of revolution. His desire for her is a form of malicious longing to despoil her faith in goodness: "I will show you," he thought, "the war for us to die in, lady. Sully your kind suffering child's eyes with it. Live burials beside slow rivers. A pile of ears for a pile of arms. The crisps of North Vietnamese drivers chained to their burned trucks. . . . It'll kill her, he thought, drive her crazy. Her eyes were already clouding with sorrow and loss. . . . He began to fall in love with her" (299). His love is only eroticized nihilism: "He was the Adversary. Shown flesh, the Adversary eats; presented with inner space, he hastens to occupy it. The Adversary is a lover" (378). Seducing her and betraying her to the military authorities, he is responsible for her being beaten to death.

Murderous men became chic. Can violent intimacy be nothing more than a greedy form of male consumerism? Piling up a bodycount is the subject of Bret Easton Ellis's *American Psycho* in which the ladykiller about town is a yuppie whose other hobby is shopping. Ellis's Patrick Bateman murders by torture: he uses a nail-gun to pin a college girlfriend to the floor, dismembers some victims, keeps a severed head in his refrigerator, and kills one girl slowly by feeding her to a rat. But he rarely fails in label-driven style: "I'm wearing a Joseph Abboud suit, a tie by Paul Stuart, shoes by J. Crew, a vest by someone Italian and I'm kneeling on the floor beside a corpse, eating the girl's brain, gobbling it down, spreading Grey Poupon over hunks of the pink, fleshy meat" (328). The yuppie as cannibal, Patrick Bateman literally enlarges himself by feeding on this woman; she fuels his being. Ellis wraps the aberrant in commercial products; brand-name mustard and his upmarket bestseller each in their way domesticate disorder and lend it a stylish edge. Just when you thought this novel had sunk safely out of sight, it was resurrected as a film in 2000. Given so much literary violence against women, the justification for retaliatory literary violence by women would seem clear. The fiction and poetry of retributive violence is enormously varied.

"Get your cut throat off my knife": Diane Di Prima's one-line poem, "Nightmare #6," could be the battle cry of the "new" woman determined not to give an inch to what she calls in her "Prayer to the Mothers," "the metal men who walk / on all our substance, crushing flesh / to swamp." The most powerful woman poet among the Beats, Di Prima evolved an explosive language, as forceful as expletives, to describe violence as fit retaliation for disappointments or fears inflicted by men. But more than retaliatory violence is at work for women who strike back by using specifically female experiences as weapons. Di Prima's use of abortion is a case in point. In "Brass Furnace Going Out: Song after an Abortion," Di Prima's persona speaks to her fetus: "I want you in a bottle to send to your father / with a long bitter note. I want him to know / I'll not forgive you, or him for not being born / for drying up, quitting / at the first harsh treatment / as if the whole thing were a rent party / & somebody stepped on your feet."

Aiming for a cool, Olympian fury, Di Prima's poems nevertheless make it clear that violence is an intimate and complicated relationship in which the reversal of relationships within the family or between lovers invokes a relationship of catastrophic disillusionment. The aborted fetus in "Brass Furnace Going Out: Song after an Abortion" serves as a poetic symbol of male failure, a weapon against a feckless lover, and the price a woman is willing to pay for retaliation.

Can retaliatory sextalk be a form of public speech? Can it make the transition from the conceits of poetry to political rhetoric? In a world distorted by the perception that the urge to harm is genetically encoded in men and a biological fact, retaliatory violence by women can emerge as part of a seamlessly constructed world view in which the world is completely hostile, and self-protection and defense require striking back.

Violence by women in the real world is most acceptable when it is shown as payback for the violence of men. Easily justified against male predators, violence has legal sanction as self-defense and, not surprisingly, finds legitimating political narratives of self-protection. For example, in her feminist argument, *Against Our Will: Men, Women and Rape,* Susan Brownmiller declared all men were rapists. Twenty-five years later, Randy Thornhill and Craig T. Palmer in *A Natural History of Rape: Biological Bases of Sexual Coercion,* claimed rape is the genetic destiny of men. They had no problem generalizing human behavior from evidence gathered partly from studying the scorpion fly. Brownmiller, although accepting aggression as male destiny, denied that destiny makes women victims.

Brownmiller claims that women can counter their "conditioning" for passivity with training for war. She describes her own emotions on taking an intensive program in jujitsu and karate: "I learned I had natural weapons that I didn't know I possessed, like elbows and knees. I learned how to kick backward as well as forward. I learned how to fight dirty, and I learned that I loved it. . . . We women discovered in wonderment that as we learned to place our kicks and jabs with precision we were actually able to inspire fear in the men . . . we *could* hurt them" (403–404).

Retaliatory violence is a form of self-affirmation for Brownmiller, a recognition that helpless passivity is not the only option. Brownmiller offered her book as journalism and made a claim to documented truths. But it is also an interpretation of the anti-world of primal misogyny in which pathological behavior by men is to be expected and any form of violence by women is warranted. Her interpretation redraws the boundary between self-defense, which is condoned, and violence for gain or self-expression that is not related to actual self-defense. Violence and self-defense form an interactive, self-reflexive dance. Because all men are rapists, each man is presumably only a representative future felon, deserving of the most extreme retaliation or even a preemptive strike.

In a universe of men out to violate innocence, violence by women would be a rational choice. In the fiction of violent intimacy it is rarely a simple choice or one that pits a woman against her tormentor in a final showdown. Retaliatory narratives show a variety of devices for displacing rage, achieving distance from one's own emotions to exercise a cold power, and denying the acute humiliation and pain of victimization. In the process, tales of violent intimacy effectively revise traditional iconic images of woman as innocent victim.

Some accounts of violence by women work out a complex poetics of reversal in which qualities of trust and love, once celebrated to magnify innocence, are deliberately set aside. Innocence and trust are repudiated as the actual source of trouble. In the turnabout, that icon of innocence, the young girl, is reinvented. The iconography of the young girl as virginal Persephone in a field of wildflowers, epitomizing purity and gentleness, is entrenched in western literature. In the new literature of violence by women, it is inverted by an outrageous countericonography of the young girl as predator. Once the most romantic of victims, the young girl emerges in recent work as a perpetrator of terror engaged in attacks on conventionally assigned roles and boundaries in an adventure in self-definition.

The *jeune fille* as predator is represented as a consciously mobilized and calculating character whose self-fashioning occurs by tactical use of a process of serial inversions: trust reverses to suspicion, social expectation reverses to violation of norms, liberation of self is achieved by destroying formative aspects of self, victimization is inverted to victimizing. To achieve these inversions, the violent heroine reverses the narrative of violated innocence to one of willed determination to seize control. To accomplish this, genre-twisting and narrative-twisting techniques for imaging, symbolizing, and describing experience utilize language games to achieve shocking results.

An avant garde writer with a devoted following, Kathy Acker in *Blood and Guts in High School* brings us the new *jeune fille* in Janey, who "carried dangerous weapons and used them . . . and acted as outrightly violent as possible. Shitted on the streets. Attacked strangers with broken bottles. Hit people over the head with hard objects. Kicked the guts out of people on the streets. Started fights and riots. I could barely stand being so happy" [Janey said] (42). Janey's "happiness" is played out as a kind of street theater of transgression, a literature of disgust and violence as sweeping in imaginative power as it is painful in the harsh, obscene, and graphic inversions it produces.

The sexual wildness of woman, according to Acker, ranges from murder to bestiality and recasts mythic figures of odd sexuality into a world view based on the desire to invert expectations of sexual conformity: "One way: Clytemestra's addiction draws, or Cressa's: 'counterfeit wood monster bull cock fuck sex'" (114). Janey emerges from the western mythic tradition of female trangressors.

The edgy language-twisting of Acker's experimentalism carries into a linguistic and literary context themes that are also at work in the media driven "truth" culture of the trash-talk show where only aberration sells. The treatment of once-taboo subjects ranging from incest and prostitution to pornography ties this radical, extreme literature of violent women to the mainstream forms supported by the media and popular nonfiction. The epitome of transgression for the *jeune fille* is consensual incest. Although father-daughter incest in actuality generally involves the victimization and abuse of the girl, it is imaginatively projected in terms of the young girl's mastery of the sexual drive as purely manipulative or as a destructive tool. In this reversal, the daughter projects herself as the aggressor who knows the vulnerabilities of men.

Want to attack the patriarchy? Show that the emperor, or at least the patriarch, has no clothes! In the literature of transgression, a world view based on violence and disgust as core experiences prevails, making it possible to treat incest in a way that seeks to redefine it. Incest was the last sexual taboo until *fin de siècle* America adopted the truth culture exemplified by the incest memoir as a best-selling form. Kathryn Harrison's *The Kiss* provided a "real life" documentary of father-daughter involvement as a thermometer of family disorder. The difference was that rather than presenting the destruction of the daughter by her father, it titillated with soft-porn intimations of mutuality.

How much power over the patriarchy can be derived from undermining the father's capacity to destroy through the damage he can inflict on his daughter by incest? Can the daughter represent what has happened not as her victimization, but as *her* tactical use of incest to achieve power through sexual manipulation? Those bizarre calculations can be projected as cartoons that mock the seriousness of incest.

The patriarchy takes a hit in *Blood and Guts in High School,* when ten-year-old Janey's rock-star father, who is also her "boyfriend," is just another sex slave featured in cartoon doodles in her notebooks. Janey draws pictures of her father with an erection filling the page; another has him in sperm-soiled briefs. Knowing he has found a girlfriend and may want to "leave" her, "Janey fucks him" to try to reassert her control, "even though it hurts her like hell 'cause of her Pelvic Inflammatory Disease" (10). She includes a line drawing of her labia with the caption: "My cunt red ugh" (19). Externalizing and objectifying sex by treating it as a doodle drawn by a detached observer is an aspect of the need for dominance, the need to talk about "body slavery," but to be above it all by force of externalizing it as a "subject."

The school notebook, filled with obscene doodles of her father's genitals and her own, incorporates incest into the everyday boredom of a kid in math class and into ordinary routine. What used to be seen as the kind of self-erasing masochism imposed by a habituation to abuse is presented as Janey's self-creating, nonchalant recognition of the cost of doing business. The effort is to redraw, recast, and invert the experience of incest since childhood so that it appears an affirmation of her will. By seizing this cynical ground, the young girl strips the father of the position of powerful victimizer.

What would happen if a young girl, so victimized by rape and rejection that she becomes mute, grows up to act upon and express her rage? Another way to retaliate is to ally oneself with other victims of entrenched power, whether male or female, and to beat the power of the patriarchy at its own game. In the brilliantly crafted novel *Defiance,* by Carole Maso, brother-sister incest reflects not only the abuse of the girl child but a shared position at the bottom of social ladder where both are regarded as immigrant trash. Radical social defiance and shared exploitation replace the expected treatment of incest as the violation by an older brother of his eight-year-old sister. Rape is seen as a metaphor for power that can be leveled against either sex.

Bernadette and Fergus J. F. K. O'Brien come from an impoverished Irish American family in Boston. Fergus as a child is mocked for his inability to read and abused by a parish priest who beat him, broke his arms, and forcibly raped him. Fergus burned down the priest's church "to kill God" in his own attack on patriarchal power (118). He uses Bernadette sexually, giving her a ring to seal their "marriage" and telling her to remain silent about what has occurred. His act and request drive her into a childhood she will spend as a mute, refusing to speak at all and tearing out her hair. In doing so, she appears as much of an outcast as her brother. Yet she loves him as the only person who ever truly cared for her and joins him in hatred of established power. The heroine who passes from victimization to violence can emerge as an almost superhuman and calculating force. Milestones in her passage involve mastery of the deformation of sexual intimacy.

Prostitution provides a paradigm in some novels for inverting self-hatred and self-doubt into aggression. Prostitution can be represented as reversing power relationships, enabling the prostitute to see herself as exploiting male desire for her own gain. A woman may erase her individuality by selling her body, but she projects the self-hatred accompanying the experience in contempt for the john who pays. Prostitution in such fiction is inflated as almost a world view based on the prostitute's exploitation of sex. For example, Janey's forays into prostitution are made with a philosopher-pimp whose capacity to twist reason creates a logic for degradation and physical decay: "Disease and mental instability cause health. The men who have taken the most extreme risks, who have done what may have disgusted other people or what other people have condemned are the men who have advanced our civilization" (64). His views provide her with a logic that supports her transgression.

Prostitution as a world view requires a prostitute whose primary objects of disgust are the john, the patriarchal culture he represents, and the structures of privilege. Maso's Bernadette outdoes her dyslexic, dysfunctional brother by her qualities of mind as a brilliant mathematician and physicist and her potential for upward social mobility. At the age of twelve she is a homely and brilliant Harvard undergraduate who is a prodigy in physics but despised and ridiculed by the privileged young men around her who humiliate and enrage her. She realizes she can profit from the mixture of envy and revulsion she arouses in them. She becomes a prostitute, a "poor prop they used to ejaculate into . . . She started charging an ever-increasing fee. Let me tell you about a small silent auction. A minor prostitution ring, with yours truly furious and mute at the center. Come one, come all" (109). Rage and power surface in Bernadette's pleasure in charging her Harvard johns, and in destroying the pregnancies they cause. She enjoys her four abortions and discards the birth control pills she is given after each.

In the reversal of the young girl as a Persephone amid her wildflowers to field commander, subordination is only a stage on the way to dominance. To counter the force of social proscriptions against assertiveness, much less aggression, women characters run to the reverse extreme, adopting an inflated, grandiose view of themselves as the dramatic heart of disruption. Lady Macbeth's plea—"unsex me here!"—surfaces in the current theater of gender-bending violence when prostitution and homosexuality intertwine in a female literature of disgust. Language-twisting takes the forms of skewed rhetoric employing extremes of obscenity and eschatological speech. Genre-bending and gender-bending are used to produce effects that combine violence, obscenity, and extreme representations that take the iconic use of the prostitute to the limit.

Prostitution and revulsion at female subordination intertwine in *Up Your Ass,* a play written in 1965 by Valerie Solanas. Solanas is usually described as both a writer and a "streetperson." She became a counterculture celebrity when she shot Andy Warhol. She had sent her manuscript to him in the hope that he would make a film of her play. When he lost the manuscript instead, she retaliated with gunfire. Her play opened in San Francisco thirty-two years after it was written. The play's main character is a lesbian hooker, described by Judith Coburn as a surrogate for Solanas, whose interaction with drag queens and middle-class wives carries a message: "When I get on my knees, I get paid" (47). In the first act a glamorous "Cosmo girl" searches the street for turds she will use for dinner and tells a female panhandler, "The turd's for me. Everybody knows that men have much more respect for women who are good at lapping up shit" (Coburn 47).

Solanas, who previously wrote the *SCUM [Society for Cutting Up Men] Manifesto,* has "been taken up by punks; anarchists, and surrealists—who hate Warhol—as well as young radical feminists, gender benders and assorted fans of Kathy Acker and cartoonist Diane di Massa's homicidal lesbian terrorist" (Coburn 47). The play's all-woman cast appears "in male drag playing drag queens" (Coburn 47).

Gender-bending and circling from "male" to "female" carry another message besides the one cited by Coburn as a "send-up of heterosexuality." It speaks directly to the possibilities for the woman writer for whom smashing female icons, particularly the "Cosmo" girl of magazine-cover fame, sexual differences, and language may all coalesce. Obscenity is used to attack the idea of charm, over-the-top costuming challenges the notion of stylish beauty, prostitution mocks any compensation from sex but money, and the use of seduction to retain control ridicules the idea of female vulnerability. All are portrayed as instruments of self-affirmation. Not unlike some passages in Hubert Selby Jr.'s, *Last Exit to Brooklyn,* such efforts provide extreme examples of disgust as bitter tragicomedy.

Counterculture portraits of the artist as a young girl may invoke comparisons with a literature of nihilism and homosexual hardship. The vision of Acker's Janey echoes the *noir* vision of Genêt's *Our Lady of the Flowers*. In *Blood and Guts in High School*, Jean Genêt appears as the character Genet, a famous writer who meets and befriends Janey. He tells her a story about a young man who is so taken with the picture of a sailor who turned over military plans to the enemy that he goes to Tangiers in search of the sailor. Attracted to the sailor's treason as an act of "defying the populace," Genet says to Janey, "I know this Sex of traitors, deviants, scum and schizophrenics exists. They're the ones I want" (129). Genet reinforces Janey's own brutal vision by serving in the novel as an articulate and celebratory voice for nihilism, but Janey believes she outdoes Genet because he "does not know how to be a woman" (130). To be a woman you have to do more than "slobber" (130).

Homosexuality serves as metaphor for a spectrum of impulses that blurs clear distinctions between male and female and diverts attention from the war between the sexes. It focuses on resistance to conventional notions of sexual power or "the patriarchy." A spectrum of affinities between male and female homosexuals who want to defy the status quo provides aesthetic metaphors that break down sexual differentiation. Similar to the treatment of sex, speech, and violence in Shakespeare's portrait of Lady Macbeth, such metaphors use aggression and masochism as flip sides of each other. Lady Macbeth calls upon the rulers of night to "unsex" her, but she also demands of her husband that he prove his potency through murdering the fatherly Duncan and usurping his throne. The falling together of male and female in the thirst for power and her pleas to the "ministers of night" to "turn [her] woman's breasts to gall" place Lady Macbeth in the company of those whose language of sex, power, and violence uses verbal techniques that promote uncertainty and instability. Lady Macbeth breaks down under the pressure, unlike the play's "weird sisters" whose mastery of spells and verbal equivocations control what happens.

Language-twisting brings intense verbal energy and interest to intimate violence. Twisting communication achieves distortions of speech to mislead, support fantasies of power, and conceal the planning and perpetration of violence. Deceptive speech and prolongation of the process of planning and doing violence lend the quality of a thriller or a mystery to novels that are largely about sex. Established uses of speech are challenged by a violence used as a form of experimentation in style.

Acker's experimental style includes extreme fragmentation of time and language. The novel begins in the present and moves back toward ancient myth, dead languages, and unfamiliar alphabets. It attempts to universalize its message through a variety of lexicons and communicative forms ranging from obscene drawings of nudes, sexual organs, and pages of concrete poetry to visual symbols and foreign alphabets. Letters explode out of control of defined lexicons just as images leap from the page. Within the novel, syntax falls apart even as sexual cartoons are scribbled by the high school writer.

Obscenity is the simplest form of language bashing. It can break communication into an eschatological vision of life reduced to bodily wastes. For Acker's Janey, "Shit!" and "Fuck!" are more than verbal tics; they mark the equation of all the body's products with each other and all the individual's works with all his or her actions. Sexual fluids merge with the fecal flow in an eschatological vision of universal immersion in the body's processes of need, ejaculation, and elimination. Oral, anal, and genital sexual expressions also break down differences in sexual expressions or stages of development into an undifferentiated response. This process drives a "poem": "I don't know what or who's happening" is the title/caption for a page reading "puke googoo me yum shitshit shitface me" (106). By reducing speech to nonsense and relationships to body fluids, Acker's Janey levels the ground linguistically and denies other forms of differentiation. Male power is undermined by reducing male and female to the same eschatological flow, claiming sexual transgressions and exploitation are equally a choice, and either can serve as a bond in a hostile world. Acker buries such questions in this eschatological flow of language, style, and expression. All that is weak, retiring, or repulsed loses distinctness in the stream.

Obscenity and eschatology constitute only one way in which language is used to support the denial or inversion of power. Grandiose power can also be achieved by the use of language for the opposite purpose of cleansing violence of impurities of ugliness or emotion. By rendering it free of rage, violent, blood-and-guts episodes seem to achieve a pristine and intellectual quality far from eschatological visions or depths of disgust.

Descriptions of brutality can be woven from a precise and meticulous representation of violence as a rational choice expressed in logical, mathematical forms. For example, Joyce Carol Oates's novel *Marya: A Life* offers a heroine whose greatest fear is of losing control, of being like her mother who loses herself in drunkenness, anger, superstition, and ineptitude. Instead the more violent Marya describes herself as going "into stone" and studies techniques of intellectual argument. Similarly, Maso's Bernadette is beyond rage. She "is [always] outside it. All mind and violence, and nothing felt" (139). Maso's techniques for rendering her violent heroine's cold logic involve giving her an Olympian vantage point: "This perch in the trees from which I have told everything, all along. All the distance in me, always" (146). She has made a " vow to retain the upper hand, to never again relinquish control . . ." (146). A prodigy in physics who is a Harvard professor, she uses mathematics as a descriptive calculus of her progress toward killing two of her students and lovers. Dehumanizing herself and the objects of her violence, she uses algorithms for calculating the pace of her sexual dominance and murder of the students to reinforce a cold power.

Controlled violence and control of language are interchangeable in a literature that employs sophisticated narrative techniques to achieve portraits of women who craft and calculate their violence. In addition to the use of lexicons of both obscenity and intellectualization, language and rhetoric are skewed to lend violent intimacy a lyrical beauty. To counter the force of social condemnations of the ugliness of aggression, women characters can appropriate aesthetic claims of high, poetic tragedy. They may inflate or mythologize themselves as embodiments of legendary female figures—Medea, Medusa, Lady Macbeth, or, in the American grain, Lizzie Borden.

Merging with the larger-than-life destructiveness of mythic female ancestors is necessary for a violence perpetrated not only to attack a specific target but also to achieve an omnipotent triumph over all the forces of convention and inhibition arrayed against the violent woman. The struggle with inner inhibition and the forces in the outer world—dependency, poverty—that underpins the subordination of women also serves to support a tragic vision elevated by grace and beauty of statement to lyric poetry.

Communication-twisting involves a use of language to seduce the reader into accepting nihilism as a form of chilling beauty. Violent and disgusting acts are so beautifully conveyed as to erase the capacity to determine their intrinsic ugliness or to perceive moral distinctions between right and wrong.

Bernadette invokes, along with her family's low immigrant status, an ethnic Irish heritage of great poetry. Maso brings high romantic lyricism into her novel through allusions to Yeats's "Crazy Jane Grown Old Looks at the Dancers." The poem describes two lovers killing each other:

When she . . .
Drew a knife to strike him dead,
I could but leave him to his fate
For no matter what is said
They had all that had their hate;
Love is like the lion's tooth. (299)

The poem eroticizes violence as intrinsic to love, an unavoidable aspect of intimacy that can be celebrated along with passion. "Did he die? Did she die?" are questions the poem will raise but never answer because the outcome is less relevant than the celebration of love in all its passions. But Yeats's poetic conceit in this poem comes true with a vengeance in the literature of violent women.

Through murder, the woman committed to violence enacts a drama imprinted with her effort at self-discovery and self-description. The need to create oneself as larger than life, to write in blood a tale of one's own triumph, converts murder into a demonstration of both power and definition. Maso's heroine defines herself as controlling both life and death: she sees herself as virtually death incarnate. She has fantasies of reunion in death with her brother, Fergus, who died in the army and who speaks to her from beyond the grave. *Defiance,* written in form of a memoir on death row, celebrates love and destruction as interchangeable.

Poetry again provides an aesthetic vision of death for Bernadette as well as romantic support for her fantasies of reunion. In her *liebestod,* a mixture of rage at own violated childhood and longing for her brother Fergus enables her to see him allied with the power of death. Invoking Yeats's "Who Goes with Fergus?" she associates her brother with Yeats's beautiful evocation of a mythic Fergus who is a reassuring and transcendent force. That mythic figure relieves her of the torment of "hopes and fear," or even of dwelling on the anguish of love, because Fergus is all-powerful and "rules the shadows of the wood," the seas, and "all disheveled wandering stars" (49).

Ethnic, class, and personal trauma meet in Maso's interweaving of the poetry of death's transcendence with all earthly terms of victimization, rape, ethnic oppression, and sadism. In the radical personalization of all forms of subjection, sexualized murder is the final term.

Maso uses Bernadette's narrative of violence to bring together varieties of language manipulation. Bernadette's exploitation of poetic metaphor is balanced by her use of mathematics to describe an unavoidable calculus of stages of degradation, integrating algorithms in her plan. The calculation supports a vision of sex as pornographic staging. In that drama her timing and the calculation of sequences and effects are underpinned by scientific accuracy. She stages murder as a sequence of sadomasochistic role-playing games ending in a climactic, snuff-porn scenario.

Pornography is a form of language-twisting that can turn lyricism into obsession, eroticizing power and control as pleasure. Bernadette twists communications with her student victims into mind/body games of authority, dominance, enticement, and seduction. Her position as professor of physics, her understanding of both mathematics and forbidden erotica, and her lust to kill equate seduction, calculation, and murder and are represented in the novel by algorithms as well as romantic lyricism. Added to this mixture is her class anger. Those physics students who come from the WASP aristocracy are designated victims. Bernadette reverses conventions of sexual and class domination, of male to female, ethnic outsider, and entrenched establishment, by being the brilliant Irish American from poverty who humiliates students she sees as emissaries from American elites. She controls their minds through their bodies, seducing them into craving to be controlled. She imposes physical discomforts: she orders them not to urinate before class, prevents them from leaving to do so during class, and insists they must accept her control as essential to learning physics.

Heterosexual and homosexual sex intertwine representations of a personal physics of pornography obsessed with both the mechanics of sexual control and the staging of theatrical games that destabilize distinctions in age and sex. Just as her victimization by incest unsettled the relationship between child and adult, so stages of sexual development collapse into each other in a confusion of anal, genital, and oral encounters that ensnare her students at every point. Bernadette enacts her sexuality as a manipulation that both arouses desire and withholds contact. Sheathing her body in a latex jumpsuit and her hands in latex gloves, she both excites and attracts young Alexander's desire, denies him touch, and forces him to lick her breasts without real contact in an eerie recapitulation of an infant's futile nursing. Her latex body condom expresses an implicit refusal to let contact, much less penetration, infect her body with the poison of another's touch.

Controlling the mechanics of pornographic repetition, Bernadette stages sexual situations, using costumes and role playing to turn her rich, brilliant, and adoring student into someone who derives pleasure from his own pain, degradation, and silence. A magnet for her class anger and an object on whom she reenacts the violation she experienced as a child, Alexander undergoes various forms of humiliation—he is hooded, dressed up as a dog on a leash, made up and costumed in drag, tied up, handcuffed. Aroused and rejected, he craves submission as she depersonalizes and uses him as ruthlessly as she was used by her brother in the tree house where he raped her and later as a twelve-year-old prostitute who was a "doll who . . . had all the power" (109). Alexander, Bernadette claims,

> begs to be suitably costumed, armored, regimented, strapped, masked, sanctioned. He wants blackouts. He wants feathers or ball bearings or bells, a high fashion of lace and leather, gauze and foams and party hats. . . . He loves to be told, to be arranged, to be configured into positions for maximum tension and resistance . . . bedecked and feathered.
>
> He loves the game . . . the ceremonies of semen and blood. Tree house. Accomplices in this grim task of pleasure—Comeback, my dove, come back. Forbidden worlds open. He begs to be exploited. Ruined. As he has

exploited. As he has ruined. . . . He says in the last eloquence on the day of the night he shall perish: sputters in the smoldering air—"*take me to the edge tonight.*" (195–197)

Poetic allusions to "Who Goes with Fergus" and "Crazy Jane Grown Old" are twisted by their use as aesthetic cover for the explicit mechanics of sexual degradation. The novel uses communicative forms ranging from poetry, to algorithms, to pornographic sadism as deceptive and inventive equations of all terms of power. Retaliatory violence for what she has suffered emerges as Bernadette's driving motive for murder. Yet her target is not anyone who wronged her but someone from the despised world of privilege who is drawn to her and to all he was raised not to be. Alexander's innocent faith in her love for him seals Bernadette's power.

Reenacting the violation of unsuspecting innocence as a predator and humiliating a son of privilege she despises, Bernadette redeems her sexual and social victimization.

In the murder of Alexander, whose abjection she associates with the purity of his "extraordinary heart," Bernadette repudiates both feeling and innocence: "Somedays I think I'd like to remove his guts and blood, everything but the heart. Have him perfected. Mindless finally. Stuffed and stopped in fondest position: on hands and knees. Turned inside out" (197).

Bernadette captures the media spotlight. The explicit detail of her snuff scenario slakes the media's thirst for bizarre and brilliant images. Class war, sex war, inversions of sexual roles, elaborate costuming, and the offbeat, surprising status of the murderer—a brilliant, Harvard professor whose victim is a gifted and wealthy student in drag—have star power. Bernadette becomes a celebrity for staging murder, but also for refusing appeals of her death sentence. Like Gary Gilmore who demanded to die, and Timothy McVeigh, who gained added attention for demanding or exalting execution as a proof of heroic leadership, she uses death seductively and coercively in her scenarios of "blood and semen." She forces the state into complicity in her *liebestod,* her suicidal fantasy of power, reunion with Fergus, and control through death.

An alliance with death as the most powerful aggressor is achieved through using the resources of language to equate power with killing or dying. Literary romanticism, with its oceanic sense of reunion beyond the grave, inventive scenarios of violent sexuality, and media chatter, with its fervor for celebrity killers and the explicit details of their crimes all combine to ensure Bernadette's death grip on aesthetic, sexual, and public discourse. Moreover, the very form of *Defiance*—it is written as Bernadette's memoir before her execution—extends her control even further. The memoir form enables a personalization of all the novel's themes, ranging from ethnic and economic discrimination, to gender-bending and bias, to class anger and the retaliatory potential offered by upward mobility. Bernadette revolts against her own sexual degradation by humiliating and murdering a WASP aristocrat.

What normalizes extreme, bizarre equations between love, social interaction, and murder is the power of women writers to sexualize every aspect of human conflict and develop immediate, personal metaphors for abstract conditions. Poverty and rage at social disparity are eroticized by both Acker and Maso. Acker's Janey accuses President Carter of sexual crimes and violence as part of her "attack" on patriarchy. Maso's Bernadette uses sexual violence as a political attack against the Establishment's privileged son.

Representations of violent women underscore the personalization of political animus which is discussed at length in chapter 4. Each relationship seems to replicate in its interactions all the despised prescriptions of established power or patriarchy. Women novelists like Acker and Maso treat the violence of women as a large, tragic theme, capable of shaping experimental forms. Incorporating visual elements and borrowing and transforming literary allusiveness, both writers experiment with techniques such as fragmented narrative, the incorporation of other literatures or, in Acker's case, languages. Ethnic subordination, child abuse, and the plight of an underclass of street kids and runaways are expressed as sexual violation by incest and countered by a complex orchestration of narratives of denial and displaced but retaliatory violence.

The heroine as an *übermädchen*, an archcriminal beyond ordinary notions of good and evil, surfaces in A. M. Homes's novel, *The End of Alice*, in which a young woman college student becomes fascinated by the horrible rape and decapitation of a girl named Alice on the street where she lived

as a child years before. Here the justification for her fascination and decision to become a sexual predator herself is resentment at all restrictions.
Her parents, fearful that the vicious pedophile might strike again during
her childhood, had kept her under virtual house arrest until the killer was
caught. Her ambivalence about the prison house of safety is expressed in
her obsession with both Alice's death and the psyche of the killer; she becomes entrapped in his mind and in his prison life. She becomes his pen
pal and stalks him in Sing Sing as best she can from outside to observe his
daily routine, yet she also stays in the same motel room in which Alice was
killed years before.

Is violence a resolution of ambivalence about the life of risk and the
claims of safety? Homes's heroine expresses her own ambivalence about the
death of Alice Sommerfeld by deciding to become a predator herself. She
rapes and humiliates a twelve-year-old boy. The heroine displaces her rage
at restriction onto a violation that expresses her desire to escape norms of
decent behavior and the confines of femininity. To do so she allies herself
with a malignant aggression that honors no limits. The public sphere for
her is swallowed so entirely by personal, violent fantasies of control that she
colors the world around her with her private obsession, convinced that the
only way to avoid victimization is to victimize.

Another way to break the wall between public and private is to treat
both as a joke. The snickers, puns, and jokes that shaped the descriptions
of the arrest and trial of Lorena Bobbitt are matched in serious literature
by the disputes of policy and law as carving out a comedy of bad manners.
Characters mimic the controversies enshrined in political movements per-
sonalizing every issue. Comedic violence about the retaliation of women
raises the question: is modern politics always personal, always about personal destruction? The treatment of retaliatory violence can be presented
as a joke in which the aggressive woman is the furious but silly force who
has wrecked every stable value with feminist demands. The push for
women's rights and liberation is presented as an ironic joke, the backwash
of a once vibrant liberal culture. Violent women can be represented from
the perspective of cultural decline often attributed to that constituency
identified as the "angry white male."

Men who hate contemporary America and confuse it entirely with women found a vivid target in the Equal Rights Amendment, which summed up for them everything from the destabilization of family life to the claims of all minorities for equality. Ironic comedy shapes the only fictional representation of the dispute over the Equal Rights Amendment. From a conservative perspective, the very idea of legislating the equality of women is an absurdity—a product of the decline of public issues and a degeneration of values that inflames a fight to the finish.

John Gardner, a medievalist, is one of the few American novelists who invokes the old faith that "except in the life of a hero, the whole world's meaningless" and explores what happens when the hero's antagonist is his sister and their combat is over the Equal Rights Amendment that challenges his ideals of masculine heroism. Gardner's darkly comic novel, *October Light* searches through the operative myths of national greatness for a surviving American heroism rooted in those Anglo-Saxon certainties that shape a Vermonter's world view. Sally, an eighty-three-year-old feminist and James, her seventy-year-old farmer brother, mirror two heroic strains in the American consciousness; the one intoxicated by progress, the other devoted to the land and deriving its values from the endless repetitions of nature. Belief in progress and change and willingness to work the land together opened up the American wilderness. Have they diverged into radically different and mutually destructive male and female cultural and political stances?

Gardner's brother and sister are old-time individualists caught in the sexual warfare of modern America in which "angry white men" are considered a voting bloc. James's life with his widowed sister intensifies his certainties: "He knew the world [was] dark and dangerous. Blame it on the weather. 'Most people believe,' he liked to say, 'that any problem in the world can be solved if you know enough; most Vermonters know better' . . . He'd had one son killed by a fall from the barn roof, another—his first born and chief disappointment—by suicide. He'd lost, not long after that, his wife . . . he was better than most men at taking [death] in stride . . . he understood what with stony-faced wit he called 'life's gravity,' understood the importance of admitting it, confronting it head on, with the eyes locked open and spectacles in place. . . . All life—man, animal, bird, or flower—is a brief and hopeless struggle against the pull of the earth" (10–11). The flowering of his fatalism is his antifeminism.

Sally rebels against the pull of her fate, her age, her sex. This WASP as Yankee princess has never had children; instead she has traveled with her generous, quiet husband, tried her hand at business, and become a Democrat in a Republican family. But she feels cheated, resenting her lack of sexual opportunities, her husband's silences, and the weight of everything she hasn't done. She is in love with the action-packed world that is now available to her only on her color TV. Finding her infatuated with its values, James shoots the TV through its glassy face. When she defends the Equal Rights Amendment, James grows furious and chases her up to her room with a stick. There she stays to assert her inalienable right to free speech. James rigs up a gun in a web of string to fire on Sally if she leaves her room. Sally rigs up an apple crate to fall on James if he comes into it. Heroic in their determination not to lose to the other, they are willing to fight to the finish.

Entertainment violence, discussed at length in chapter 5, reinforces the irreconcilability of their interests and, in *October Light,* represents the degeneration of public discourse. Locked in her room reading a commercial thriller, *The Smugglers of Black Soul's Rock,* Sally finds even her plight is perversely reflected in the novel she reads. Intertwining with *October Light,* the thriller holds a distorting, fun house mirror up to it. It reverses the relation of the reader to art. Once the reader whose life was anger and compromise looked for fictional heroes great and firm enough to take him out of his smallness. Sally, whose flintiness is on the grand scale, finds herself consuming a fiction of marijuana smugglers whose only value is self-interest and whose misogyny never rises above low-level antagonism.

Gardner's defense of maleness rests on his faith that men have been losing out to the aggression of women since the primitive hero entered the age of the Christian knight only to be tamed there and rendered ripe for eventual destruction. Heroism there depended on a chivalric code that demanded the great-hearted man be capable of a worship of woman as the helpless creature his might must protect. Love as service to a lady, power as a tool to protect the weak, charity, and free-flowing generosity are ironically etched by Gardner in the devotion of the Sunlight Man (in his novel *The Sunlight Dialogues*) to the sweet, gentle woman he marries only to find she is crazy, violent, and convinced of her own omnipotence. As he labors to save her from madness, she burns his face and destroys his career. Henry Soames in the beautiful novel *Nickel Mountain* is a big-hearted man who marries a young, pregnant girl, cares for her, and loves her child as his own. But this modern Joseph has heart trouble and eats himself to death as he is displaced from his business by his wife. Coming of age, she turns out to be an ambitious businesswoman. The knight of chivalric charity finds himself done in by his own mythology of the helpless princess. In defending the Equal Rights Amendment, Sally champions all the forces James feels have defeated men and made "trouble" into law.

Sally is mocked by Gardner as the silly old woman whose best ideas come from the evening news. She is Gardner's example of the American woman as force and fury, the powerful, controlling principle hiding in liberal tolerance, political correctness, and instant sympathy for the underdog. Through her, Gardner trivializes the values of the America she represents and elevates misogyny into an attack on the United States of assaultive femininity.

Gardner's angry men feel displaced by women in the new America. The smuggler Captain Fist in Sally's thriller has only two choices: "to turn on [women] and on everything that reminded him of them with rage and scorn, or accept them, be swallowed up like the rest of us in effeminate softness and confusion—give into a world so feminized that revolutionaries with slogans of death and home-made atomic bombs are softly analyzed, generously understood. Imagine a whole planet of big-boobed girl Congressmen" (380–81). James Page, raising his gun to kill a bear, thinks he hears the bear speak in his wife's tearful voice, "Oh, James, James," and shoots above the bear, wrecking a lifetime of shooting to hit the mark (434). Unlocking his heart, the female voice wrecks his "manliness" and makes him vulnerable.

Violence as comedy is treated with far greater nuance by women writers. With a light and witty irony, they convey how it feels to be caught in the crossfire of urges, deciding whether to kiss or fight. Ambivalence about violence can be projected in the choice of a woman poised between directing violence outward or against herself. Comedic portraits show women who are conflicted over whether to maximize or minimize aggression, or concerned that if they unleash their rage, they will lose control of it. A witty treatment of destroying one's own aggression as a vamp, a woman on the make, to achieve peace by forgoing the hunt for men can be found in Daniela Gioseffi's poem, "My Venus Fly Trap is Dying." Gioseffi uses a surprising, "botanical" image of the *vagina dentata*. The poem concludes:

> But this Venus Fly Trap
> is too much for me.
> It will have to die
> tossed into the waste can
> with the bright red lipstick,
> the blood red nail polish
> I no longer wear.
> This Venus Fly Trap doesn't
> photosynthesize peacefully
> It's trying to become an animal
> and I
> trying so hard to be a tree
> can't bear it.

The ambivalence described by Gioseffi with wit and charm has a dark, ironic counterpart in an oscillation between aggression and suffering. Extreme and tragically violent fiction annihilates suffering with violence. Comedic fiction balances less severe versions of both impulses in irony.

Women on a seesaw between overt violence and chronic self-destructiveness play with the oscillation by focusing on its visible signs and artifacts. Vamp lipstick and clothes, obscenity or proper speech reflect alternations short of murder. Maso's Bernadette, tearing out her hair as a child, rendering herself bald and refusing to speak at all, violates the grooming and deportment that would make her acceptable. This kind of self-punishment seems to enable a sense of control over the violent forces such women see as the hostile universe surrounding them and evident in all the abrasiveness of others whom they cannot subdue. By harming themselves before others might, they seize control of the hostility they feel surrounds them. Sadomasochism expresses a vision of oneself as both abused and abusive; through self-victimization, one assumes control of the process and identifies with the aggressor. For such women, masochism is an expression of guilt; sadism is an identification with the aggressor.

Identification with the aggression of men and guilt over their own combativeness toward men often lead women to punishing violence against other women. The desperate struggle for control and power evident in both traditional and experimental narratives finds a corollary in the emphasis on emotional control and the adoption of contempt for other women.

Violent intimacy is often depicted by probing ambivalence. Some heroines hate women who lose control while identifying with them as women subject to the same pressures. The result is often a troubled misogyny in which it seems essential to break down the relationship to other women. This often occurs in stages: in the first, the need to gain control is emphasized. In the second, one attacks other women who are victims or who have retaliated against men in self-destructive ways.

The primary mechanism for emotional control over ambivalence is intelligence. Joyce Carol Oates's *Marya: A Life* shows the genesis of a woman whose aim is self-mastery. The first step in a woman's quest for dispassionate logic is often rejecting the emotionalism exemplified by her mother. Marya's childhood was spent amid drunken talk among her father's friends and her mother's brutalizing rage, drunkenness, superstition, and inability to take charge of herself and her children. After her father is murdered in a labor dispute and her mother abandons her, Marya lives with her uncle's family where she is sexually abused by her older cousin. While that is consistent in this literature with accounts of early violation that provide the justifying narrative for violence against men, Marya deals with her sequential hardships by increasing her control over her own emotions and attacking other women who lack self-discipline.

Post-feminist portraits of violent women provide positive and negative images of one's own emotional identity as a woman among other women. For example, as a young woman Marya becomes an amanuensis to a dying priest from whom she learns philosophic dueling: "To be able to argue so powerfully . . . she wonders if it is an entirely masculine skill, an art of combat by way of language, forever beyond *her.*" She quickly surpasses the priest and her association of intellect with maleness. She builds a professional life on intellectual argument and polemics and successfully outwits men in professional confrontations. It is only other women who remain able to provoke uncontrollable emotions in her. Angered in college by another girl whose wealth and looks inspire envy and whose beautiful earrings Marya has stolen, Marya simply floors the girl with her fists when she demands her earrings back. As an adult, Marya punishes other women by having affairs with their husbands. The acquisition of men and what she once believed a male intellectual style substitutes acts of appropriation for direct confrontation with other women.

Violence in intimacy is often layered and complex, using male-female relations as the occasion for scripting violence between women. A narrator who tells of a woman's killing of her lover tells the tale of the crime, but in doing so she may provide a portrait of her own ambivalence in how she deals with the female killer and her male victim. In the process, the narratives the writer and the killer each weave about the same crime can provide a stark account of generational change.

Accounts of real crimes dramatize the changes in manners and mores that pit women against each other in values. One woman's use of her own intellect against another woman who has murdered provides a measure of how the war between the sexes affects people of the same sex whose disappointments in men might be comparable but whose retaliatory tactics have differed. The treatment of violence in literary narratives of actual crimes reveals a mingled attraction to and revulsion at violence on the part of women who, in different ways, have experienced men as a hardship. The disapproving narrator of another woman's crime story may serve two functions. She is the voice of traditional female morality, understandably outraged at violence, but also personally upset and intrigued by a younger woman who was not content with mere complaint and who struck back. Her account may reveal the attitudes of an older generation of women whose resentments, however great, were kept in check and expressed covertly.

The reporter-writer as player in the narrative of crime shapes the life of the criminal and her victim by her own interpretation. Diana

Trilling's *Mrs. Harris: The Death of the Scarsdale Diet Doctor* pitted the life and mind of Mrs. Trilling against those of Mrs. Harris. It was not entirely surprising that Mrs. Trilling chose the crime as the subject of her first book in years. When Jean Harris was tried for killing her lover, the Scarsdale Diet Doctor, sparks flew from a gallery of women journalists whose company Diana Trilling joined each day in court as an emissary of high literary culture. Not since the Charles Manson trial had exposed the violence of Leslie Van Houton, Susan Atkins, and her girlfriends, who exulted in murdering the pregnant Sharon Tate, had a murder case so captured the imagination about what women could do to and for each other.

The case became a magnet for both antifeminist and feminist advocacy. It was, after all, not too distant from the time at which violence by women, justified by self-defense, was creating a new kind of pioneer heroine. Joan Little, a black woman imprisoned for robbery, had won fame in 1977 for stabbing her jailer to death as he tried to rape her. That year, in Michigan, Francine Hughes had responded to years of her husband's abuse by saturating his bed with gasoline and setting it afire while he slept. Each woman had been acquitted; each had become emblematic of the refusal of rape victims or battered wives to remain passive victims. As the "aging" mistress about to be displaced by a younger woman, Jean Harris, the elegant fifty-six-year-old headmistress of the Madeira School in Virginia, on trial for the murder of her sixty-nine-year-old lover, Herman Tarnower, seemed to bring that spirit of revolt to the world of privilege.

For many who followed Mrs. Harris's trial, the question of her guilt or innocence was less important than the legitimacy of what had happened to Dr. Herman Tarnower. Mrs. Harris seemed to stand for those women who no longer wished to bear passively and decorously the psychological tortures of abandonment. Could she do for the emotionally battered what had been done for victims of physical violence? Would a jury view her confusion as compassionately as it had, in the celebrated cases of Little and Hughes, the desperation of the disadvantaged? Elegant, slim, and articulate, would she be every older woman's champion against those aging husbands and lovers on the prowl for trophy bimbos?

On trial, Mrs. Harris outraged such expectations. Her apparent refusal to permit her lawyer, Joel Aurnou, to voice any criticism of her lover, her avowals of love for Tarnower, her denial of jealousy, her arrogance, her preference for self-dramatization over her own freedom: all made it clear that she was far more complex than a standard-bearer ought to be. Inspiring a dozen books, Mrs. Harris led readers into a labyrinth of the confused mores of the time and a chorus of women writers who each wanted something different from her. The conflict between generations was evident in the opinions of women who as writers sat in judgment on her. Would the sexual forbearance of one generation collide with the overt violence of another? Would women who had harbored grievances silently or saved revenge for nonviolent retaliations speak up? Generations of women seemed to march into court with Mrs. Harris, including those matriarchs who were well-married, filled with a certain conviction about sexual attachment and social climbing, and who saw Mrs. Harris as a troubling mixture. When Mrs. Trilling, the celebrity literary critic, produced her judgment of the newly minted celebrity criminal, what sparks would fly?

Of the books about the case, none was more magisterial than Diana Trilling's *Mrs. Harris: The Death of the Scarsdale Diet Doctor.* The product of her assiduous attendance at the trial, the book provided such a startling sifting of fact and emotion about Harris and Tarnower that it represented most clearly the condemnation of one woman by another. Trilling's journey through the maze of Mrs. Harris's life and her own bitter severity both became evident in the story of Mrs. Trilling's assent, offered and withdrawn, as she measures Mrs. Harris against the evidence and tries her in the court of her own ideals. Mrs. Trilling's Harris and Tarnower were lovers fueled by ambition, taking their ethic from the American dream as they helped each other climb the social ladder. She saw Jean Struven Harris as a lovely Episcopalian from a modestly situated Cleveland family that, impressed by her energy and ability, sent her to the best private schools. Graduating from Smith *magna cum laude,* Jean Harris married a man of modest means, had two sons, divorced, and supported herself and her children as a teacher, headmistress, and executive before becoming headmistress of the Madeira School, where she was known, not without affection, as Integrity Jean.

Herman Tarnower, a Jewish boy from Brooklyn, was the son of an Eastern European immigrant. He graduated from Syracuse University in a six-year program leading to a doctorate in medicine, specialized in internal medicine and cardiology, and established a practice in Westchester in the 1950s. There, Mrs. Trilling says, he "fixed his eye on the German-Jewish social peaks" at whose apex was the Century Country Club. Alone, he determinedly made a fourth at bridge at the home of wealthy German-Jewish widows, but "with a charming Gentile like Mrs. Harris at his side his continual social advance must have been assured." In turn, Jean Harris, who had moved among but was not of the circles of WASP privilege, found a place in the company of sophisticated, affluent Jewish couples. "Mrs. Harris was able to be of great social usefulness to Tarnower even while she was made to feel what was entirely so, that it was Tarnower who opened the social doors for her."

Mrs. Trilling writes from an Olympian point of view above the struggle for social advantage. Her perspective was that of a respected critic of formidable harshness toward what she regarded as cant. She also wrote as the wife of the celebrated scholar, Lionel Trilling, and assumed the mantle of his Claremont Avenue intelligentsia. In her thoughtful, densely intelligent appraisals of Mrs. Harris and her lover, and in the authority of her previous writings, Mrs. Trilling established fair claim to represent the values of that "class-less" class, those academics and intellectuals who eschew "worldliness" for the life of culture and an ethic outside the marketplace. Mrs. Trilling sets out to analyze possible relationships between the life of culture and morality and life in the world, but her intellectual poise breaks down under the weight of a sweeping contempt for those women who require money and position.

Mrs. Trilling believes Mrs. Harris, an academic, "had no business knowing or wanting to know so many wealthy people." She accuses her of materialism, although Mrs. Harris lived on what she earned and profited little from her affair with Tarnower. Mrs. Trilling says that "the way in which taste is exercised is the firmest clue we have to how someone pursues his life in culture and therefore to the style of moral being he would legislate for us if he had the power." But she allows these lovers no "taste," responding to Mrs. Harris's mention of T. S. Eliot with the disdain of a woman who has found poachers on the family preserve: "Why had these people moved in on Eliot this way?" She dismisses Tarnower's small house as in "ostentatious bad taste," and describes it confusingly as a "Japanoid manifestation." She envies Mrs. Harris's slimness. Her distaste seems out of proportion to anything described as she concludes in a tone better suited to *Ecclesiastes* than to a book by one human being about others: "Could he or Mrs. Harris have known, could they have endured to know, how inglorious were the social heights to which they'd attained?"

Mrs. Trilling's sweeping disapproval prevents her from continuing her appraisal of Tarnower's social climbing and of the changes that occurred in his tastes after wealth and position were achieved with the bestseller, *The Scarsdale Diet*. Surely Tarnower's growing preference for Mrs. Tryforos, Mrs. Harris's rival, may have been social as well as sexual. It was not Mrs. Tryforos's existence as his mistress but her emergence as Tarnower's public companion that was the point of contention between Mrs. Harris and her lover. That he should have a decreasing need for a woman like Mrs. Harris, who had contributed to his book, and an increasing desire to display Mrs. Tryforos suggests he felt his search for social *éclat* was better served by the visibility of a young woman whose assets were physical and whose presence confirmed his sexual vigor. The man who had everything else required a young, trophy woman on his arm. Mrs. Trilling had no clue that in current mores ambition could be transferred from the old standard of money and position to a new one of sexual plenitude.

Mrs. Harris knew better. Tarnower had already made and withdrawn an offer of marriage years before, justifying his change of heart by a good-times ethic: "I didn't want to worry about which retirement home your mother was in . . . and I didn't want to watch you die of cancer, and I didn't want you to play nursemaid to me." Yet in practice he could not let go of Mrs. Harris any more than she could let go of him. He sent her his manuscript, he took her on vacations, he supplied her with enough amphetamines and antidepressants to create a drug dependency and tie her to him, if only as her supplier. When she came to him on the night of the killing, anxious and suicidal, he could not comfort her, finally telling her to "get out" because she was "crazy." In remaining and refusing to go, Mrs. Harris, wittingly or unwittingly, became his nemesis in a drama that could be seen as a moral fable.

Mrs. Trilling and Mrs. Harris share a moral acuity that establishes both as alien to the slickly self-aggrandizing ethic that characterized Tarnower. Mrs. Trilling considers Mrs. Harris a Puritan, but she speaks as one of the saved to one of the damned. Take her response to the pathetic "Scarsdale letter." In it Mrs. Harris informs Tarnower of her state at the time she had returned his $35,000 engagement ring with a charming note, after he had withdrawn his offer of marriage. She tells him she had given up her children's scholarships, notifying their school that she was marrying and moving away. When Tarnower changed his mind, it took her two years to have the scholarships reinstated, and she had to meet the additional expenses from her gross yearly salary of $12,000. Mrs. Trilling responds, addressing her remarks directly to Mrs. Harris:

"She should herself be reminded that this supposed extreme of poverty was not too uncomfortably shared throughout the academic profession. Between 1966 and 1969 the basic salary of a full professor at Columbia College was $14,000 and it was only in 1969 that it was raised to $16,000. And those were days in which we climbed a long hill to reach this exalted rank."

Does this really do more than remind us that it is easier to live simply as the wife of a gifted and respected man, in an intimacy so complete one can refer to his professorship in the plural pronoun, than to be lonely, jilted, and further penalized in the amount of two scholarships? Surely if the elect choose to instruct the less fortunate, they should do so more charitably, secure in the knowledge that a convicted murderer has already lost her claim to success in any moral competition.

Mrs. Trilling's magisterial excesses are part of the drama of her portrait of the crime; they document the intense personal response aroused by the tragedy of Tarnower and Harris. Mrs. Trilling's severity is balanced by intellectual honesty and patience in sifting through the facts of the trial. Her comments on the guilty verdict delivered by the jury reflect her standards of fairness: "I'm afraid that on the basis of what I heard and observed in Mrs. Harris's trial, I find it entirely possible that Mrs. Harris murdered Tarnower. But 'possible' is not enough on which to convict a person of so serious a charge or any charge. Had I been on Mrs. Harris's jury I could not have voted as it did . . . And yet, though I question the verdict against

Mrs. Harris I have no doubt at all that deep in her mind and heart she wanted to kill Dr. Tarnower. I think her fury at him was murderous. . . . But if there'd ever been a time when the wish was conscious, this was no longer so. And it's conscious action that is judged in a court of law."

By force of her personality, Mrs. Trilling underscored the essential disparities between the life of authority, with its stabilities of affection and place, and the life of romantic risk. She condemned Mrs. Harris's very idealism with a certainty that fused her moral and psychological views into this lyrical fatalism: "I think there remains a level, deep enough, on which she's always the brave wide-eyed provincial in a metropolis that should never have been opened up to her. There are people who were born to stay home rather than to follow the beckonings of their imaginations: the Emma Bovarys and Anna Kareninas of this world. If this is the counsel of their despair, it's also the counsel of their ultimate salvation."

Mrs. Trilling sentenced Mrs. Harris to the fate of the sentimental heroine doomed by her own craving for romance, assigning her a tragic role she carefully scripted in her representation of the crime. But what distinguished Mrs. Harris from such romantic heroines was that she was alive, writing her own script, and crafting it as a very different act of optimistic affirmation.

The narrative density of the trial was evident in the role Mrs. Harris wrote for herself as she stood trial for murder. With her own freedom at stake, she presented the narrative of the crime as a tribute to her lover, producing a more idealized version of the relationship than any Mrs. Trilling, distracted by materialism and money, could imagine. Like those aggressive heroines of Henry James (she has the sense of surfaces of a Madame Merle, the moral Puritanism of an Isabel Archer, the generosity toward a flawed lover of a Milly Theale), Mrs. Harris saw possibilities for self-transcendence through violence. The measure of Mrs. Harris's romantic idealism cannot be taken without an appreciation of the extent to which she wrote the script for her trial without regard for her own self-interest in obtaining an acquittal. Who determined that she would not make a psychiatric defense (such a defense saved Francine Hughes) or follow other lines of argument than she did? Who decided that her lawyer would request the jury not to consider a lesser charge but to find her guilty or acquit her of second-degree murder? Mrs. Harris's behavior, her apparent effort to "take over" her case, and the desire not simply to win an acquittal but to be judged both innocent and beloved, suggest that she was using the courtroom to accomplish some psychological goal not congruent with merely evading punishment.

Mrs. Harris, I think, used the courtroom to stage her final public appearance with Herman Tarnower. She put the presentation of their romance ahead of her personal freedom. She cast Tarnower in the role of her savior, struggling to take from her the weapon that would end her life, and therefore dying so that she might live. Her description of their final struggle for the gun bespoke the physical intensity of their encounters. Tarnower's death had clearly killed the feeble, fawning side of herself she must have wished to destroy in her suicidal anguish. Her queenly arrogance toward the prosecutor, her mastery of her case, and her need to appear flawless, suggested she was shedding the vulnerable side of herself. In her commanding demeanor, her perfect grooming, and her unfailing loyalty to Tarnower, she claimed him. She may never have been his wife, but in court she became his widow.

Mrs. Harris created a narrative of love and union reaffirmed by Tarnower's death. She sealed that script in an armor of arrogance and propriety that could simulate the values embodied in the motto of the Madeira School: "Courage in adversity, finish in style." Did either Mrs. Harris or Mrs. Trilling finish in style?

Mrs. Harris spent fifteen years in the Bedford Correctional Facility before her exemplary behavior and heart attacks earned her freedom from the punishment the judicial system considered due a woman convicted of shooting the man who had abandoned her. Shortly after her incarceration, she was physically assaulted by another inmate and required infirmary treatment. In meeting what Saul Bellow called "the reality instructors," she gave more gracefully than she received.

In the years that passed before her parole, Mrs. Harris taught other inmates to read, improved their grammar, counseled them, and used her incarceration to maintain her position as a woman who could be among the felons without ever being one of them. On her release, she wrote a book evaluating the penal system from the perspective of women and arguing for greater rehabilitation efforts and fewer restrictions on parole. Her exemplary life earned few accolades. In 1994 when she flew to Toronto to appear in a "Unique Lives" series, she was denied access to Canada as a convicted felon. When she tried to promote her book and the cause of helping women prisoners gain parole and a respectable life, the usually courteous Larry King ignored her efforts and her cause and tried to interrogate her about Tarnower's death. She continued to maintain that Tarnower died in a heroic effort to save her from killing herself and tried to talk about the plight of young, disadvantaged women prisoners and their children.

Mrs. Trilling, in contrast, prevailed as a literary widow, protecting and advancing her husband's reputation until, long after his death and near the end of her own long life, she published a memoir, *The Beginning of the Journey* (a sendup of the title of Lionel Trilling's only novel, *The Middle of the Journey*). In it she revealed her longstanding contempt for his failings. He drank, "although his personality was disagreeably altered by even a single cocktail" (17). Equally annoying, she complained, was the fact that he slept well and soundly, enjoying an "inviolable sleep while I lay stiffly awake [imagining] hostile intruders" (123). She saw his sleep-filled nights as an act of aggression against her. She condemned the "overzealousness" of his tennis game, his withdrawals, and his remoteness (283). All these had kept a smoldering anger alive in her. She believed she had taught him to write. Was she simply devoting the harsh severity that marked her writing to him? After a long and respected life as Professor Trilling's loyal widow, did she become his character assassin?

Husbands and wives often find in their children resourceful and remorseless allies in their wars with each other. Some women use children as instruments of their rage. The murder of a Utah multimillionaire by his grandson at the insistence of his daughter garnered national celebrity as it became the subject of extensive news coverage and two miniseries. The murder tied the relationship between the millionaire, his wife, and their children into a tale of the interaction between generations of women that led to the death of the family patriarch and the "betrayal" of one sister by another who turned her in for ordering the death of their father.

Money, social climbing, and rage between husband and wife, mothers and children became the focus of two books, each of which focused on a different narrative of the crime and each of which became a television miniseries as the motives of violent and manipulative women moved to center stage. Depending on the account, the murder was seen as a bizarre tragedy of generations and social climbing or a stark tale of the power of women to destroy their husbands and sons.

Franklin Bradshaw was shot one Sunday morning in August 1978 by his grandson, a prep school junior, at the insistence of his own daughter, Frances Bradshaw Schreuder, a convert to the Episcopal Church, a resident of Manhattan's Upper East Side, and a member of the Board of Trustees of the New York City Ballet, which she treated with the veneration of an acolyte. Schreuder had manipulated and virtually tortured her son to kill her father, but the genesis of the murder was in her relationship with her own doting mother and envious sisters and her hopes for her own young daughter. Did Bradshaw deserve what he got or was he, along with his sons and grandsons, the victim of a raging wife and venomous daughter? The war between the sexes merged with a war between the networks as NBC and CBS presented made-for-television movies based on two best-selling books that offered different visions of the crime.

In the tale of generations, manners, and social climbing, Frances's mother Berenice, who wanted only what the family could afford, was a paragon of devotion to her daughter. Shana Alexander presents Frances Schreuder as the renegade child of a workaholic father and a mother enraged with her husband for depriving her for years of the benefits their wealth should have conferred. Berenice's family feeling was focused on her angry and ungrateful daughter, Frances, who seemed to enact both her own anger and fantasies of escape. Alexander's book, *Nutcracker,* is written as a cautionary tale of maternal indulgence, social frustration and the perils of social climbing.

Evil Frances tried and failed to escape the work and family ethic first through education (she was expelled from Bryn Mawr for drinking and stealing), next by marrying a European charmer who seemed to offer a life of sophistication (she was twice divorced and without support), and finally by siphoning money from her mother to create a setting of success, choosing her religion, the location of her apartment, schools for her children, and the lifestyle of her daughter to place herself in New York society. Using the Bradshaw money to propel herself onto the Board of Trustees of the New York City Ballet, she hoped to underwrite the cost of the *Nutcracker* and to arrange for her daughter, whom she had pushed into the American Ballet School, to dance the lead. Frances decided to kill her father when she learned he was writing a new will that would disinherit her, inhibit the flow of money from Berenice, and prevent her from securing her position on the ballet's board.

Alexander directed a savage eye on the disparities between the world Frances wanted, epitomized by the *Nutcracker* fantasy, and the one she knew. Spending her days in bed in filthy nightgowns and stinking from a lifelong habit of not bathing, Frances lived in an almost total social isolation, buying $10,000 earrings and $1,000 nightgowns she never wore. By underwriting fundraising dinners and much of the cost of George Balanchine's last ballet, "Frances was moving into a new world of culture and beauty," although she could not pronounce Balanchine's name correctly. Tolerated more than accepted by the wealthy New Yorkers she met, Frances earned the following ratings, delivered with cold malice: "Her white mink looked secondhand." "She reminded me of Tara—decayed and neglected." "A woman who was really brought up with money wouldn't wear a long white dress with black shoes and an old bag." No matter. Frances as parricide had become the ballet's Lady Bountiful. She saw her dancing daughter as the instrument for releasing herself from the wreckage of her life.

Berenice the enraged and Frances the malevolent who emerge in Alexander's treatment seemed to count on Frances's graceful young daughter to become the *Nutcracker* princess both off and on the stage. Raised by a British nanny who supplied an upbringing of cleanliness, good manners, and proper speech otherwise unavailable in the home, the child was the idealized version of both Berenice and Frances, a vision of perfection neither could achieve. Frances was determined to promote that image of her perfected self at any price, even the sacrifice of her son by making him a killer.

At Mother's Request, by Jonathan Coleman, focuses with sympathy on the son who is the designated killer of his grandfather and the victim of his mother. This is a narrative of grandfather and grandson that parallels Alexander's story of frustrated women with a portrait of devalued and exploited men. It offers a male perspective that focuses on the evil that women do to men. Seventy-five-year-old Bradshaw has a troubled dignity in Coleman's version. Working seven days a week, rising early for a regimen of one hundred push-ups and fifteen minutes of rope jumping for his ten- or twelve-hour workdays at his auto-parts warehouse on the seamy side of Salt Lake City, Bradshaw was a harsh parody of the American ideal of plain living and thrift. For a briefcase, he used a ragged Coors carton he salvaged from someone else's garbage pile; his clothes were thrift shop workpants and T-shirts. One winter, when the zipper on his jacket gave out, he wrapped the jacket around himself with a rope. He clipped the blank portions of letters for his own stationery, inserting the scraps into an old typewriter that had lost bits of its letters. His files were orange crates and cartons culled from the refuse of fruit markets and grocery stores. Yet he presided over an auto-parts empire and had parlayed an undergraduate education in geology into controlling 40 percent of all the oil and gas leases in America. At his death his assets were in the tens of millions, some of it scattered among the orange crates or tucked into outdated auto-parts catalogues in a filing system not even he had mastered.

Languishing in their shabby house in a working-class neighborhood, and irritable in her ten-year-old Oldsmobile, Franklin Bradshaw's wife Berenice only suspected they were wonderfully rich. Unable to pry from her husband either money or an accounting of his worth, she resorted to begging his foreman to buy her a new car from company funds, to stealing, and returning to work in the warehouse at seventy-four to facilitate her thefts while also earning an hourly wage. A vivacious woman who valued her good looks, she had married Bradshaw when he was a college football player and she was a social success. She had not taken kindly to the birth of three children in rapid succession, a late-arriving fourth (the lethal Frances), economic hardship early in marriage, or to her husband's refusal to acknowledge or spend the money he had. Winning approval from male cronies for his plain living, Bradshaw seemed to enjoy outraging Berenice's love of comfort and good times and keeping her at a high pitch of anger and unhappiness.

Berenice raised her children to feel like misfits in the Mormon world in which they all lived and her husband had flourished. She exploited her two older daughters as helpers, referring to Marilyn, the oldest, as "the other mother," and refusing to acknowledge the physical weakness of her younger daughter. Her only son Robert, who wanted to be like his father, was cruelly scapegoated. When he began to have seizures as a ten-year-old, he was sent to his basement room in the care of his sisters and never medically treated. While Berenice lamented over what Franklin didn't do for him, and her daughters pleaded for medical intervention, Robert descended into madness and spent most of his adult life in state mental hospitals where, several years after a lobotomy, he died. His sisters never recovered from what had happened to him and grew into sober, responsible women. Marilyn admired her father's business ability and wanted a place in the management of the firm, which earned her Berenice's enmity. In her youngest child, Berenice found an ardent ally.

Frances received a love that reflected Berenice's disgust with Bradshaw. She was raised as his opposite: where he and her older sisters were hardworking, honest, and reliable, she was incapable of sustained effort, dishonest, and vacillating. She had witnessed the demolition of her brother and the unrewarded virtue of her sisters. Berenice had sent them to local schools and taught them to make their own clothes, but Frances was sent to Bryn Mawr with an expensive wardrobe. There the renegade behavior that had been rewarded in the past flowered into criminality: she forged checks she stole from classmates, took what she wanted, and was expelled.

Although Frances proved to be Berenice's ultimate weapon against Franklin, she was one that backfired. Lacking her father's strengths, Frances nevertheless proved as withholding and stingy as he was. In an odd parody of her father's wealth without consumption, she entered into orgies of acquisition without using anything she bought. She had jewelry and fine clothes yet wore the same filthy things day after day. She rented huge mansions in the Hamptons in which she lived in isolation. She shared her father's need to withhold from Berenice what she needed most: gratitude and admiration. She repaid the endless stream of money

Berenice sent with unreturned phone calls, open insults, and indoctrination of her own children to regard Granny with as much contempt as they visited upon Gramps.

Ironically Frances's bond with Berenice was expressed in her dealings with her own children, which recapitulated Berenice's neglect and exploitation of her sisters and brother. Frances scapegoated her oldest son almost from birth, failing to provide him with essentials. She locked him out for weeks at a time, refusing him access to his home and clothing and forcing him to fend for himself. He built a "nest" of cardboard boxes in the stairwell of their luxury apartment building on the Upper East Side and lived there. Her rejection of him escalated until she behaved as though he did not exist. He sank into unreality as his uncle Robert had done before him and was hospitalized after committing a brutal crime while having delusions. Exploiting her younger son, Marc, as her housekeeper, cook, and confidant, Frances alternately induced his obedience by her total reliance on him and by threats of suicide, but also by threats of locking him out if he refused to do her bidding. Just as her mother had pinned her fantasies of a socially exciting life of irresponsibility and good times on Frances, so Frances pinned her dreams of glory on her own young daughter.

Frances's daughter was clearly raised to redeem Frances from her social disabilities: her bizarre isolation, her bad smell and poor grooming, her "uncultured" Utah parents. Having hired a nanny to raise her properly, teach her to bathe daily, and keep her room immaculate, Frances pushed her to become a ballerina who might one day command center stage as a perfection of girlhood in that ultimate showcase, Balanchine's *Nutcracker*. Two generations of female ambition focused on this girl who was to transfigure Berenice's simple love of good times and music and fulfill Frances's dreams of being admired.

The solution to the puzzle of who killed Franklin Bradshaw mirrors the development of violence as manipulation, withholding, and bribery. For two years after the death of Bradshaw, the police had no evidence against Frances or Marc. Frances's plan for killing her father had been well executed by Marc, who had secretly flown to Utah, shot his grandfather, and come back to New York in what appeared to be the perfect crime. But

Frances was as stingy as the father she had killed. She ignored Marc's pleas to dispose of the murder weapon that was the only evidence against them. Instead, she gave it to a friend to whom she owed $3,000 as a way of not having to pay him. Her delight in withholding his money from him even after she had access to an immense fortune rendered her friend vulnerable to the efforts of her sister Marilyn, who had offered a $10,000 reward for information leading to the solution of the crime. Marilyn was sure that Frances had killed their father and had years of rancor fueling her desire for justice. She made it her business to sympathize with the friend's anger at Frances for not paying what she owed him. Eventually he delivered the gun to Marilyn for the reward. Frances's need to exploit Marc without limit led her to adopt a defense at her own trial centering on naming him as a vicious killer who planned and executed the crime alone. Finally, Marc realized that nothing he could do would make her love him.

Pushed by detectives who had begun to feel sorry for him, by the prosecution, and by the magnitude of his life sentence to confront his mother's willingness to sacrifice his life for her own, Marc testified against her for the right to an early parole. But not even that was all.

The war between Berenice, Frances, and Franklin transcended Franklin's death and Frances's conviction. Berenice continued to champion Frances and began to attack her daughter Marilyn for siding with Franklin against her and Frances and for turning the murder weapon over to the police. She accused *Marilyn* of destroying her family. Disinheriting Marilyn, she made Frances, who was in prison, her sole heir. In response, Frances frequently refused to accept her calls or mother's visits. She knew from watching Berenice that frustration made for the tightest of relationships.

The generational bond between mother, daughter, and granddaughter focuses the murder of Franklin Bradshaw in a violence script in which each of the two mothers used her daughter as an idealized version of herself. Frances lived out Berenice's fantasies of revolt, even as Frances's daughter embodied Frances's dream of grace and social brilliance. What seems like a murder for economic gain—an inheritance eventually estimated at forty million dollars—turned into a revelation of murder as a family style in which a husband and sons are sacrificed to madness or murder while women remain to fight it out among themselves or to support each other. Berenice and Frances can be seen as violent women whose savagery is evident in their destructive effect.

Nonfiction crime narratives like *Mrs. Harris: The Death of the Scarsdale Diet Doctor, Nutcracker,* and *At Mother's Request* provide accounts that reveal the relationship between generations of women along a spectrum of grievances against men, ambivalence about each other, and the erosion of passive acceptance as a response to the provocations of men.

Intimate relationships are the world writ small. Representing them on the knife-edge holds an enlarging mirror up to those malignant interactions between men and women and within families that make out of intimacy both a torment and a wellspring of violence. Deformations of kinship are projected in incest, deformations of sex are projected in prostitution, violated fidelity is projected in narratives of betrayal, denial, or condemnation. All provide extreme illuminations of what can and does go wrong. More important are the means chosen by women in these narratives to deal with humiliation and injury and to shape their stories, often spinning their situations into triumphal tales. By doing injury to the iconic innocence of the young girl and projecting the young predator as an alternative, by claiming prostitution as a form of retaliation against men, by exploiting sexual manipulation and the blurring of sexual differences, heroines use violence as a means of redefinition of what it means to be a woman.

None of the narratives discussed in this chapter supports the notion that payback is a simple choice for women. Virtually all the women enact a retaliatory violence in which the victim is not always the person who abused them. Instead, their violence is directed at the effects of male authority and often displaced onto another, sometimes random target. They revise the tormenting concepts of innocence and trust they see as sources of their humiliation. The effort to redefine what a young woman is leads to celebrations of the young girl as predator. Grounded in the culture of misogyny, this literature of revolt often bears its mark. Serious fiction dramatizes and condenses male authority into the abusive father or brother, the john, or the pimp and locates the rebellion of women using language and murder to deny and destroy male power.

Language and perspective are primary instruments of revolt. At one extreme violence is presented as a rational choice; at the other it serves as the climax of lyricism or outpourings of obscenity, as a literary and allusive formalism or violent pornography. Through the denial of innocence and the protected and nurturing roles once played by women—the mother, daughter, wife, sister, lover—a new set of core roles is harshly affirmed. The prostitute emerges as a figure of power, the victim is represented as a killer, the abject street kid becomes a revolutionary writer in command of many lexicons of rebellion, the young, overprotected women a predator, the long-suffering mother a virago. Sexual talk is used as a form of inflammatory speech with public implications. In the skewed and distorted rhetoric of displaced retaliatory violence, the actions of the girl or woman are not only self-justifying in the hostile universe they invoke as their home. They use the female passage out of vulnerability as the product of evolutionary change and development, the inevitable consequence of the erosion of male authority. It is a deformation of the empowerment of women that springs out of their experience of malignant forms of male power. In intimacy on the knife-edge, a violent woman carves from that hostile world an angry vindication.

A mixture of realism and imagination meets in one woman's bizarre retaliatory violence. By staging her own gangbang, one woman tried to seize control of the profound victimization of gang rape and present it as evidence of her own omnipotence. Can the victim outdo her attackers and outwit fear by dictating the script of her "rape"? Can she control trauma by enacting it? Like self-mutilating people who cut or burn themselves deliberately so as to control their pain, can a woman outdo sexual fear by seizing control of the feared scenario of gang rape?

Sex: The Annabel Chong Story is a documentary film by a twenty-two-year old self-identified "feminist" and college student who wanted to establish and hold a world's record for the "biggest gang bang" and made the film to secure her title. On January 15, 1995, when Ms. Quek staged her own gangbang scenario, she was on camera for a continuous ten-hour period while having sex with 251 men. The documentary, opening in New York on February 11, 2000, recorded selections of her experience and subsequent interviews with her friends, none of whom could explain why she did it. In *New York Magazine* the film received special treatment among the other movie ads (February 14, 2000, 145). Ms. Quek stands in a photograph on the movie page in a black T-shirt, with "gang rape" printed on it, smiling in colorful earrings and bright makeup, promoting her documentary.

Averaging twenty-five contacts per hour, Ms. Quek had a different man about every 2.4 minutes for ten hours. Intrapsychic and social interactions merge as neither personal interaction nor fantasy nor Ms. Quek's merchandising patter keep aggression and victimization in different boxes; one is indistinguishable from the other in her "show." Her control mechanism is her camera. It secures her image of the staging of "rape" as a spectacle and reconciles her contradictory narrative of victimization and consent, keeping at bay anxiety over opposing concepts of herself. Is she victim or perp? One becomes one's own "attacker" in a fantasy made real. Twisting communication opens a Pandora's box of spin in which the effort to deny and appropriate power by utilizing the camera as an instrument of control focuses on the conflation of victim and attacker in a media-driven culture.

The paradox of power presented by equating victim and attacker is amplified by its close connection to those inseparable companions, the sadist and the masochist. Once largely identified as male and female stereotypes, they can now find themselves equally condensed into power images. By shifting power from one to the other, the meaning of sexual aggression is inverted from simply giving or receiving pain to an eroticized oscillation between the two. Condensation of the contradictory visions of oneself as "feminist," gangbang victim, impresario, and star wards off the anxiety of self-contradiction and vulnerability and permits the presentation of images of control that undermine clear separations between victim and perpetrator. All retaliatory violence involves a transformation in the identity or role of the woman involved from victim to agent of destruction. However, Grace Quek's documentary illustrates the power of violence to consolidate both roles and, by doing so, deny the differences between the victim and the perpetrator.

A kind of *folie à culture* is underscored by the curiosity aroused by the film, as if Quek, her audience, and the large pool of men willing to be part of the film all shared a stake in the bizarre redefinition of the victim and attacker and the spectacle made of the gangbang. The two-hundred-fifty-one men who directly participated in gangbanging Ms. Quek, the theater that screened the documentary, those who saw it, as well as the magazine that featured a photograph of her and highlighted a précis of her story, are all part of a new collision between individual and social pathology involved in staging gang rape as a media event. The normalization of the aberrant and bizarre by wanting to "set a record," and the use of film to achieve a reversal of victim-perpetrator status scripted in the language of a competition on the model of "Ripley's Believe It or Not," establish a woman's use of media as a central device in the redefinition of both the pathological and the socially acceptable. It normalizes a retaliatory violence in which the victim has seized control of the terms of her victimization, formalized and selected its significant aspects, and redefined it as triumphal, as her own star turn.

The obsession with the passage from vulnerability to power or the quest for control of others renders many narratives of the violence of women of picaresque adventures. Each experience seems to constitute a stage or milestone on the passage to violence in a universe ruled by a sexualized aggression that devours all differences, reversing the roles of predator and victim. The attack on the lover, the murder of the father, and the lust for the role of predator are all peak experiences in the destruction of both taboos and stereotypical female roles involving love and intimacy.

Language plays a major role in the violation of taboos against violent, immoral, and grotesque action. Extremes of distortion permit vile actions to be described as beautiful or appropriate in a hostile and degraded world. Morality appears as the obsession with wrongdoing dramatized in the compulsive commission of crime or transgression. Fears of entrapment and punishment are lost in narrative arabesques of denial and control that redefine brutalization. From the literature of retaliatory violence in intimacy, the violent woman emerges as a dramatic embodiment of modernity, a representation of what has changed. The imaginative richness of deceptive or coercive speech, the vividness of experiential detail, and the force of violated traditions all enable a narrative power great enough to script payback as a strategy for winning the war between the sexes. Linda Greenhouse has written that "family law is the battleground of social revolution" (*New York Times,* September 2, 1988, B6). But the treatment of intimate violence in powerful and serious literature speaks to a time in which intimacy is competitive aggression and sex is understood as combat.

CHAPTER 3

MOTHER LOVE ON THE ROCKS

WANT TO HEAR ABOUT CHILD-FREE LIVING? THE *NEW YORK TIMES* THINKS you do. "More people don't have kids, don't want them and wish everyone else's would just go away," it announces on the front page, promoting the magazine cover story in the July 23, 2000, *Magazine,* "The Backlash Against Children." Interviews with habitués of anti-child chatrooms and clubs persuaded reporter Lisa Belkin that she had uncovered "a parallel and expanding universe where the printable names for children include "crib lizards," the name for traditional families is "SITCOMS (Single Income, Two Children, Oppressive Mortgage), and "child-free" couples are called THINKERS (Two Healthy Incomes, No Kids, Early Retirement)"(32).

Hostility to children as a subject rises when cultural definitions of responsibility are in crisis and self-absorption rules. Destructive egotism is at work on both sides of the "are kids worth it" issue. Lisa Belkin's characterization of the troubles between parents and the "child-free" seems to describe the issue only in terms of a competition between the greedy. On one side there are parents who feel entitled to demand benefits for raising children and inflict their children on others in pricey restaurants and movies. Opposing them are the "child free" who feel deprived of employment benefits and tax credits available only to parents and who are irritated by unruly kids who violate their peace and ruin the atmosphere in elegant restaurants or at serious films.

Invoking competing claims of victimization and violated rights, Belkin represents the conflict over the desirability of children as free of class and gender differences. She treats the matter as a sanitized war between factions who each lay claim to entitlements and victim status. Kids are used as footballs in a game of competing material interests and rights in which the sex and class of the players does not matter. Belkin's article lingers on cost-benefit calculations and never addresses the impact of women on the issue. But it illustrates what the literature of child murder makes clear in serious and darker ways: how we represent the desire to be with or without children is colored by cultural ideals of the time and speaks to larger social concerns.

Child murder comes to the fore as a subject of interest when cultural attitudes about motherhood are in crisis. The relationship between mothers and children records changes in how mothers respond to both the burdens and compensations of caring and reveals the cultural attitudes that affect how they see their lives. The ways in which the media treats women accused of killing their children tells us something about changing attitudes toward family life. The power of writers to open up the moral and psychological complexities of women who kill their children reveals even more.

The literature of child murder constitutes an attack on the role postmodern academic theory has assigned to women and their children and has obscured its mixture of personal and social meaning. Lacan's rather arcane vision of the Mother-child dyad as a psychic state he calls the "Real" also eliminates from serious concern the role of women. Lacan idealizes the mother-child dyad by describing it in abstract terms as pure "nature," an indissoluble bond of need and satisfaction without recognition of the differences between mother and child. Both exist in the "wordlessness" he calls the "presymbolic," the time before an infant or child (aged from birth to one and one half years) acquires a sense of separateness from its mother. Lacan sees this psychic state as one of absolute "presence," the domain of the Real. But to accomplish that level of abstraction, Lacan defines the mother-child dyad from the perspective of the infant who is without any idea of "self" or otherness apart from its mother. That state is one of pure "presence," a bliss of need and satisfaction lost with the child's discovery of its separateness and its entrance into "culture" and language.

Lacan's configuration of the mother-child dyad as absolute presence reflects a larger abstraction of the feminine in terms of the "unrepresentable" such as "Nature" or the "sublime." That idealized psychic state of the real takes the perspective only of the preverbal child for the whole of the dyad, assuming the mother's satisfaction of the child's needs provides fulfillment and substitutes for her own expressive language. This view may fulfill Lacan's conception that the mother-child relation is the opposite of the social and political world that he believes does require the representations of language, not the satisfaction of being. But his Real has, of course, nothing to do with reality, much less literary realism, which fully recognizes the role of the mother and the variety of expressive, verbal talents she brings to her own motherhood.

Mothers script their relation to their children quite differently and with great variety. From the Palestinian mothers who claim they have dedicated their infants to "martyrdom" as homicide-suicide bombers to women whose professed motives for eliminating their children may be purely personal, women provide varying and inventive narratives even for their destructive bonds with their children. How a woman scripts her tie to her child is always politically charged, because the relationship between a mother and child is at the heart of that wider social world whose sense of stability, coherence, and meaning is based on the persistence of mother love and the vision of woman as nurturer.

From ancient times, child murder has constituted a social as well as well as personal crisis deeply connecting the stability of the family to societal cohesion. Euripides's *Medea* describes child murder as an invasion of the Greek body politic, claiming it was previously unknown in Greece before Medea, who is from the Middle East, introduced it. Repugnant because of the helplessness and innocence of children, the death of children at their mother's hands also calls into question the bedrock of family stability on which social order is partly based, the limits of mother love, and the impact of that loss on the larger world. *Medea* implies that mother love is a less powerful emotion than self-love. Medea's murders are also extreme examples of a new and terrifying social instability that will flow from women who subordinate loving their children to using them to outdo men in ruthlessness.

Medea's actions are in part the result of her will to win the war between the sexes, to outdo Jason in the competition between egotists that defines intimacy in the play. What is legendary is her refusal to comply with the social expectations that demand she accept the tragic consequences of being abandoned by the man for whom she has given up her father's kingdom and her life as a princess and whom she has made a hero. She kills her children to hurt Jason for leaving her by depriving him of what, after himself, he prizes most. Euripides's Jason is a consummate egotist, willing to take all that Medea has given him and then consign her to lifelong wandering as an exile so he can marry the princess of Corinth and eventually become king.

But Euripides's Medea is a more complex figure. She is in turn pained, thoughtful, and finally violent. Her pitiless intelligence thinks through her disruption of family, state, and even religious conventions and her decision to inflict on Jason the life he wishes to inflict on her. Her sense of language is deep and extends to the inauthenticity of Jason's prayers and his verbal attacks on her. When Jason asks the gods to avenge the murder of the children, Medea only jeers: "What god or power divine hears thee, breaker of oaths and every law of hospitality?"(756). She correctly predicts Jason's death in the future as a homeless wanderer. Her own prospects literally soar as her magic chariot flies her to Athens where she will continue her potential to disrupt both the state and Greek conceptions of dynastic and family order. Just as Medea's murder of her children crowns a series of murders that destabilize the kingdom of Corinth, so her violations of mother love epitomize the destruction of social order. At the same time, by killing her children she kills all that remains of her vulnerability and establishes her fitness for the ruthless battle of wills she must win to have power in a male-dominated world.

Prizing conquest and power more than maternal love destabilizes life not only in the legends of the ancient world but also in their contemporary counterpart, the infotainment chronicles found in the daily news. In our own time, the sexual revolution and desire of women for sexual freedom and power redefined the issue of child murder as newsworthy. Women have traditionally expressed their wildness through sex. In the

early days of the sexual revolution, those woman who needed sexual conquests and power became a magnet for the conflicts of those anxious over
what would happen to the family if married women wanted to remain free
for sexual experimentation. Turmoil over the sexual revolution helped turn
public discourse about child murder into an illustration of the irreconcilable differences between motherhood and sexuality, between performance
as a mother and sexual success in pursuing multiple partners. Newspapers
were quick to treat cases of child murder in terms of the mothers' penchant
for what was condemned as sexual excess. Even in contemporary fictional
child murder narratives, it is often the sexual cravings of women that are
seen as threatening and the cause of disruption in the modern family.

Much of the thinking about social order has depended on the inviola-
bility of the tie between mother and child that secures the family as an institution. Theories of social order have involved theories of sexual
difference in which the nature of women, epitomized by the self-sacrifice
of mother love, made no claim to a powerful will, the desire for sexual adventure, or competitiveness with men. A classic formulation of the double
standard provides a baseline against which contemporary media attitudes
can be measured. Adam Smith's lectures on jurisprudence explore fidelity
and acquiescence as the duties of wives, not husbands. Jane Rendall as-
tutely describes Adam Smith's statement of the double standard: "The first
duty of marriage, for Smith, is the wife's obligation to fidelity. Its foundation lay not only in the sense of injury felt by a husband, or the utility of
securing legitimate offspring, but in the sympathy felt by a spectator with
the jealousy of the husband"(63).

As Smith wrote: "The indignation of the public against the wife arises
from their sympathy with the jealousy of the husband, and accordingly they
are disposed to resent and punish it. . . . The laws of most countries being
made by men generally are very severe on the women, who can have no rem-
edy for this oppression. . . . A wife might also feel a sense of injury [at her
husband's infidelity]; yet because the man was generally acknowledged to be
the superior, the injury to his honor was the greater"(63–64). Rendall concludes: "There was here no attempt to suggest that natural justice required
any principle of equality. . . . Smith offered not an abstract, but a naturalis-

tic account, using the two themes of a wife's obligation to fidelity and the perpetuity of marriage to trace the history of the marital relationship"(64).

Secured by woman's docility and mother love, the family served as a bulwark against the ruthless appetites of the marketplace that was exclusively male terrain. Would the sexual revolution challenge social order? If women entered the sexual marketplace as competitors for freedom and pleasure, would children seem to them only drags on their performance as players?

Media accounts of women who murdered their children illustrated changing expressions of cultural anxiety as the sexual revolution began and eventually prevailed. In the early skirmishes of the sexual revolution, the killer mother was represented as doing so because she was a sexual player. The positioning of sexual performance in opposition to maternal performance is part of the narrative of fear the media posed in the question: What if mothers decided they would rather have fun and profit too? When a woman betrays her husband, sacrifices her children, and uses sex to achieve upward mobility, she charges into those hot skirmishes in which the sex war and the class war intertwine. In what John Updike called the "post pill paradise" of the sixties, women seemed armed and dangerous.

Media accounts of actual crimes in which sexually adventurous women were convicted of killing their children plunged the accused mother into a crossfire of sexual and class antagonisms that often aroused more fury than the crime itself. Sexual and class antagonisms surfaced with particular force around the 1965 murder of two children from an unraveling family in Queens. Alice Crimmins was a too-beautiful working-class wife who had separated from her mechanic husband, Eddie. When their children— Eddie who was five and Alice who was four—disappeared, the police suspected that Alice had done away with them to escape the drudgery of caring for them and to enjoy herself as a single woman. The media agreed. As male detectives pursued her sexual life relentlessly, news accounts documented that her amusements included several sexual partners, among whom was a wealthy older man whose presence added greed to sex as a motive for wanting the children out of the picture to ease the way to marriage.

Although she continued to claim her innocence, and little definitive evidence was found against her, Alice Crimmins was indicted a full three years after the deaths of the children. After a series of trials, appeals, and overturned verdicts, she was convicted of killing her children and served time. The media was swifter than the law in its judgments. The *New York Daily News* tagged her "the Queens housewife with hamster morals" (Jones 275). In news photos and stories, Alice Crimmins emerged as a woman more interested in sex than a Catholic mother ought to be. Her sexual life seemed to be blamed for the children's death, whether she had killed them or not. One of the jurors who convicted her is quoted as saying, "A tramp like that is capable of anything." Her "own attorney said she was 'amoral' and acknowledged that the jury had been forced to listen to a lot of 'filth'" (Jones 275). Ann Jones describes the outrage of the reporters covering the story: "'Even if Crimmins hadn't killed her children,' said one reporter, 'she had plenty to feel guilty about.' *If* she had been a faithful wife—and mother—whose primary concern was her home, her husband, and her children, there probably would have been no estrangement from her husband. . . . *If* her husband had been at home that night, the children might never have been abducted . . . [and] murdered" (Jones 277–78).

Although the murder of children is infinitely worse than having an affair, it was sex that seemed unforgivable. One reporter later concluded: "The Alice Crimmins case . . . was perceived as frightening because the women's movement was just coming into existence when the case broke, and the implications—a housewife grown rebellious and out of control—terrified those who felt a stake in maintaining the status quo" (Jones 279).

Crimmins had transgressed class expectations as well as the double standard. Twelve years after the death of the children, and during her time on a work release and furlough program, she was still being pursued by the press. The *New York Post* entangled her sex life with her betrayal of her working-class background, documenting that "she has spent many balmy summer days of her prison term—on a luxury cruiser at City Island," and printing photographs of her "looking remarkably attractive for her 37 years" in a bikini on her companion's yacht. When she married her wealthy older lover in 1977 with the permission of the Corrections Department, the outcry was vicious (Jones 279). One of jurors on her case declared:

"They should lock her up and throw away the key" (Jones 279). His comment appeared next to a photo of Alice, chic and sleek, entering her husband's white Cadillac.

Public opinion in the media and public prosecutor's office aroused anxiety that women no longer considered maternal self-sacrifice a major asset and wanted to amass the kind of sexual capital that could prevail in the marketplace. The literary panorama behind media representations of Crimmins's crime was a blend of cultural themes long in the making. Such themes had typically been applied to men and did not directly challenge the double standard. The social narratives that supported them seemed to arouse both the fantasy and anxiety caused by women behaving "like men." Jack Kerouac's *On the Road* (1959) hyped balling on an endless roadtrip as a male style in which women were willing but inconsequential participants. Paul Goodman wondered why women were attracted to the Beats, who were not good prospects as husbands and fathers. Tom Wolfe's sixties journalism mocked the family as MOM&DAD&BUDDY&SIS for its plain vanilla boredom. What would happen if MOM wanted to go on the road herself?

Crimmins's pursuit of sex and money and her abandonment of working-class, family style expressed, for the unsympathetic, the horror of a mother behaving like the men who were busily mocking marriage and family in counterculture art. Her kind of perversity seemed guaranteed to destroy children even if the children were not murdered. Her case became the billboard for the fear that in a sexually free, luxurious lifestyle that included yachts and Cadillacs, children would inevitably be crushed between the claims of Eros and entrepreneurship.

Literary representations of women who could not survive as mothers did far more than illustrate sexual politics. While media and journalism focused on the externals of crime, creating sexy, cartoon villains out of women like Crimmins, novelists opened up the dilemma of mothers who had internalized *both* the desire for freedom and disapproval of it. They loved their children but resented them too. Literature here supplies the complexity of experience, placing through its command of form, language, and theme the intersections of culture and character in a wrenching and lethal ambivalence.

Performance murder over the enactment of one's own identity as a mother opens up dilemmas of female identity as part of the heritage of generations of women revived and reaffirmed in a mother's treatment of her own child. Emerson's dictum, "the world, this *other me*" often comes true with a vengeance in the relationship between mother and child (*The American Scholar* 55). The mother may see the child as part of herself and use it as a vehicle for her own self-expression. Her violence against the child may dramatize her vision of herself and her place in the scheme of things.

Creating portraits of ambivalence about having children involves mastery of complex and deceptive communications in which language is used to conceal feeling and to simulate and fulfill expectations of normalcy. A mother may use such simulations of expected behavior to control rage, reassure herself, and fit into a community that will not readily accept her egotism, anger, or self-hatred. Such mothers may alternate between extremes of self-justification and self-disgust, or even open rage and denial of anger.

The novelist's task is to make a child murderess more than a demon or even a demonic icon of revolt. She must be sufficiently real to embody the terror and revulsion her act arouses but sufficiently sympathetic for the reader to want to know her as a literary character. Before the murder, representations of such mothers can show their ambivalence toward the child in the form of a passive aggression—they are not simply inept but also agonizing and raging over their failure to perform as mothers. They have what seems to be a sudden awareness that they cannot carry on in the old ways. The disaffected mother dramatizes the internalization of change through both her failure at motherhood and rage at what she believes she must do for her child. Her internalization of traditional norms of behavior, self-hatred for not meeting them, and rage at her situation are frequently embedded in extended visions of generational changes within the family.

Performance murder is a pattern that develops in the context of such conflicts. It erupts from the change in attitudes toward mothering from one generation of women to another. Janice Springer Angstrom (along with her husband Rabbit Angstrom) embodies transforming sexual roles in one of the remarkable novels of the contemporary period, *Rabbit, Run* (1960) by John Updike. Rabbit, the faithless twenty-six-year-old father of two, who works as a vegetable-peeler salesman, still dreams of self-transcendence through sex, and Janice, the girl he married as a high school senior because he got her pregnant, are a matched pair: both resent the roles tradition has assigned them. The novel carries the hedonistic Beat ethos of *On the Road* into a working class world of early marriage, minimal education, and family obligations in which the sources of joy and regeneration that drove Rabbit to Janice are precisely the origins of her misery. The novel explores what happens when a couple marries to do the right thing and follows the old family path, only to find they are in a world that has changed all the road signs.

How can changes in women be measured? The differences between three generations of women in the novel provide a remarkable answer. *Rabbit, Run* shows transforming American Moms. "Momism" flourishes in the generation of grandmothers, those American housewives who are controlling, relentlessly involved with their children, and unwilling or unable to recognize their separateness. Mrs. Springer, Janice's mother, is an effective, hardworking woman who maintains a clean, orderly, thrifty home and a working-class lifestyle despite her husband's financial success. She has expressed whatever longing for the good life she had by giving it to Janice, by demanding no effort or accomplishment from her. She has infantilized Janice by never holding her accountable for anything and taking charge of her problems. She blames Rabbit and his mother for everything that goes wrong in her daughter's marriage. Janice depends on her mother's strength and fears her judgment of her.

Rabbit's mother and sister Mim are angrier counterparts of Mrs. Springer and Janice. Mrs. Angstrom envies Mrs. Springer's money and is full of contempt for Janice as the tramp Rabbit had to marry because he had made her pregnant in high school. Stroking her son's grandiose sense of entitlement as a high-school basketball star, she blames Janice for his failures because she *let* him make her pregnant. Mim, her daughter, won't make Janice's mistake of falling for men. She is a cool, high-priced call girl, an unsentimental materialist who sells sex.

Neither Mrs. Springer nor Mrs. Angstrom has reproduced her kind. Although Janice followed the path of fifties respectability laid out by her parents, marrying to give their older child a name and home, she is a child-woman who is proud of her ability to stay inside the lines while coloring with her four-year-old son and is fearfully aware of her inability to care for her home, her son, or her infant daughter. She expects Rabbit to take care of her and ask for nothing in return, indulging her as her mother did. When Rabbit runs out in anger, she turns to the bottle for comfort. The third female generation, baby Rebecca, pays the price. The change in generations is dramatized by a killing.

Janice drowns Rebecca in a scene that incorporates a saga of generations in which the relationship between Mrs. Springer and Janice helps bring about the death. Janice strives to simulate her mother's competence in her relationship with her infant daughter but in doing so expresses her own identification with the infant's helplessness, stench, and dependency. To set the scene: Rabbit has stormed out in anger, leaving Janice alone with their son and infant daughter. Janice has been drinking whiskey for hours and feels clever when she decides not to try to change the baby's wet diaper because she is too drunk not to stick her with a pin. But Janice's caution vanishes when her mother telephones, realizes how drunk Janice is, and says she will rush right over. Janice is terrified of her mother discovering the apartment is cluttered with dirty dishes and clothes, whiskey bottles and glasses, crayons and coloring books. Worst of all, Rebecca begins to wail and Janice finds her "nightmarishly smeared with orange mess" (241). Her interaction with her infant daughter under the pressure of her mother's coming reveals her displacement of all her rage and self-hatred on the baby girl:

> "Damn you, damn you," she moans to Rebecca, and lifts the little filthy thing out and wonders where to carry her.
> "Oh you little shit," she murmurs. . . . She strips the baby . . . and carries the sopping clothes to the television set and puts them on the top. (241–242)

Janice teeters into the bathroom to bathe Rebecca:

> She is proud to be carrying this to completion; at least the baby will be clean when Mother comes. She drops gently to her knees by the big calm tub and

does not expect her sleeves to be soaked. The water wraps around her fore-arms like two large hands; under her eyes the pink baby sinks down like a gray stone.

With a sob of protest she grapples for the child but the water pushes up at her hands, her bathrobe tends to float, and the slippery thing squirms in the sudden opacity. She has a hold, feels a heartbeat on her thumb, and then loses it, and the skin of the water leaps with pale refracted oblongs that she can't seize the solid of; it is only a moment, but a moment dragged out in a thicker time. (243)

The drowning expresses the internalized interaction between Mrs. Springer, Janice, and Rebecca. Infantilized by Mrs. Springer, Janice is driven by fear of her mother to deny she is too drunk to help Rebecca. She identifies her own inadequacy with the child's filth, treating the soiled baby as the failed part of herself. Drunkenness is the metaphor for the state of anxiety and denial of self-hatred in which she is operating. The filthy baby in that context is less a separate person than Janice's own self-image, a projection of all that is dependent, stinking, and frustrated in herself. She is trying to clean up that dirty self, to eliminate it. The death of the child represents a partial suicide, the destruction of her weakest, most despised, dependent, needy self in a mothering, cleansing water. The drowning is a culmination of the roles each of them has played: the rescuer (Mrs. Springer), the child in need (Janice), and the failure (Rebecca).

Mrs. Springer deals with Janice by expecting nothing of her, relying on her own competence, and trying to do her own job and Janice's too. Janice has mastered a coercive dependency that keeps her mother closely watchful of her, but she fails to control Rabbit and prevent him from running out on her for other women. She has internalized an awareness of both the value of competence and her own inability to conform to her mother's standards or to make a pleasurable life for herself. Her dependency and sense of failure are bound together, personified in the stinking daughter she must clean to save face with her mother and the drunken, buffered anger in which she lets Rebecca slip.

Janice's drowning of Rebecca underscores her interaction with her mother in its style. The water in "the big calm tub" feels "like two large hands" (perhaps not unlike her mother's) into which she is delivering the child. Putting the child in the water of extinction, Janice tries to release a hated self-image that combines her own dependent needs and her anger that her mother can no longer hold her own life securely in the grip of her capable hands. Through the active expression of letting the child go, Janice registers her revolt against expectations of motherhood. Her alcoholic haze provides a buffer against the brutality of her act. Only through severing herself from her mother's example through committing a terrible and irrevocable act can Janice end her angry need for her mother's approval. Killing Rebecca breaks the chain of mothers and daughters.

The portrait of Janice is a complex revelation of performance agony in a time of uncertainty and transition. The social panorama in which *Rabbit, Run* goes forward is a period of acute change. Ending with the burial of Rebecca and with Rabbit running from the gravesite, the novel prefigures the rise of Janice who will no longer be expected to have any more children or behave like a mother. The death of the daughter is the price of her liberation. Subsequently, in the novel that serves as the sequel to *Rabbit, Run,* Janice transfers her dependency from her mother to her father, adopts what has in the past been seen as a male style, accepts a job from her father, has an affair, discovers orgasm, and runs out on Rabbit and her son.

How did the solid housewives of the forties and fifties fail to reproduce their kind in the postwar generation that comes of age at the beginning of the sixties?

Mrs. Springer's brand of "Momism" flows from the pre-gratification world of economic depression, war, and economic strife in which women confronted the facts of their lives with a harsh and unsentimental realism. She represents those serious, hardworking women who have helped lift their families by force of their own relentless effort and thrift and whose thirst for pleasures was expressed vicariously through showering their children with comfort and care. She can afford an upper middle class lifestyle, but makes no attempt to have one. Wearing socks and men's shoes, she displays her varicose veins and heavy legs without self-consciousness, secure that her value comes from the life of effort and accountability she has protected Janice against.

In contrast, Janice is a consumer of fantasies of perfection as both mother and wife against which she measures herself and finds herself wanting. She has little capacity to assess realistically what life might hold. Janice spends hours watching TV sitcom wives and mothers, those well-dressed and well-groomed icons of the nineteen fifties who seem to have effortlessly mastered it all: good looks and assured performance. They wear high heels, attractive clothes, and pearls as they vacuum their clean, well-furnished houses, talk with their children, and welcome home husbands who are glad to be there. Janice is made anxious by their ability to give dinner parties she cannot conceive of providing. In leaving her baby's stinking, filthy clothes on the television set, she virtually crowns those idealized mothers on the tube with her own gross reality.

The death of the child from the collapse of devotion to self-sacrifice, work, and nurture is the dark shadow that tracks the sixties narrative of turning from the past to search for peak experiences and freedom. The demise of the generation of Mrs. Springer and Mrs. Angstrom, their creation of a generation of daughters and sons who are either unable or unwilling to deal with children as they and their husbands did, and the sense of catastrophic social changes in the family cast the culture into the social torments, racial animosity, abandonment, and drug addiction of the sixties that will burn down the House of Angstrom in the sequel, *Rabbit Redux*.

Updike's polished and rich narrative presents the killing of Rebecca as a performance murder—the price of destroying motherhood as an ideal because it seems unfulfillable. It is built out of the multiple scripts for women's lives in the novel: Mrs. Springer's Momism, Janice's dependency; Mrs. Angstrom's angry power, Mim's independence. The drowning is depicted as an accidental murder that is not completely accidental. Alcohol and fear mitigate the intentional clarity of Janice, but both are belied by the clarity of psychological forces that drive Janice's rage and self-loathing toward killing Rebecca. Updike's coloration of child murder performs two major functions: it permits Janice the "out" of an accidental, uncalculated act that enables her to survive as a character in subsequent novels. Yet it also permits the killing of the infant daughter to serve as the bedrock of all future transformations, the dysfunctional departure point against which all must be measured. The House of Angstrom serves as a microcosm of the family in an age of angst in which the pressures on sexual identity and expectation are barometers of social and political upheaval. The drowning of the infant daughter, Updike's version of Janice's original sin, is a transgression against protective mother love that sets in motion the spirit of violence and dysfunction in the series of Angstrom novels that follow American culture through the nineties.

Performance agonies over caring for a child are sometimes presented as justifications for the child's death. The mother lays claim to an altruistic murder by insisting that the problems the child will face are great enough to warrant killing her. What future for a child could be worse than death? Communication-twisting is often required in order to offer death as preferable to life and dramatizes the mixture of fear and will to power of women who feel unable to control or protect their child's life. Self-disgust at their own helplessness is projected on a broad social panorama of conflict and interacts with issues of class or race or both to project child murder as a form of triumph over one's own helplessness. The destroyed child has no independent existence to such women, but instead seems to be the "*other me*," the weak and despised part of oneself that must be cut away.

In the last century, "Old Woman Magoun," a short story by Mary E. Wilkins Freeman, describes a grandmother's poisoning of her motherless granddaughter who is on the brink of puberty to prevent her from being claimed by a man who has won her in a card game with her gambling father. The game of chance that worked against the girl comes to seem to the grandmother another expression of the malignant and irresistible will leveled against them by a corrupt and powerful patriarchy. In the twisted logic of the tale, the grandmother's murder of the child is presented as the only possible victory against male power; she attempts no other response. In giving the child a poisoned apple, the grandmother reenacts the crime of disobedience that expelled Adam and Eve from Eden, driving them into a world of painful labor and trouble. By killing her granddaughter, the grandmother sees herself as driving the child into the heaven of a chaste death where no man can claim her. The story closes with the grandmother's "triumph." The murder, represented as entirely altruistic, seals her victory.

What would happen if a murdered child came back to confront her killer? The voice of contemporary outrage is that of the victim come back to demand compensation and force a traumatic flashback of violence that rebounds against the wrongdoer. If the dead could return, even killing a daughter could be scripted as an *ongoing* relationship between mother and child, a complex narrative of distributive justice in which life and death, possibility and nothingness, are pitted against each other in a contest of values. The question of what was the right thing to do establishes a type of performance murder that turns the mother-child relationship upside down by claiming murder is the best way of caring for the child and justifying it as an altruistic act.

In Toni Morrison's extraordinary novel, *Beloved,* Beloved is a murdered child who comes back from the dead in the flesh to confront her mother, Sethe, who killed her to protect her from life as a slave. American slavery establishes the claims of justifiable murder and grounds her internalized hatred, self-hatred, and deprivation in a broad social panorama of oppression. Although the novel is generally taken as a political document that fully justifies a slave-mother's murder of her daughter, I believe it also raises rich and stunning questions. Even its historical source seems pointed. The novel is based on an actual case in which Margaret Garner killed her daughter in 1857 to prevent her from living as a slave. Garner, of course, could not know that the South would fall in eight years; the child would not have become a woman under slavery. Morrison, of course, has full knowledge of what was to come. I see Morrison's novel as based as much on a knowledge of the future as on Sethe's past as a slave and as rich in the meaningful ambiguities Sethe's error spawns.

Can child murder really be justified by slavery? A slave-mother who kills her daughter to prevent her from experiencing life as a slave can lay claim to an altruistic murder. Nevertheless, her murder can also make claims of injustice against her. Killing one's own child passes on the blow of oppression inflicted by enslavement and places oneself in the position of white society in violating the lives of innocents, controlling those lives, and assuming the burden of dealing with the ongoing rage of the wronged. What connects the public sphere to private recesses of inner life can be presented through the mother's conscious and articulate guilt about her own violence.

Guilt drives the narrative justifying altruistic child murder. White guilt and maternal guilt contend for ownership of the primary culpability for killing. Sethe, who claims she slit the throat of her infant daughter for the child's own good, must prove the value of what she did to the victim in *Beloved*, weaving child murder into the specific threats and experiences of slavery, racism, and deprivation. In the process, it becomes clear that the intensity of guilt felt by the mother expresses how unjustifiable she feels her act was.

Sethe describes her act as creating a "smile" below the jaw in the baby's neck. She does so to prevent her from knowing life as a slave woman and from exposure to her mother's inability to protect her: "If I hadn't killed her she would have died and that is something I could not bear to happen to her" (201). The depersonalization of the infant and the denial of her independent life as more than a problem seem embedded in the denial of her birth to begin with. Sethe's daughter, Denver, and her murdered child, Beloved, are flip sides of a mother's will to give birth and death. Sethe traumatically reenacts *Denver's* birth when she first sees Beloved: Her "bladder filled to capacity," she urinates and . . . as it went on and on she thought . . . like flooding the boat when Denver was born" (61). Her "water breaking" imagery suggests the dead infant has never left her own body, but has remained as much a part of her as a fetus. Denver and Beloved are both drawn to Sethe, but Denver loves her protectively while Beloved demands payment due. "Denver was alarmed by the harm she thought Beloved planned for Sethe, but felt helpless to thwart it. . . ." (104). Beloved is associated with imagery of blood, infantile feeding, and wailing tantrums—all of which are presented in terms of her will to revenge. Beloved tells Denver: "[Sethe] is the one I need. You can go but she is the one I have to have" (89).

Traumatic guilt drives Sethe's compulsion to feed Beloved at the price of her own starvation; fury drives the child's insatiable hunger to devour the mother. Sethe gives Beloved all the food she has, starving herself to provide a surfeit for Beloved, who is permitted to control her through violence: "When once or twice Sethe tried to assert herself—be the unquestioned mother whose word was law and who knew what was best—Beloved slammed things, wiped the table clean of plates, threw salt on the floor, broke a windowpane. She was not like them . . ." (242).

When Sethe and Denver run low on food, they starve while Beloved grows bigger. They are locked in combat that makes Denver comment, "The job she started out with, protecting Beloved from Sethe, changed to protecting her mother from Beloved. Now it was obvious that her mother could die and leave them both and what would Beloved do then? . . . Neither Beloved nor Sethe seemed to care . . . (Beloved lapping devotion like cream)" (286).

Child murder is represented as an ongoing relationship in which the child can be figured as an aspect of oneself. She is both the needy infant who must be nursed and cared for and the parasite who will never stop draining food and life. The child is both victim of the mother who cannot care and a victimizer, serving as a reminder of humiliation and torment. Sethe makes no distinction between Beloved and herself. "I AM BELOVED and she is mine," she declares (248). Beloved is part of Sethe, a representation of herself as both outraged victim and destroyer.

Mother and daughter serve as different facets of self that have been compartmentalized to keep them apart. This splitting between mastery of life and victimization by it, between strength and weakness, is projected in the parasitic imagery of host and invader, of feeding and starving, control of all the food there is and deprivation. Eating and starving replicate the terms of infant life and death, but they also invoke episodes of traumatic victimization. Sethe claims her milk was "stolen" in an attack by white men who suckled at her breasts. In such images of a parasitic white world, Sethe projects the attempted theft of the slave's capacity for protective love. Killing Beloved enabled Sethe to gain control of her own victimization by delivering the blow herself, wresting from white society the power to abuse, exploit, or starve. Beloved is the victimized part of herself.

Performance anxiety over her inability to protect and care for Beloved is allayed by the logic-twisting in which the performance of murder is presented as the highest expression of maternal love. This communication twisting is an essential part of child murder. Despising herself for being helpless and overpowered by the white world, she ends that self-hatred by eliminating the child who embodies, in its unmet needs and demands, her own frustrations. Sethe revolts against victimization by killing the child who represents the weakest aspects of herself.

That the "altruistic" murder was generated by rage at her own weakness is underscored by the extent to which living with Beloved is worse for Sethe than killing her, precisely the opposite of the argument for the good of the child she has made. It is feeding Beloved that is starving Sethe to death. Beloved's devouring demands for compensation reflect the extent to which Sethe's guilt is an active and ongoing two way street of justification, remorse, and self-punishment. Beloved beats out a fugue disproving Sethe's guilt-tormented claims of altruistic murder. Yet is equally clear that Sethe's murder of Beloved is also a partial suicide.

Slavery was the national form of partial suicide, but *Beloved* is a contemporary novel that, intentionally or not, is most fully realized in its rendering of the price paid for child murder as a crushing ambivalence about oneself. The effort to kill the victimized part of herself has turned Sethe into a killer guilty of the slave owner's dehumanization of the child whose independent life she could not recognize as having value in its own right The slit throat of the baby carves no "smile" but a two-way line of communication between mother and daughter. Killing is a process of communication that sends messages of rage and self-hatred, all that prevents the self from being whole, integrated, fulfilled. The splitting and demonizing of a hated portion of oneself ironically named "Beloved" incorporates an agony of ambivalence and conflict over the performance of both mothering and killing. Having murdered the child she saw as no separate being but as an extension of her own needs and capacities, Sethe killed that capacity to love, and "be loved" that requires self-acceptance. Internalized rage, rage as destabilizing self-hatred, defines the world of Sethe and places the question marks at the end of Sethe's last word in the novel: "Me? Me?"(273). The possibility for a whole, integrated, self is a question elaborated in a novel in which Sethe's internalization of white oppression makes her feel a failure and causes her anger to turn against herself.

Claims of altruistic murder took a new and bizarre form in the performance crisis of Andrea Yates. Her murders erupted from the extreme high goals of self-sacrifice of this born-again Christian married to a born-again Christian engineer. Andrea Yates had five children despite severe, repetitive bouts of postpartum depression and psychosis. Her disengaged husband was happy to have her home-school all of them, despite a recent bout of postpartum psychosis and the withdrawal of medication that helped prevent episodes of unreality. The determination to home-school all her children guaranteed she would be the constant companion and caretaker of her children for the next sixteen or seventeen years. She methodically drowned each of her children, forcibly holding the older ones underwater. Her long history of mental illness and support from those who had suffered from postpartum depression failed to enlist compassion from the prosecution. Her conservative religious idealism was the opposite of the sexual indiscretion that surrounded Alice Crimmins and reflects the difference in social context between the sixties and nineties.

Yates's act was drawn into a nineties controversy. On one side was the increasingly influential Christian fundamentalist, male view of the legitimacy of demanding a large family and home-schooling of even a mentally ill woman. On the other side was the outrage of those who were horrified by her murders but whose framework was individualistic and therapeutic rather than theological and who were moved by the suffering of a woman who had internalized both fundamentalist ideals and self-hatred for not meeting them. The controversy was bolstered by a Texas justice system that wanted nothing to do with postpartum depression or any female form of psychosis. Nor did it appear to take seriously either professional testimony or personal accounts by those sympathetic to Yates's obvious travail, many of whom had suffered bouts of postpartum depression themselves or were professionals who specialized in women's mental health. Tried by a prosecutor seriously considering the death penalty, Yates's case polarized the expert testimony in the opposing explanations offered by the prosecution and defense but reflected the defense's fear of the influence of Texas conservatism and fundamentalism.

Yates was described as in a psychotic state by the defense psychiatrist Lucy J. Puryear, M.D., whose psychoanalytic training and specialization in women's health would, it was feared, outrage Texas conservatives and was not mentioned. Dr. Puryear described interviewing Yates following the event when she "seemed lost in her own thoughts." In response to the question "What is going on inside of you now?" Yates conveyed her "fixed belief that Satan was trying to send her children to hell, and that she herself might be Satan or was Satan's agent. Her last loving act as a mother was to save her children and send them to heaven" (4).

The prosecution's expert, Park Dietz, had no interest in the mental state of Andrea Yates. He was well known for his rejection of the importance of knowing what mothers were thinking when they killed or whether their motivation was delusional. Dietz had a view of his role as projecting the behavior of the perpetrator from his analysis of the crime scene, not from understanding the motivations of the mother: "Forced to make a choice between interviewing a defendant and viewing crime scene physical evidence, he states he would forgo the interview" (Puryear 1). His view of the irrelevance of anything but physical evidence is "antithetical to the way psychoanalysts think about the mind and human behavior" (Puryear 4). Meyer and Oberman cite Dietz's general view that "no amount of stress alone can account for women killing their children." Puryear noted that Dietz questioned Yates after she had received heavy doses of antipsychotic medication that took her far from the mindset in which she drowned her five children: "The prosecution argued that she was organized and deliberate and knew what she was doing was wrong" (Puryear 4). Yates's shame at her inability to fulfill the demands of home-schooling five children, homemaking, and selflessness surely exacerbated her conviction that she was Satan's agent but that torment aroused no compassion in the prosecution.

Yates's long history of mental illness, postpartum psychosis, and recent release from a mental hospital did not prevent her receiving a life sentence in jail. It is hard to imagine how anyone could recover from the murder of her five young children, even if she were incarcerated in a first-rate psychiatric hospital. But the crime and the discussion surrounding it highlighted extreme opposition between male and female views of the crime and even a larger cultural divide.

The crime, prosecution, and media coverage threw a harsh light on the cultural collisions between Christian fundamentalism and a therapeutic world view. That cultural context of the Yates tragedy colors the discussion of the war between the sexes. Just as Andrea Yates's psychosis involved self-hatred and her belief that sending her children to God was the best protection against her Satanic agency, so the male fundamentalist response might be to accept her as utterly lost. The relevant male fundamentalist is Rusty Yates, who stood by his wife through the trial, but immediately after was determined to cut his losses and run out. Andrea Yates's supporters condemn her husband's inability to understand his role in pressuring her to have so many children and in fomenting her self-hatred at her inability to live up to his expectations. They are raising funds for an appeal of her sentence. According to *Newsweek*, Rusty Yates refuses to contribute to her appeal. He says he moved out of their house because, "I don't want to spend my time cutting tree limbs." He gives an appeal only a 30 percent chance of success. An "anonymous donor agreed to pay the roughly $50,000 cost of preparing a transcript of her trial," which is the first step in her appeal. "Rusty says he's paid all he's going to pay. 'I've lost money in this, not made it. I've given all that I want to give.' His pastor . . . says he remains involved in the church: playing basketball, attending men's prayer sessions and becoming involved in a religious singles group. Yates says he's still considering suing his wife's doctor and the mental hospital that released her less than a month before she drowned the children" (*Newsweek*, October 7, 2002, 6).

Yates's women friends see Rusty Yates as a large part of Andrea's problems. They cite his insensitivity and the fact that now free, he has not moved back into the trailer he had once considered good enough for his wife and children at the height of his religious fervor. He has moved into a country club condominium community that is luxurious by local standards, and he wants a divorce. No one could blame a man for not wanting to stay married to the woman who killed his children, but his cool unwillingness to shoulder responsibility for driving her to meet his needs when she was so incapable of doing so seems clear. And there is that fundamentalist singles group where wife number two might be waiting. The real-world twenty-first-century fundamentalist Rusty Yates and Updike's fictional sixties swinger, Rabbit Angstrom, have something in common after all. Are they brothers on the run from culpability? About to flee the burial of his daughter, Rabbit screams to the mourners: "I didn't kill her. . . . You all keep acting as if *I* did it. . . . *She's* the one."

The performance agonies of women who cannot accept their rage at the restrictions motherhood imposes are often expressed in terms of the oppressions of race and class. News accounts reveal how women script child murder in claims of victimization or represent the death of the child as beyond their control. Ambivalence over their own aggression and rage along with the ability to simulate traditional maternal values, spawns communications that twist their own murder of the child into the story of their victimization. Susan Smith charged her killing of her children with racial, sexual, and class antagonisms. In news accounts and a novel inspired by her actions and trial, performance agonies sifted through racial prejudice came to the fore.

A native of Union, South Carolina, Susan Smith emerged in the media as a churchgoing former honors student, a white woman who was separated from her husband, working as a secretary, and caring for her two sons, three-year-old Michael and fourteen-month-old Alex. Struggling to pay basic expenses on her salary and child support, she was dating the richest bachelor in town and hoped to marry him. Her mother had divorced her working-class father and married a stockbroker. Susan Smith seemed determined to take the same path. However, her wealthy boyfriend wrote her a letter announcing he was leaving her because he was not prepared to take on a ready-made family. On October 25, 1994, she strapped her children into their car seats, drove to the John D. Long Lake, and pushed her car down a boat ramp, watching as the children struggled in their car seats, drowned, and sank out of sight. Afterward, she appeared distraught and claimed her car and children had been hijacked by a black man who forced her out of the car. Her story sparked a massive manhunt that received worldwide attention and nonstop media coverage.

Susan Smith's racist lie polarized black and white communities and managed to dupe everyone for a time. When she eventually confessed she had drowned her children, the public and police were infuriated by the tremendous effort they had expended to search for the fictitious carjacker and perhaps even by the readiness with which this religious young, white mother had been believed. Smith had told authorities, and at her trial her attorney reaffirmed, that she had intended to drown herself along with her children, but "found herself rolling the car with her sons into the lake instead" (Pearson 45). She was sentenced to life in prison.

Novelist Richard Price, who had gone to South Carolina to research and attend the Susan Smith trial, used the case as an inspiration for *Freedomland* but moved the location of the crime to urban New Jersey and placed issues of race, class, sexuality, and motherhood into a more complex relationship with each other. Moreover, he brought media coverage into his novel as a central part of the crime narrative. The result is a fascinating, imaginative interpretation of the crime. Structuring his novel around the relationship between a black detective, Lorenzo Council, who investigates the murder; a reporter, Jesse Haus, who capitalizes on the story; and Brenda Martin, the mother who is responsible for the death of her four-year-old son, Cody, Price provides multiple narratives of the meaning of child murder and its exploitation in the media.

Urban edginess surrounds Brenda, whose white working-class enclave is surrounded by a black ghetto of housing projects rife with drugs, crime, and despair. Between the two neighborhoods is a refuse-strewn area known as Martyr's Park. A single, unmarried mother, she was told by the father of her child he was returning to Puerto Rico. Brenda moves easily between white and black communities, works in a "Study Club" for children in the black projects, and seems comfortable with her counterparts, black single mothers and children who, like her, are stressed by poverty and bleak prospects. One night she shows up in the local hospital, beaten, cut up, glass shards, and metal still in her hands and knees. She seems incoherent and desperate, claiming a black carjacker overpowered her, threw her out of her car, and drove off with her son.

Investigated by Lorenzo, the savvy black detective who suspects she killed her child and tries to convey the sympathy that will elicit her confession, Brenda is nevertheless known as a good mother completely devoted to her child. Accordingly, Lorenzo does all he can to find the child in case there really was a carjacker. The police descend on the black-occupied housing projects, searching for Cody. The community's leaders are furious at their treatment by police, both black and white, who harass them with searches, claiming that the life of a child is at stake and there is no time for niceties. Racial animosity and a media frenzy are stirred by the search, by community leaders enraged by the treatment of innocent black people, and by white rage.

Using social disorder as a metaphor for the mother's turmoil, Price explores her motives for murder in terms of the interaction of racial, family, and class despair that divides the neighborhood but ironically unites both blacks and whites in common experiences of hardship. A despairing loner and former junkie who has a child largely to define and anchor herself, Brenda stopped using drugs and made her child her life. Trying desperately to make raising him enough for her, she finds herself unable to continue a life with no pleasure in it for her. When she falls for the lover of a black woman friend and begins an affair with him, she cannot endure Cody's relentless needs.

Racial conflicts and disturbances within the self interact in the novel, binding social and private life, outer circumstances, and inner realities. Brenda's lie looms over everyone, mushrooming out of control, causing protests in which people are hurt and one man is killed. The hunt for the child and the deaths caused by the lie intertwine. Trying to open up Brenda's feelings about black people, Lorenzo finds a tangled ambivalence. In Brenda's past, during a brief stint as a teacher while she was on cocaine, her students, most of whom were immigrants who were people of color, brought her back to a sense of responsibility by their efforts to learn English and to work. The father of her child is Puerto Rican. Her work with the women and children in the Study Club suggests a closeness. Her new lover is black. Yet she believes African Americans are: "the *other . . .* it's *safe* to put out for them because they're not quite real to me. And if I had to guess? I'd say I'm not quite real to them either" (403).

Race, self-image, and self-knowledge interact in complex ways. Brenda's lover, Billy, is a well-educated black man who worked on Wall Street for a while but has lost his job. She is drawn to Billy's mixture of striving, decency, competence, and hunger and begins an affair with him after many years of celibacy: "It was like instant pain for me. Like a reminder of *why* I had structured my life around my son, focused my love on my son. But it was too late. . . . I had *held* someone not a child after all those years, and it was too late to go back. I had overabstained and now I was in trouble" (406–7). Her lover's sensitivity calls her back to a need for love, much as her students once called her back to a need to work, to respond to their ambition for a decent life in the States. But the need for love is itself dangerous, awakening possibilities she cannot meet for a life that integrates her own dependency and Cody's.

Drugs, the medium of exchange on the streets of the ghetto, invade her interaction with her child as she administers Benadryl to put him to sleep so she can meet Billy. Once the companion who gave structure and meaning to her life, her child now seems her jailer: "I'd think he was asleep and I'd just make it to the hallway, you know, tippytoe, and it would be, like, at the last second, 'Mah-mee, Mahmee . . . ' She used a braying sing-song. And I'd be like, 'Get to *sleep!* Brenda shouted it, eyes wide and gelid" (409).

The narrative Brenda weaves of her crime presents her relationship to Cody as a tale of emotional parasitism in which she is persuaded that Cody's survival requires her complete sacrifice of self. Nevertheless, she is able to see herself from Cody's point of view: "And how fast would *you* fall asleep, you have this, this *giant* hanging over you, this half-insane giant who didn't *love* you anymore, didn't *want* you anymore; this person who used to treat you like the sun, the moon and the stars, but no more, no more. . . ." (409).

There is life enough for one only in the duo of mother and child. The well of mother love is gradually drained dry by the child in an unavoidable parasitism. As Brenda attempts to retrieve a piece of life for herself, Cody's life diminishes. One night he tells her, "I know where you're going and I don't want you to go. . . . If you go you'll be *sorry.*" Says it just like some jealous husband: 'If you go you'll be sorry.' I almost didn't go. If he had only sounded more babyish or more pathetic, maybe I wouldn't have, but it was so hard, his voice, and it scared me. It like repelled me out of the house" (411). When Brenda returns home she finds Cody dead; he drank the bottle of Benadryl. Symbolically the child's death completes the draining away of her life. Unable to escape either her sense of responsibility or her desperate loneliness, Brenda rides an emotional roller coaster speeding from love for her child to resentment of him, to guilt over his death, which she is sure she caused by giving him Benadryl instead of herself.

Race also functions in Brenda's own crime narrative as a way to resolve performance agony. Torn between love and resentment of Cody, she disowns the crime of child murder by blaming it on the "other," permitting her to remain the "perfect mother" in the eyes of the community, and to claim victim status for herself. Racist accusations and denial of responsibility go hand in hand. Communication twisting permits her to blame a "black carjacker" and deny the magnitude of her actual sense of guilt but also to project the thirst for life that drove her to Billy as something "other" and outside, something that hijacked the direction of her life and threw it off course.

The excuse that the killing was part of a failed murder-suicide attempt offered by Susan Smith's attorney at her trial comes true in Price's novel: Brenda knows she murdered Cody and she sentences herself to death. Price scripts Brenda's narrative as one of murder-suicide in which the identity of murderer and suicide keep changing place. Cody killed himself and is technically a suicide, but Brenda is sure she killed him, and so she kills herself, making his coercive suicide, the fulfillment of his threat to her, a form of murder too.

The ongoing quality of the destructive relationship between mother and dead child is also expressed in the possibility that Brenda sees her suicide as leading to a reunion in death with her child. Although reunion fantasies are not explicit, they are embedded in the feeling that life was not possible for Cody without her or feasible for Brenda without him. They are united by a double suicide in which death serves as the continuation of their bond.

Performance agony is evident on a broader scale in the social ramifications of the narrative Brenda weaves around her crime. Her initial effort to blame a fictitious black carjacker, is recapitulated in her belief that her love for Billy hijacked her from the self-denial she had practiced that sustained their life together. Her carjacker lie is as lethal as the Benadryl she introduced to Cody: one of the marchers is killed in a protest by the black community against the way it has been treated. Billy, who helped bury Cody, is in serious trouble with the police. Brenda's inability to accept her needs or to meet her child's disrupts the stability of the city. Conversely, in the logic of the account, the stability of the community depends on parental subordination to the needs of the child. The community was unraveling because it could not protect its children from drugs and crime, from dealers selling crack from the benches surrounding the projects or recruiting its children to help them. The focused tragedy of deception, failed desire, and hopelessness epitomized by child murder drives toward the center of communal experience in a vision of cultural crisis.

Child murder and racial violence are stuff of the infotainment news devoted to the principle "If it bleeds, it leads." The media have made the dysfunctional a source of endless photo ops. In Price's novel, Brenda becomes a media celebrity at every point: as the victim of a carjacker, as the killer of her child, and as a suicide. Every facet of disorder nourishes the news, making the reporter the only one who grows fat on the eruption of the community and the deaths of Brenda and Cody. Price's reporter comes from the same well of urban disorder, but she is the only one who knows how to use it for profit by weaving and manipulating all the competing strands of the narrative for maximum interest. Each escalation helps keep the ongoing trauma news.

America is indivisible from the infotainment news that provides violent spectacles for the arena of public discourse. Urban America is encapsulated in the novel as "Freedomtown," an abandoned amusement park that has exhibits and rides based on major moments in American history, most involving disasters. America as a theme park about the bizarre, the disastrous, and the catastrophic is an image for our obsession with entertainment violence and dysfunction. Once a place of family amusements, it mirrors in its decay the erosion of the family and the capacity to find happiness there. Brenda has buried her son's body with his favorite action figures in front of a replica of a boarding house being consumed by flames in the Chicago fire. Cody had thought a female figure trapped at the window of the burning house was an angel; his remains are found just below her in a shallow grave. Private and public disaster are projected in this image of the home going up in flames, of the destroyed mother and child, of all the crises of motherhood wrapped up as a media event in the new America of entertainment violence.

In "An Analysis of Anxiety," Freud wrote that "intrauterine life and early infancy form a continuum to a far greater extent than the striking caesura of the act of birth would lead us to believe" (77–78). His elegant formulation of birth as a "striking caesura" comes true with a vengeance as it becomes clear in the fiction of child murder that pregnancy, birth, and death are part of a continuum and the splitting off of mother and child in childbirth is only a pause in their narrative line. Narratives of child murder all enact a complex interaction among mother, child, and culture. The separation of mother and fetus through birth is used to underscore their interconnectedness and serves as a metaphor for a continuation of the dynamic exchange in which the formation of two identities is at stake. The boundaries between one and the other are ill defined so that their separateness and connection depend on the twists and turns of the narrative line. A paramount question is always one of shifting borders and uncertainty about where one life begins and the other ends. Fantasies of child murder move to the forefront when cultural definitions of appropriate boundaries between mother and child are confused, when mother and child seem merely extensions of each other.

Portrayals of child murder suggest how much the mother experiences her relationship with her child as an aspect of her self-image. This creates a conflicted symbiosis in which she is torn between the need to preserve that intense connection and the need to free herself from it, much as the child is torn between dependency and the urge to separate. The ability to achieve a balance is governed by the mother. Traditional definitions of the good mother are distorted by a destructive egotism. The perfectly devoted mother seems to reward a dependent, regressive child with feelings of approbation. She keeps at bay whatever anxiety she may have over the wider demands of work or love on an adult basis. The mother pulls the child in; the child is secure until competing claims threaten the arrangement. When the mother's impulse to separate grows strong, both the mother's and child's stability seem threatened. The child seems to the mother a destroyer; the child, unfit for independence, is enraged.

Performance murders spring from mothers' self-hatred at the inability to fulfill the opposing claims on them. Denial of a separate existence is also projected in a destructive and malignant egotism that uses the child as a mirror of either the mother's hated self or her idealized self. Either way, the child is not a separate individual. In *Rabbit, Run,* the child can be stinking and wailing and in constant need, a projection of dependency and ugliness. In *Beloved,* she is a magical hallucination, physically perfect with poreless skin, rising from the water of the river as if she were Venus rising from the sea. Her idealized physicality along with her absolute power to mesmerize and to command attention exploits metaphors of infantile grandiosity and symbolizes Sethe's need to believe that she was right to kill her to enable a magical "rebirth." Whether idealized as young and as beautiful as Beloved or demonized as befouled with feces like Rebecca, the child sums up the split between the all-good and all-powerful combined mother-child duo. That the perfection of Beloved is associated with her wish to destroy Sethe highlights a large general question.

What happens when the mother's performance anxieties cause a different split? When the self-hating mother who cannot approximate her own ideal of female perfection feels bound to a daughter whose youthful perfection intensifies her own self-hatred? The negative bond between a mother who is grandiose herself and craves feelings of omnipotence, but who feels her own potency waning and finds in the child's growth a drain on her powers, provokes a different crisis. Omnipotent and impotent become polarized in the figures of mother and child. The splitting reflects extreme and opposing self-images that threaten stability and give rise to a third possibility in the meaning and motivation for child murder. What if the mother attempts to enhance or regain her own power by reclaiming the life of the child, by reconciling the mother-child duo in one being?

The woman who kills her daughter may see her act as a form of reclamation, combining and unifying impotence and omnipotence, passivity and control, inadequacy and adequacy. Ironically the opposing energies of the relationship sustain it. The child will not stop demanding because it is constantly rejected and denied; the mother's efforts to satisfy its needs only exacerbate the insatiable need for more, and fuel the mother's resentment. Casting the child as a despised or idealized aspect of self scripts the mother's need not for the individuation or separation of the child but for self-enhancement, reassurance, and incorporation of the child's youth. The relationship between mother and child and the line between two identities emerges as a kind of border war in which real distinctions are ground to bits between self-hatred and grandiosity.

Performance agonies are most intense when the mother expresses them as competitive rage against her daughter. Such relationships may constitute what could be called an interactive violence in which the mother feels an envious rancor toward a daughter whose very existence she sees as depleting her own. In this sense, murderous rage is expressed through a vision of the child as a parasite who grows more insatiable as it grows up.

Anne Sexton's "Mother and Daughter" sees a daughter's coming of age as the theft of a mother's own life:

> Linda, you are leaving
> your old body now.
> You've picked my pocket clean
> and you've racked up all my
> poker chips and left me empty
> and, as the river between us
> narrows, you do calisthenics,
> that womanly leggy semaphore.
> Question you about this
> and you will sew me a shroud.
> and hold up Monday's broiler
> and thumb out the chicken gut.
> Question you about this
> and you will see my death
> drooling at these gray lips
> while you, my burglar, will eat
> fruit and pass the time of day (12).

Sexton's persona in the poem describes her daughter's life as itself stripping her of all her assets and "killing" her. But the daughter will not simply "eat fruit" and escape unscathed for doing so; instead, she will be bound to the death of the mother by "causing" it. The accusation that her daughter will be responsible for her death and will "sew me a shroud" casts the daughter in the role of a murderer who is responsible for her mother's suicide. This is a reformulation of the mother-child duo based on a negative bond in which neither should live without the other. This is not unlike Richard Price's treatment of Brenda and Cody; he cannot survive without his mother who is like an essential organ of his own body, a living part of himself. Cody's suicide, if caused by Brenda, also kills her by leading to her own suicide. Death ties them together forever. Sexton actually used her anger and suicidal longing as weapons. According to her daughter, she delivered this poem to her daughter after finishing it, an act that followed many other examples of an interaction between them based on Sexton's morbid rage (Gray Sexton 144–45). Sexton's suicide fulfilled her own prophecy, perhaps attempting to establish her own death as a legacy of guilt for her daughter.

Alternations between omnipotence and worthlessness are expressed in the complex use of guilt as a coercive expression of power. Just by breathing and living and growing up, the daughter is cast in the role of a killer. To not kill, the daughter will have to die, as if the daughter were the part of the body that controls aging, a part that, if destroyed, would halt the ravages of time.

Poems by Sylvia Plath suggest that fantasies of child murder and suicide may contain much more. Plath's poems make use of the variety of meanings suicide can hold: reunion and retaliation fantasies shape suicide in "Daddy," and rebirth fantasies recur in the serial suicide attempts in "Lady Lazarus." Child murder reshapes such fantasies so as to increase the allure of death. In Plath's "The Edge," murder is seen as an enfolding of children back into oneself, reversing the experience of depletion through childbirth. The children in death are "returned" to the mother, even as the mother in death is released from the torments of living. Murder-suicide, a frequent theme in both actual and imaginative accounts of child murder, offers reconciliation though recombining mother and child, and blurring "the edge" or border between life and death. Plath writes in "Edge":

The woman is perfected.
Her dead

Body wears the smile of accomplishment,
The illusion of a Greek necessity

Flows in the scrolls of her toga,
Her bare

Feet seem to be saying:
We have come so far, it is over.

Each dead child coiled, a white serpent,
One at each little

Pitcher of milk, now empty.
She has folded

Them back into her body as petals
Of a rose close when the garden

Stiffens and odours bleed
From the sweet, deep throats of the night flower.

The moon has nothing to be sad about,
Staring from her hood of bone.

She is used to this sort of thing.
Her blacks crackle and drag. (93)

The imagery captures related ideas of stability, monumentality, and completion. The mother in death achieves the status of Greek sculpture. The dead children are like serpents each at a dry breast, evoking the mother who starves her child. The poet uses milk as a metaphor for feeling as well as nourishment. Dead and no longer needing anything from the mother, the children achieve a kind of perfection too by losing their separateness and being folded back into the body of the mother. No longer separate and demanding "serpents," they are "roses." Presiding over this reunion with the mother's body is the female moon, which is seen, like the Greek statue, as hard, a "hood of bone" with black spaces for eye holes and mouth hole, impassive, and dark as in a skull or death's head.

The child who dies is often a repository for extreme anxieties over self-image as the mother may alternate between efforts at being the perfect mother and her sense of worthlessness because she cannot tolerate her life with her child. The mother sees the child as an extension of herself and not as a separate individual. Birth is not something permanent, but a reversible condition in Plath's poem. Freud's "striking caesura," the break in the rhythmic line, can be rewritten according to the heartbeat of the poet.

What happens when beauty is defined in terms of the controlled abandonment and destruction of the child's soul? Communication-twisting and child murder have combined to produce a new and horrifying narrative of the beauty of cruelty in which the child is placed in the service of the mother's idealization of her own performance as a woman, as an artist beyond ordinary conventions, or even as a mythic figure in her own right. The perfection of description available to the accomplished poet carries the search for appearances of beauty as well as normalcy into the verbal realm. The verbal brilliance of Plath, for example, aims for and achieves a sculptural elegance of statement for a series of images that link horrible prospects and beautiful writing.

Antagonisms between mother and child based on the mother's need for reassurance about her own performance may appear in narratives of great beauty, drawing on poetic skill to achieve positive distortions that present the vile, cruel, and horrifying in an aesthetic context. Like Plath's use of imagery of sculpture or roses to describe the death of children as a beautiful and pleasing act of reclamation, the use of an aesthetics of violence and abandonment is a characteristic of some destructive mother-child relationships built on violence. Language serves as a buffer to experience. Gorgeous writing narrating a tale of the violence done to a child by a mother who is a gifted writer may offer layers of speech designed to mask both the brutality of the mother and the legitimate rage of the daughter.

In a powerful first novel, *White Oleander* by Janet Fitch, the beauty of the poisonous plant with its fragrant white flowers projects a mother-daughter bond in which the mother, a poet, uses ethnicity, legend, and poetics to elevate a narrative of murderous aggression into one of elegance and power. The role of language-twisting looms large in a mother's primal violence involving the virtual design of a child who will look like a younger version of herself, the attempted annihilation of that child's individuation, and the murder of a lover that underscores the price paid for crossing her.

The mother's performance anxieties are resolved by a grandiose and destructive egotism that seeks to create and use a daughter who will be a purely admiring clone of herself. That need is enacted through relationships based on control. Choosing a man to father her child who so resembled her he could be her twin, Ingrid is a mother who carries self-absorption to the point of trying to raise Astrid as a daughter who will serve as an extension of herself. Since the satisfied child becomes a separate person, the way to accomplish a perpetual bond is through applied cruelty. Ingrid tells her she has no home or life but with her, and then subjects Astrid to serial abandonment. When Astrid is three, Ingrid leaves her with a neighbor for the afternoon and disappears for a year. Ingrid's explanation is simply, "I was used to having time to think, freedom. I felt like a hostage" (373). Or "you, you just wanted, wanted, wanted. Mommy Mommy Mommy until I thought I would throw you against the wall" (373). Ingrid provides her daughter with epigrammatic justifications for her own cruelty: "Love humiliates you, but hatred cradles you. It's so soothing" (34). Aggression is her own technique for "cradling" the child she raises to admire her ruthlessness, to see it as a legendary force.

A larger literary culture of violence provides an aesthetic and cultural context in *White Oleander.* Ingrid sees herself as a heiress of all the Vikings who hacked their gods to pieces, hung them on trees, and pursued their vision by voyaging to new, strange places. She sees ruthless ferocity as the essence of purity and beauty. Believing all power and control emerge from cruelty, she uses her poet's notebook to record her goals: "Spread a malicious rumor. Suggest suicide to a severely depressed person. Tell a child it isn't very attractive or bright. Throw handfuls of useless foreign coins into a beggar's cup" (212). Language and act coalesce in her work for a movie magazine in which she cuts and pastes interviews, using a knife and claiming: "I'm peeling . . . the skins of the insipid scribblers." When the publisher bends to see her work, she slashes his arm.

Language is used to redeem violence from ugliness in a hip Los Angeles world where creativity, murder, and celebrity are intertwined. Ingrid's grandiosity is expressed through her appropriation of great villains: she works for a tabloid called *Caligula's Mother* and identifies with Milton's

Satan, whom she praises for his endless hatred and refusal to submit to God. In the horserace of life, she puts her money on Medea—at the racetrack she bets on a horse named Medea's Pride and wins. Just as Medea poisoned the beautiful blouse she gave as a wedding present to the princess Jason wanted to marry, so Ingrid coats the doorknob of her lover's bedroom door with a deadly mixture. Touching it will kill the man who abandoned her or perhaps even his new lover. Murder is the winning ticket for Ingrid, but it is also the key to success in the world of media, magazines, and poetry slams.

Contemporary literary culture makes celebrities of those, including writers, who act on brutal urges and, conversely, of killers who redeem themselves through writing. Actual murder catapults Ingrid's poetry to the forefront of American interest. While Astrid is exploited in a series of foster homes, ending up in a state institution for violent teenagers no one wants, Ingrid in prison is embraced by literature students, attorneys working to free her, and university administrators offering her professorships. Ingrid's triumph as a writer through murder provides a sharp, ironic satire of celebrity culture. Even the lawyer who represents her wants a stint on legal talk-shows and hopes to win, along with Ingrid's freedom, a prize post as a legal pundit on TV.

The voice of the abandoned, abused Astrid helps shape a competing narrative of soul murder that counters her mother's celebrity as killer. This enables the child's perspective on her mother's lifelong attempts to extinguish her to be fully realized as a narrative. The result is a strikingly eerie representation of the daughter's ambivalence, her final understanding of both her mother's violence, and her wish for reunion even at the price of her own life. Longing for fusion and security, the daughter claims, "I want to disappear into her body, I wanted to be one of her eyelashes, or a blood vessel in her thigh . . ." (39). Plath's poetic imagination of the suicidal mother who takes her children back into her body by taking them with her in death finds a counterpart in Fitch's brilliantly realized evocation of the pain of the daughter who might agree to give up her life to do just that.

The mother-child duo can be a duet. The tale of child-killing as soul murder, as an ongoing relationship, can be told by the daughter who has experienced and observed the roles available for women in literary tradition and contemporary life. The suicide, the murderer, the playgirl, the housewife, and the destroyer are actresses whose performance agonies take different forms. All express the collapse of secure cultural definitions of the family as the path to wholeness. Astrid at eighteen is a veteran of foster care in the variety of homes that come to represent contemporary family life. In these she has met "Women with pills, with knives, women dyeing their hair. Women painting doorknobs with poison for love, making dinners too large to eat, firing into a child's room at close range. It was a play and I knew how it ended, I didn't want to audition for any of the roles. It was no game, no casual thrill. It was three bullet Russian roulette" (265). Like Ishmael, she survives disaster to tell about it.

Soul murder and child murder are communicative and expressive forms of violence that lend themselves to a variety of narratives: of sexual transgression, generational revolt, altruistic violence, racial conflict, or literary idealizations. Deceptive forms of communication are essential to virtually all of these. Metaphoric language provides the buffer between the mother's thought, feeling, speech, and actions, mitigating the horror of the act even as it describes it. For example, Updike uses Janice's drunkenness as metaphor for Janice's need to blur the relationship between cause (putting the baby in the tub) and effect (the infant's drowning). Placing her arms in water, Janice does not expect even to wet the sleeves of her bathrobe; lowering the child into a full tub, Janice believes not that she lets go of her, but that the "hands" of the water take her away.

The language splits causal actions from resulting effects. It can be used to blur the violence of what is being done or to sharpen it. Language may serve defensive or aggressive purposes. Similarly, allusive literary references both convey the mother's grandiosity and place a veil between the mother and the repellent behavior described. Ingrid's grandiose belief that her cruelty toward a helpless child is comparable to Satan's against God or Medea's against Jason uses literary reference and association to magnify her own aggression. In other representations, imagery of reincorporating the child in oneself, of converting its needy, unruly life to the perfection of Greek sculpture confuses emotion with action, representing murder as a creative, aesthetic event. These representations draw on the evocative power of language to reinforce the communicative and expressive quality of violence and have a formal power all their own. Anne Sexton's "Mother and Daughter" is a poem of mental processes, emotions, and sequences of thought moving in two directions: inward to reflect the view of the growing daughter as a parasite gnawing at the mother's life, and outward as aggression against the self-esteem of daughter who is punished with violent language just for living and growing. Expression of aggression is the model of the mind of the poet's persona whether representing the devouring quality of suicidal thought or the murderous anger at her daughter. In literary representations, splitting the idealized and demonized aspects of self creates a vacuum filled by the use of the child.

All literature confers on language, fantasy, and dream the felt effect of action. But representations of child murder seem uniquely fabricated to fill the vacuum between the idealization or demonization of the self with narratives of the child's death. The distinctive energy of the fiction of child murder may come from its representation of the mothers' actions as a dysfunctional effort to repair their own self-esteem. When Brenda in Price's *Freedomland* compassionately imagines her child seeing her as a giant torturing him with her withdrawal of love, she expresses both her guilt over the child's death and her belief that his death validated her omnipotent power over him. Conversely, the mother may script her life as being destroyed by the powerful demands of the child who is draining her strength, much as Sexton's poem describes. In this sense the mother's suicide is a destructive act aimed in part against the daughter.

At the parting of mother and child Freud projects as the "striking caesura" of birth, the break in the continuity of the poetic lifeline between mother and child is not an emptiness but a source of narratives about aggression. A mother may script her actions as a murder or suicide or as a "partial" murder or "partial" suicide. Lacan defined absence as a state of indeterminacy between "intrusion" (too much presence) and "loss" (too much absence) and felt those poles could never be breached. But in the literature of child murder, oscillation between demon and ideal, self-love and self-hatred, grandiosity and worthlessness close the gap and confuse sharp definitions of the separateness of the mother and child. Demon and ideal are figured in the mother-child duo that comes to represent dualities that can be bridged or reversed by the action and process of murder. Extraordinarily varied, such narratives may be scripted as accidents, altruistic acts, suicides, or aesthetic alliances with mythic powers that result in celebrity and success. What unifies them is the portrait provided of women in agony over their performance as women and mothers. Whether bent on denying transgression of traditional values or exalting their violation of them for higher causes of altruism or art, they provide tragic images of the thirst for legitimation, empowerment, and the price paid for both.

The alternation between idealization and demonization makes it possible to describe child killing as a performance murder. In some fiction, idealized maternal roles are contrasted explicitly with the mother's incapacity to perform them, whether because of her personality, unmet needs or situation. Drunken Janice compares herself with the TV mothers of the fifties; self-sacrificing, lonely Brenda is beset by dreams of love; Sethe is powerless as a slave but makes protecting her daughter from slavery all that counts; Ingrid insists only her daughter matters but disappears for a year to escape her so she can think and write—all reflect the performance anxiety of mothers who affirm norms of motherhood while also being pulled by competing cultural ideals of youth, freedom, self-affirmation, and success. But there is still another prospect implied by the desire for access to desirable men, and for youth and freedom in Anne Sexton's "Mother and Daughter." What if the performance queens of the future were to be the daughters who reject motherhood and pregnancy as forms of failure? The hated pregnancy is not only an obstacle to freedom, pleasure, and success, but also a living, growing proof that one is a loser.

Child murder is the special-of-the-day on the new media menu of entertainment violence, which focuses new fears that being a mother is a loser's game. In the sixties and seventies, Alice Crimmins was the newspapers' poster girl for women who claimed a sexual freedom that would destroy the family. Now the media and culture accept a large degree of family instability and sexual experimentation, and what arouses fear is colder than sex. Accounts of child murder feature mothers who kill newborns casually and with surprise that anyone might care. Those who make infotainment news are not products of working-class hardship or racial oppression but of mainstream, middle class America.

Mothers in the news who are convicted of child murder seem increasingly young, may be comfortably off, have the option of legal abortion readily available and parents willing to accept their sexually active lives, but neither they nor they parents seem to want to confront the difficulty posed by their pregnancy. Flat language guides the representation of how they kill their newborns, a communicative flatness that expresses performance agonies over motherhood by a virtually complete denial that motherhood took place at all.

Amy Ellwood was the seventeen-year-old daughter of two high school teachers who knew she was pregnant but were afraid she would run off with her boyfriend if they acknowledged the fact. They never mentioned her pregnancy to her. In a detailed account of Amy's behavior, Patricia Pearson notes that she delivered the baby early one morning in 1989 in the bathroom of her comfortable suburban home. She wrapped the kicking baby in a towel, put it in a bucket, and went back to sleep. She had decided that although the baby was kicking and making noise, it was a "miscarriage" (72). That is what she told her friends and the young man who was the baby's father. When she awoke, she wrapped the baby in several trash bags, put it in a cooler, put the cooler in her car, and kept it there as she drove to see friends, meet her boyfriend, go swimming, and spend time at the mall. That night, she dumped the baby into Laurel Lake, not far from her home in Suffolk County, Long Island. When the corpse was discovered by swimmers who notified the police, she was surprised. "'I couldn't imagine,' she later explained, 'why the police were involved'" (Pearson 65).

Among the first young, middle-class women to become notorious for coolly disposing of their infants, Amy seemed to represent the advent of a different kind of child murderer. She scripted her murder as a denial that the child was ever alive in the first place. Surprisingly, the community found no better way to support her than to simply embroider her denial. Patricia Pearson reports that "the pastor at [her] church wrote a letter to her judge describing what she'd done in the lake as a 'baptism'" (72). She was also praised as a good student with a college acceptance for the coming fall who should not be inconvenienced. Although she shared with her fictional counterparts a view of the child as having no separate life, she lacked, in media accounts, anything beyond a bland surprise that anyone cared about her easygoing murder. Her sentence for the crime was postponed so that she could attend college as planned.

In 1988 coolly executed, middle-class child murder seemed a rare occurrence; twelve years later it would focus fear that cold violence was the hallmark of a new generation of young women. Although accurate statistics for the number of infanticides do not exist since many incidents are assumed to go undiscovered, "the National Center on Health Statistics reported that infanticide had climbed 55% between 1985 and 1988, until it was several times the rate at which adult women were murdered. Nearly half of the child maltreatment fatalities between 1985 and 1992 involved infants under a year old" (Pearson 70). More important than figures of increasing frequency was the increasing outrage of the media in reporting such crimes.

Amy Grossberg and Brian Peterson were high school sweethearts who had gone off to college in 1996 knowing Amy was pregnant but determined to tell no one. Although both came from concerned, middle-class families and Amy was described as having a particularly close relationship with her mother, her parents never noticed that she was more than eight months pregnant. That fact was not lost on the women in her dorm, but Amy did not want to talk about it, so they respected her wish. She gave birth to a son in a motel room in Delaware with the help of Brian Peterson, who put the baby in a plastic garbage bag and disposed of it in a dumpster in back of the motel. When the act was discovered, prosecutors and the media called for the death penalty.

Both Amy and Brian claimed the child was stillborn, but forensic evidence suggested otherwise. An account by reporter Melanie Thernstrom revealed that prosecutors had evidence suggesting "that Brian and Amy's crime was less a panicked accident than a deliberate incident of first degree murder: Moments after their infant was born, they bashed in his skull while he was still alive and then left his battered body in a Dumpster to die" (20).

The Grossberg family dealt with the notoriety of the case by increasing it to provide their narrative of what happened. In June 1997 Amy and her parents "appeared on Barbara Walters's television show 20/20 . . . to convey that Amy was a good daughter. Filmed sitting on her bed in a girlish room with large stuffed animals, Amy and her mother spoke in eerily matching phrases, affirming their special closeness" (Thernstrom 20). Although the case aroused sympathy, it also provoked ongoing demands for the death penalty or a life sentence.

Amy continued to claim that she thought she had a miscarriage and could not understand why the baby was left in the dumpster. Friends reported that Amy had "told [Brian] she would kill herself if he told anyone" she was pregnant. When it became clear that Amy's defense was to blame the disposal of the baby on Brian, Brian's lawyers argued that he "was under Amy's spell." He pleaded guilty to manslaughter in exchange for a reduced sentence. Robert Hanley reported Brian testifying that after the delivery he did not believe the baby was alive and that Amy had said: "Get rid of it—get rid of it!" (New York Times, March 10, 1998, A1). Amy Grossberg eventually pleaded guilty to manslaughter to avoid the prospect of a life sentence. At the hearing prosecutors insisted that Amy Grossberg "showed a chilling indifference to [the baby's] life" (New York Times, April 23, 1998, A1, B7).

Seven months later the case of Melissa Drexler would make front-page news, arousing concern that the cold killing of babies was a trend. Melissa Drexler (see chapter 6) was dancing at her high school prom when she went to the ladies room, delivered a baby, stuffed it in the trash, and went back to the prom. She danced, asked the band to play her favorite song, and had a salad, seeming to reach a high plane of chilling detachment. Both she and Amy Grossberg fit the emerging media image of callous young, middle-class women who epitomized a generation of women who could kill their newborns without missing a beat.

The depersonalized violence of young women toward their newborns linked child murder to a complete breakdown of values. Grossberg and Drexler were emerging as the female counterparts of Eric Harris and Dylan Klebold, the Columbine High School boys in Littleton, Colorado, whose calculated killing of their schoolmates in 1999 left thirteen dead and three others permanently disabled. Harris and Klebold were said to have been inspired by violent videogames. Did they see themselves as action heroes who could make history with a dysfunctional parody of masculine power? Were Melissa Drexler and Amy Grossberg suitable counterparts? Neither girl was a serial killer but in a sense both were affected by a warped vision of the ideal young woman that counterpoints Harris's and Klebold's travesty of cool, masculine power.

Grossberg's narrative stressing her denial of her pregnancy and her determination to go on through college was a dysfunctional parody of the myth of a middle-class young girl's innocence and intelligent ambition. She was intent on hiding her pregnancy and maintaining the image of the perfect child she believed her parents had of her. Both her parents also seemed committed to denying or not noticing anything was amiss. In their interview with Barbara Walters, her mother claimed that Amy had never so much as gotten a parking ticket and finished Amy's sentences for her. Amy was focused on being the perfect daughter, not the failed college girl who'd gotten knocked up.

Cool killing of newborns is front-page news in part because it dramatizes how much the performance anxiety as a young woman who can play the perfect daughter and rising star can be allayed by a destructive egotism that explodes old notions of innocence, family protectiveness, and the need for reality testing. Striving, middle-class parents may not demand celibacy of their daughters, but the family's success ethic requires that their daughters know enough not to get pregnant. Both parents and children have a stake in using each other as projections of effectiveness and control. No longer only an icon of innocence, the young woman must be, if not virginal, then savvy enough to remain a go-getter.

Amy Grossberg aroused strong feeling because she was an embodiment of performance anxiety in an affluent but hardworking middle-class world in which early or unwed pregnancy is the mark of female ineptitude. Abortion, adoption, or marriage are realistic pathways out of that problem, but they are all alternatives that require the mother-to-be to forsake the grandiosity of believing she is beyond failure. If realism requires accepting pregnancy as a fact and even a mistake, killing the newborn and denying it was ever alive, it would seem, does not. It was such destructive egotism, perhaps as much as the actual crime, that sparked cries for the death penalty or a life sentence for Amy Grossberg. It made media coverage of the college girl who coolly disposes of her lovechild a vehicle for expressing cultural fears that female success no longer had anything to do with confronting motherhood.

The young mother's ability to deny pregnancy and birth constitutes an admittedly dysfunctional attack on postmodern theories that deny female agency. Literary fiction of child murder throws complex narratives in the face of Lacan's projection of "living process" as an irresistible affirmation of bliss without language. That Lacanian interaction without verbal construction is repudiated or disrupted by the thickly meaningful ways in which women bring their own scripts to bear on pregnancy, birth, and the child's prospects. Narratives of the mother's goals and performance anxieties speak to the experience of changing ideals of womanhood. Literary child murder returns us through violence to the close connections between realism, representation, and those changing attitudes toward women's lives that lie at the heart of a traumatic modernity.

Narratives of child murder provide both a critique of abstraction and a critique of the material condition of women at the same time. American narratives of child murder reflect a turmoil over performance of the selfless motherhood that remains an ideal while becoming ever more difficult to fulfill. As Meyer and Oberman have shown, even women whose children die because of their inability to protect them from abusive husbands or lovers are often convicted of murder along with their batterers because the expectation of absolute protective selflessness, even when under siege, remains strong. Ironically the performance agonies erupting in child murder reflect the high traditional place of mother and child in our culture through violation of their sacred status.

Performance violence erupting in child murder makes it clear that representations of the violence of women are more than snapshots of postmodern effects and easily defy the efforts of recent academic discourses to address them. The Lacanian theorist who sees gender as only a category of language or the determinist who invokes biology to claim the social irrelevance and irremediable weakness of women cannot readily deal with the meaning and motivation of child murders portrayed in fiction or the media. Nor can the post-Marxist's claim of the will to power of capitalist-dominated media spewing images designed to enforce loyalty to consumption provide a political-economic explanation for child murder. Surely capitalism would be better served by reinforcing ideologies of happy motherhood if only because households with children need to buy ever more goods to meet the changing needs of the growing child.

Accounts of child murder throw the death of innocents in the face of hollow abstraction. Intricate maternal narratives refute the nonverbal "presymbolic" conception of the "Real" or visions of the silenced feminine position. Each of the women discussed commits violence as a woman not in the "male position" but out of distinctively female experiences and goals defined in inventive narratives. These may address sexual experimentation, social protest, competition with other women, romantic longing, or career ambition. Mothers claim agency as much over the narratives they weave as they do over the lives they create and destroy. The mothers' justifying narratives of victimization or altruism or even denial of pregnancy or birth all open up the ways in which language mediates emotion and seeks to control and structure the responses of the onlooker in the public sphere.

Performance agonies that erupt in child murder are never identical, never the recapitulation of the same trauma but instead provide subjective and inventive engagements with motherhood in a culture that prizes performance, success, and public achievement. Over a spectrum of changing ideals and a variety of hated weaknesses, different aspects of female ideals are disclosed. Each of the women discussed unsettles our heritage of faith in maternal love and care. Together they expose the fear that the entire chain of generations of mothers and children is breaking. Ironically, the serious literature of child murder may reaffirm the high sanctity of mother and child by violating it so memorably. Meanwhile in the media "nice" girls who coolly kill their babies serve as poster girls for the latest maternal style.

CHAPTER 4

THE LADY IS A TERRORIST

Women, Violence, and Political Action

As a member of the Symbionese Liberation Army, Kathleen Soliah planted a bomb under a police car. She played a virulent role as one of her captors in the transformation of the kidnapped heiress Patty Hearst into Tanya, the terrorist. When Soliah went underground to escape from the police, she transformed herself into a country-club socialite living in a Minnesota mansion, the well-to-do wife and mother of traditional American dreams. It was Hearst, the heiress, who went to jail for bank robbery and became a seventies icon displayed on posters and T-shirts. Her picture toting a machine gun, taken by a surveillance camera during her bank robbery in 1974, blazoned from novelty items with the caption "I'm Patty Hearst." The terrorist who finds happiness in a mansion while the heiress travels the route to jail are on the same trip. The exchange between the all-American rich girl and what Thomas Pynchon called the "floozy with an Uzi" takes place along a two-way street. Women who travel both directions on that road express a new and different form of politics.

Conventional wisdom holds that political violence and terrorism are inspired and shaped by structural inequities, those broad social forces, such as poverty, that operate independently of individual situations or predilections. One widely recognized formulation holds that violence arises primarily when no legitimate means of protest is available. But portrayals of the political violence of women in the contemporary United States indicate otherwise. A personalization of all social issues lends political terrorism a unique meaning and configuration of motives.

Violent women activists in our literature constitute an *experiential* definition of female political power expressed primarily in the moment of violent action. Through that action they experience the passage from one state to another as the rush of power. From terrorist to lady, from lady to terrorist is the seesaw whose extremes serve to organize the consciousness of a female vision of power as the experience of transfer, movement, and change. Violent political action reflects an identity violence that envisions power as individualistic, actual, and elemental. It is marked by a radical personalization of all substantive social issues.

In "Self-Reliance," Emerson described power as a moment of extreme vitality once envisioned as the passage from "savage" to "civilized." Grandiosity achieved and sustained by amoral violence in contemporary writing eerily echoes Emerson's notion that power can itself bespeak an identity violence that resides in the moment of "transition from a past to a new state . . . in the darting to an aim," and identifies power as the amoral thrill of change. Emerson's celebration of the self was sweetened by spiritual idealism. The literature of political activism often follows a darker process of radical personalization that portrays moral life and moral agony through their violation. Activists enact an identity violence marked by richly imaginative and deceptive speech and destructive egotism. It is a violence that vitalizes the woman who commits it and moves to the status of visible crisis the struggle for identity as a terrifying agent of change.

Such a conception locates power and force entirely within the person of the terrorist who controls violent disruption. The personalization of political violence has a unique meaning for women. Apologists for modern terrorism have stressed the terrorist cell as providing a communal experience organized on principles of collective emancipation. But women could not achieve power through the community of the cell. For example, even Frantz Fanon, architect of the modern ideology of terrorism as a means of restoring humanity and creating solidarity among the colonized oppressed, nevertheless justified the oppression of women by claiming: "acceptance of their men as masters prevented Algerian men from really bowing to their colonizers. The Algerian man remained sure of his manhood because he controlled his own women so completely" (Rowbotham 237). Women were eventually pressed into service in various roles in violent actions against the French, but after their victory, Algerian men lost little time before imposing even harsher restrictions on them than had been allowed under French law. Women who had risked their lives for national liberation found that submerging themselves in a larger cause only drowned their hopes for empowerment.

In the fiction of American women terrorists, destructive egotism rules, swallowing American traditions of individualism and exploiting our Emersonian celebrations of innate power. For Emerson that force was divine, the expression of an indwelling God each person has the potential to reach. Women terrorists frequently invoke superhuman or legendary female ancestors: Wonder Woman, the Holy Mother, or Mother Earth herself. As Leslie Marmon Silko has her Native American woman say as she writes her history of radicalism, "Poor Engels and Marx . . . they had not understood that the earth was mother to all beings, and they had not understood anything about the spirit beings" (749). This is a politics that transcends ideology and formulaic dogma to focus on how power feels.

Power as the experience of taking action, as the moment of change, is expressed by stressing descriptions of the sensations of mastery and force. An experiential sublime emerges through the personal sensation of omnipotence deriving from daily encounters and intensified by organizing a life around risk. By foregoing the life of security and stability for one of daring, women reverse all expectations of domestic order. Producing, experiencing, and escaping each high-risk activity make violence a lifestyle involving perpetual motion. In transit to escape capture, the underground life exalts impermanence and instability. A vision of power in instability and transition suggests several distinctive characteristics. Power (1) is revealed only through disruptive action, (2) is present and future oriented, never permanent, and (3) produces uncertain results because of the unpredictability of the dimensions of destruction. Each of these characteristics exalts risk, but all produce one sure effect: power and force are measured by the person of the terrorist who controls disruption and experiences its rush. The issue of control is central to the formation of the radical as a destructive egotist. It is not simply that she refuses to see herself as a victim; she believes that by wielding aggression, she can harness aggression itself to her will. A major characteristic is the belief that one can control one's life only by staging or taking charge of violent events and experiencing them.

As an attack on the conventional wisdom that women require stability and support, the choice of a life of risk and danger carries with it a rejection of formulaic radicalism prized by older forms of insurgency. Devaluation of stability gives rise to an attack even on the methodical radicalism of the past or celebrations of antirational religious terrorism. A compulsion to self-fulfillment inflames the need to awaken the potential for violence within the individual who can transcend female inhibitions and emerge as a powerful will.

The terrorism of women in American fiction constitutes an assault on the denials of the agency of women as well as the static category of the linguistic "feminine position" as one of inchoate deprivation. It constitutes an assault on devaluations of the individual and the facile anti-western attacks and dehumanization characteristic of Baudrillard whose rage at the victories of the capitalist West takes the form of an orgiastic nihilism. The terrorism of women in American literature also constitutes a rebuke of Baudrillard's insistence that resistance to power is impossible. It does so by rejecting the basic presumption that individualism is meaningless, which has guided much of the thinking about culture and representation from Lévi-Strauss's indictment of the self as "the spoiled brat of philosophy" to Lacan's insistence that the self or "human subject" is a void, an unreal illusion of language, to Baudrillard's political view that the individual is only a synthetic product of capitalism, so that resistance to any dominant force is impossible.

Baudrillard's denial of individualism is central to discussions of the portrayal of individual action and political violence. Because it informs the theory of representation that has addressed the issue of terrorism, a brief mention of its tenets may be useful.

Baudrillard stresses the role of capital in producing the images, signs, and sheer consumerism that annihilate individual difference and individualism itself and eventually make any political or personal resistance to capitalism irrelevant. He sees the destruction of individual difference as a "schizophrenic" need to consume identities through consuming images. It is defined as "feminine" because it places everyone in the position of the powerless "void of the subject" that fills its emptiness and weakness with mass-produced images designed to promote more consumption. That process destroys individualism as a concept.

Baudrillard severs the connection between individual action, the rebellion against economic power that is usually central to political insurgency, and the will and the ability to express individual difference even through capitalism's approved mode, selective shopping. His conception of consumerism annihilates individual choice: "The whole discourse on consumption, whether learned or lay, is articulated on the mythological sequence of the fable: a man endowed with needs which direct him toward objects that give him satisfaction" ("Consumer Society" 35). But this centered individual consumer does not really exist, according to Baudrillard, because "the manufacturers control behavior as well as direct social attitudes and needs. The world of objects and needs would thus be a world of general hysteria. Just as the organs and functions of a body in hysterical conversion become a gigantic paradigm which the symptom replaces and refers to, in consumption objects become a vast paradigm designating another language through which something else speaks" ("Consumer Society" 45). That "something else" is presumably the "language" produced by capitalism's domination of the media.

In *For a Critique of the Political Economy of the Sign,* Baudrillard writes that late capitalism "institutes a certain mode of signification in which all the surrounding signs act as simple elements in a logical calculus and refer to each other within the framework of the system of sign exchange value" (191). In effect, whatever we buy, we buy capitalism; whatever we say, we speak capitalism.

It is not only individualism as a concept that no longer exists, according to Baudrillard, but individual agency or choice and finally even the individual: "The logic of exchange is primordial. In a way, the individual is nonexistent . . . a certain language is prior to the individual. This language is a social form in relation to which there can properly speaking be no individuals, since it is an exchange structure. . . ." *(Political Economy* 75).

Presumably, since we construct ourselves from the objects we consume, we *are* the simulated objects we consume. Accordingly, there can be no resistance to the "code" or any "revolution" in any known sense. For Baudrillard the media-dominated world of consumers consuming images makes it impossible to resist or even expose the workings of capitalist power. In this orgy of futility, all efforts only come down to collusion with the oppressor.

In *Forget Foucault,* Baudrillard writes: "In fact the revolution has already taken place. Neither the bourgeois revolution nor the communist revolution: just the revolution . . . power is only there to hide the fact that it no longer exists, or rather to indicate that since the apogee of the political has been crossed, the other side of the cycle is now starting in which power reverts into its own simulacrum . . . only the *mise en scène* of . . . power is operational . . . power . . . is now transmuted at once into a single pure sign—the sign of the social whose density crushes us" (50–51). Thus while most think that the media control the masses, Baudrillard affirms that masses "envelop and absorb the media—or at least there is no priority of one over the other. The mass and the media are one single process. Consumers consume consumption!" (*Silent Majorities* 44–45).

Baudrillard's conceptualization of the problem blasts not only the possibility of individuality but also destroys any conception of difference between the depiction of opposing sides, much less the differences between "oppressor" and "oppressed," that are central to portrayals of political action. Although Baudrillard praises Marshall McLuhan's formulation—"the medium is the message"—as the most important insight of our time, he blasts McLuhan's conception of the media-saturated world as a global village. For McLuhan that concept meant the possibility of interactive, integrated knowledge of each other. For Baudrillard, it means global domination by a media that blocks interaction and renders difference meaningless. He sees TV as "a social control" that establishes the "*certainty that people are no longer speaking to each other*" (*Silent Majorities* 21–22).

Even if someone were to speak out, revolutionary speech is impossible because the universal language is the voice of absolute power. To speak is to oppress. As Roland Barthes puts it, "Language is legislation, speech is its code. . . . To utter a discourse is not, as is too often repeated, to communicate; it is to subjugate. . . . Language—the performance of a language system—is neither reactionary nor progressive; it is quite simply fascist" (15). Speech as an individual communication is silenced in this vision. Baudrillard sees the only truly "subversive speech" as "graffiti" because it doesn't "oppose one code to another" but "simply smashes the code" as a kind of verbal terrorism (*Political Economy* 184). The result is not new meaning but no meaning at all. In the final term of his argument, Baudrillard rules out even nihilism and death: "it would be beautiful to be a nihilist, if there were still a radicality—as it would be beautiful to be a terrorist, if death, including that of the terrorist, still had meaning." If there is no life and death, what is murderous terrorism?

According to Baudrillard, even "terrorism is the accelerated form of indifference that it contributes to imposing. . . . Death no longer has a stage, neither phantasmatic nor political on which to represent itself, to play itself out, either a ceremonial or a violent one. . . . We are in the era of events without consequences (and of theories without consequences). . . . there is no more hope for meaning" (*Simulacra and Simulation* 164).

Terrorism is embraced by Baudrillard as spectacle, proof of the "unreality" of individuals, whom he sees only as undifferentiated symbols of consumption, and of the conflation of living and dying. Unhampered by a rational belief in death, freed from compassion by his embrace of meaninglessness, Baudrillard brings his mixture of anti-westernism, dehumanization and nihilism to his consideration of terrorism as largely an illustration of his accuracy of thought: "Terrorism in its unrepresentivity, subverts the power of unmasking the unrepresentivity of power . . . its blindness is the exact replica of the system's absolute lack of differentiation . . . terrorism strikes at precisely the most characteristic project of the whole system: the anonymous and perfectly undifferentiated individual, the term substitutable for any other" (*Silent Majorities* 55–56). Just as the terrorist may seek to kill whoever is available, so Baudrillard sees the innocent, random victim only as an unreal symbol, a depersonalized capitalist product.

Baudrillard comments on the early inquiry into the bombing of Pan Am Flight 103 as if it were only an illustration of his ideas:

> You might have thought Westerners would unhesitatingly back the terrorist hypothesis in the Lockerbie incident. Within the framework of the eternal struggle between Good and Evil, it was a scenario better than anyone dared hope for. And yet some vacillation was evident in the first few days (contrasting with the haste with which responsibility was claimed by suspect groups). Wasn't it better to let suspicion fall on the hardware—an unflattering version of events for Western technology, but less dangerous than acknowledging the superiority of terrorist action over all control systems? In the former case, the West's weakness would only be mechanical whereas in the latter it would be a symbolic attack striking at its vitals, a defeat in the battle with a totally elusive enemy. It would have been better then, to stick to the accident hypothesis. Sadly, no one would have believed it, since the terrorist hypothesis wins out anyway in the imaginary register. The imagination isn't sensitive to real causes or to technical faults: what excites it are chain reactions . . . —this attraction is, in itself, terroristic. What fascinates thought is this terroristic enchaining of things, the symbolic disorder of which terrorism is merely the visible epicentre. (*Cool Memories II 1987–90*, 21)

Baudrillard enthusiastically treats terror as if it were only a competition between the West's need to construct discourses of technological perfectibility and the terrorists' narrative of meaningless destruction. Baudrillard claims the true achievement of terrorism is "interchangeability between the 'spectacular and the symbolic,' . . . the uncontrollable eruption of reversibility. . . . The force of the terrorists comes to them precisely from the fact that they have no logic. Hence the stupidity and the obscenity of all that is reported about the terrorists: everywhere the wish to palm off meaning on them, to exterminate them with meaning. . . ." (*Silent Majorities* 115). For Baudrillard terrorism is a spectacle of pointless death that constitutes "a superior model of extermination and virulence operating through emptiness" (*Silent Majorities* 116 –17).

What remains after this unsavory embrace of murder is Baudrillard's affirmation of advertising, his vision of terrorism as display or invention that competes successfully with the establishment's selling of unreal images. Baudrillard diminishes the Italian effort to deal with the Red Brigades as if it were limited to a form of alternative theater: "In Rome, Niccolini manages to counter the obsessive fear of terrorism with a cultural revival. To the Romans who no longer dare go out in the evenings he offers festivals, performances, poetry galas. He brings culture down into the street. He combats the terrorist festival with the cultural, advertising festival. He will be criticized for wasteful expenditure, but the only way to fight terrorism is not to create 'solid' institutions, but to put upon the stage a culture that is as sacrificial, eccentric, and ephemeral as the terrorist acts themselves. One festival against the other. If terrorism is a sort of murderous advertising campaign which keeps our imagination on tenterhooks, it can be countered only by a piece of more effective advertising" (*Cool Memories 1980–1985,* 189–90).

Baudrillard's facile denial of any difference between living and dying and his faith in unreality are probably best addressed by his own evaluation of his philosophic enterprise:

"Fiction? That's what I do already. My characters are a number of crazy hypotheses which maltreat reality in various ways and which I kill off at the end when they have done their work. The only way to treat ideas: murder (they kill concepts, don't they?)—but the crime has to be perfect. This is all imaginary, of course. Any resemblance to real beings is purely accidental" (*Cool Memories II 1987–1990,* 21).

Social theorist David E. Apter shares Baudrillard's fascination with terrorism as a type of fictive discourse, but has attempted more formally to connect actual terrorism with discourse theory and to define the communicative aspects of terrorist violence. Where Baudrillard sees all the terrorist narratives as an implosion of meaning in unreality and meaninglessness promoted by western capitalism, Apter sees them as calculated propaganda based on deceptive speech. Baudrillard sees himself as writing "fiction" in which all his characters are ideas and he as author is also, apparently, their serial killer. In contrast, Apter sees actual terrorists as forming discourse communities dedicated to communicative violence based on calculated corruptions of truth.

Apter sees the terrorist cell as a "discourse community" (3). In his view, the cell survives through its ability to subvert entrenched meanings so as to produce incitements and moral justifications for murder. What Apter describes are actually the persuasive processes of language devoted to a rhetoric of violence. Terrorists' narratives are purposive, hortatory, and calculatedly deceptive. They are not intended as accurate descriptions, but clearly reflect a malignant use of speech as a form of moral brutalization. Apter claims: "Violence . . . creates interior meanings, especially when prolonged. . . . Seeking the moral moment in the cannon's mouth it ritualizes death as sacrifice, turns martyrdom into testimony. When death is the measure of devotion to noble causes, even the victims become co-conspirators if they accept it as some historical necessity" (1–2).

The purpose of oscillating between moral opposites such as victim and perpetrator is a kind of "boundary smashing" that Apter sees as part of a process of substituting the "anti-state" for the state, for reordering definitions so as to provide a rationale for the terrorist cell as a "discourse community" that can create a rhetoric, however spurious, of "legitimacy" (5).

Apter uses his concept of violent speech to describe the terrorist cell as a model discourse community and tries to develop a specific social model that directly addresses the relationship between speech, interpretation, and social action limited to actual terrorism: "People do not commit political violence without discourse. They need to talk themselves into it. . . . On public platforms it becomes inflammatory. It results in texts, lectures. Political violence . . . is not only interpretive, it engages the intelligences in ways out of the ordinary. It takes people out of themselves" (2). Violence is, he claims an "unmasking discourse" based on the interpretations of symbols and ideals expressed through action that claims "some moral purpose, some transcending goal, some overcoming project which will work simultaneously for the individual and for the community. It is in this sense that political violence generates not 'communitarianism,' a thin word, but a discourse community, a thick condition" (3).

Apter believes that "discourse becomes important as a way of connecting moral principle and interests. Hence the discourse constitutes a boundary between the acceptable and the unacceptable interest. . . . It is in the mutual reinforcement of principle and interest that discourse becomes both conceptually and, on the ground, self-reflexive, legitimizing, and no matter how reprehensible the act, not a matter of the 'event' alone. In this context acts of violence are never innocent. Nor are the victims, the targets: businessmen, political leaders, journalists, etc. Each becomes a role rather than a person. A surrogate for the system may be destroyed. Hence even the most horrifying acts may be perpetrated in the pursuit of some higher purpose. Extremism is testimony of provocation" (3–4).

Apter holds that "justification" for the "filthy rite" of violence is transferred to the victim who symbolizes all the forces that are claimed to provoke violence: "When people . . . try to take control by means of interpretive action, then the iconography of violence, the choreography of confrontational events, the planning of actions based on interpretation and interpretations deriving from factions becomes a process. The process enables one to shuttle back and forth between violent acts and moral binaries" (4).

The discourse of legitimacy is crucial to terrorist action. However, the discourse of legitimacy, according to Apter, is based on interpretations of truth that may be completely antirational and have no basis in fact. Its purpose is not to convey "truth," but to dramatize and mobilize belief and action. For example, the very existence of suicide bombers is used to justify claims of the desperation of the "oppressed." The terror they inflict is also cited as "evidence" that "proves" the greater terrorism of their foe, even if that foe is simply passive and has done nothing to provoke them. The despicable nature of suicide-homicide bombing can be alleged to be a proof of its just cause. As Apter writes, terror is "outrageousness [*sic*] in its truth claims, it is ruthless in the disjunctive break it seeks with 'normalcy'" (5). Its logical inversions may involve a rejection of all political categories.

Apter's best example of antirationalism is radical, fundamentalist Islam, which "replaced socialism and communism as well as both exploited and rejected democracy. . . . In Algeria the most militant fundamentalists claim[ed] the right to rule based on electoral principles, while publicly proclaiming their intent to abolish democracy if they win power" (6). Antirationalism is key for Apter because "what makes [such insurgencies] important is not their status as doctrines, but as discourses—fictive and logical reconstructions of reality" (6).

The totalitarian nature of that "fictive" discourse seems of little concern to Apter, as is the tragic loss of innocent life that its "discourse" produces. Like Baudrillard, Apter appears to favor the terrorist and dehumanize the victims while celebrating actual violence as an effect of speech. Apter's discussion of terror has overtones of what Tom Wolfe called "pornoviolence," a sense of murder as an erotic interchange and manipulative, deceptive speech as seductive propaganda.

The act of violence communicates for Apter through its symbolic power as an intimate relationship. For him, the innocent civilians who die do so as symbols of the hated other; the "martyred," suicidal killer is, for him, equally symbolic. Apter sees the suicide bomber and his victims as co-conspirators in a pornographic drama: "Martyrdom—[is] a way to die with drama and artistry. The excitement of the act is sexual as much as political, the body as weapon. And afterwards the mourners. On one side are the families and friends of the victim-victimizer and on the other those of the victim-surrogate. One celebrates martyrs as part of a social text" scripted to establish a "close connection between killing and sexuality" (6).

The erotic power of killing and dying for Apter is itself a form of pointed communication meant to destroy "hegemonic discourses, the power of the abstract conceptualizers who use knowledge as power, or as in Foucault to challenge abstraction in the service of professionalism and expertise" (8). Therefore Apter sees irrationalism and deceptive, hypocritical speech as attacks on the social order. Language is "perceived as hegemonic" and a legitimate "object of violence" (8). Illogic and language-smashing impose a new form of absolutism: nihilism.

Terrorism as discourse relies, for Apter, on a conceptual framework appropriated from an array of theorists including Guy Debord "on spectacle," Jean Baudrillard "on simulacra," and Pierre Bourdieu on "symbolic capital." All of these are used to serve his interest in blurring the distinctions between inventive language and actual situations of violence.

Can reality be redefined as merely the remains of violence? Apter's fusion of discourse theory and sociological analysis of terrorism depends on seeing political reality as the residue of the "unmasking discourse" of violence. In that view, expressive "acts" reveal "unmasking" as an "overcoming project" that works "for both the individual and community." Apter writes: "It is in this sense that political violence generates not 'communitarianism,' but a discourse community, a 'thick' condition" (3).

Apter's work can be seen in the context of the representation theory of Baudrillard that denies differences between reality and representation, claiming all reality is only a simulation, all language the symbolic product of capitalist power. This sweeping, contemporary form of nihilism contributes to his judgment that "modern nihilism . . . language smashing . . . [and] violence as spectacle" make language and narrative more important than ever (8). "Indeed with this evolution both language and discourse become more important than less because language itself, perceived as hegemonic, as a form of hierarchy, itself becomes the object of violence" (8).

These ideas, familiar from Baudrillard's celebration of terrorism as evidence of only "symbolic disorder," are sickening as a description of actual events in which people are killed or wounded and are further demeaned by also being described as players in a terrorist's pornographic drama. The vision of a "social text" created by a discourse theory of violence should not degenerate, as it usually does, into a view of human beings as only words and social chaos as merely a page-turner. That not only denies our humanity but also prevents us from considering the narrative of violence as confronting the agony of depersonalization and identity crises revealed in the more individualized expressions in fiction. Moreover, the literature of political violence by women constitutes an attack by narrative realism and the individualism evident in dramatic characterizations against all the forces that consign action to an unreal symbolic order. It is as if realism takes its revenge on abstraction in the experiential narratives of political violence by women.

Baudrillard ignores and Apter minimizes these possibilities by presenting the act of violence as merely a spectacle that mocks established values or power. Apter's phrase, "language smashing," approximates Baudrillard's use of the term "graffiti" to describe the kind of language that can "smash" the unreal language spewed by capitalism through the media or by the terrorists' counternarrative of devastation and nihilism. Baudrillard, writing about actual terrorist episodes, sets up a false equivalency between the "advertising" of brand names and the "advertising" he believes is constituted by spectacles of terror. Obviously there is no equivalency between buying toothpaste and murdering people. Packaging the antirationalism of terrorists' rhetorical actions as an attack on the rationalism of those in power is itself a form of "graffiti" or "language smashing" without much claim to descriptive accuracy if only because the techniques of reason and language used in attacks on western logic are, as Jacques Derrida has noted, precisely those used to defend it. Narratives of terrorism that emerge in American novels of political violence by women cut to the heart of the personal, familial, and cultural dimensions involved.

American fiction, memoir, and self-report provide such enormous correctives to dehumanization that they constitute the revenge of the individual on facile theories about individualism's demise. The absence of self, the purely symbolic nature of the individual, or the meaninglessness of life and death are disproved by the effort to enact power and define it as a living, individuating process.

The social construction of violent women in American narratives addresses the close connection between narrative and violence, discourse and action, but it does so in the reconstruction of the individual identity of women. Such changes in interaction, feeling, or self-concepts affecting domestic as well as political life, as well as women's development of communicative violence, are not concerns for either Baudrillard or Apter. Neither addresses the ways in which private life and the public sphere interact in the meaning and motivation of the individual woman who commits unprogrammatic political violence. These are subjects of immense concern to the American novelists who depict the violence of women activists and even to the actual women who have attempted assassination and violence and provide their own explanations for their acts. In these contexts, neither the abstraction of the feminine position as remote from the symbolic code, nor the conceptualization of the individual as a vexed linguistic "void of the subject," nor the "commodity fetishism" of those female images manufactured by late capitalism according to Baudrillard have much meaning. Those abstract formulations are exploded by women whose passage toward violent action emerges from their elemental experiences as women and serves as a catalyst for change.

Realism about women returns as the shock of violence by women bent on revising their lives. Through seizure, appropriation, and revision of narratives and the exploitation of stereotypes, women activists weave violence narratives to restore to the depiction of women the allure of risk, change, and rage and to seize agency through action. American narratives of violent women also reach far beyond to new, cosmopolitan combinations. They can exploit what Baudrillard calls the "sign-world," the media, and purposefully manipulate both their own self-images and how others view them. They draw on American traditions of pragmatism and its vision of the power of will. By doing so, they seize control of American intellectual traditions that emphasize individual will, interpretation, and perspectival truth. They ground narrative in a strong intellectual tradition of pragmatism focused on both consciousness and material reality. They claim agency over the narratives they weave according to their subjective will and the unmistakable impact on physical reality conferred by violent action. An emphasis on personal experience returns through violence that lodges a physical assault on abstraction.

The dramatic situations found in the fiction of women terrorists open up the narrative of violence to a larger view of aggression as a process of self-discovery described from the dark side. Their violence occurs along a gradation of change and mediation with the public sphere. They enact passages from revulsion at violence, to inhibition over it, to exultation in its performance. Their changing relationships to those around them, their self-concepts, and their incorporation of multiple roles and guises culminate in an identity based on destructive egotism.

Communicative violence sends a message that conjoins terrorism and speech in a woman's interactions with others and sense of the larger public world. In an American culture of freedom, protected rights of protest, and empowerment for women, it would seem to have no place at all. Its very presence in our literature opens up otherwise suppressed narratives of rage, pathology, and unrest. Fears of political and personal instability merge in those representations of women terrorists as the mystifyingly disruptive daughters of the most benevolent of patriarchal cultures.

In Philip Roth's *American Pastoral,* an indulgent father's nightmares about his own violent daughter merge with news accounts of Bernadine

Dohrn, Angela Davis, and others—violent women willing to destroy all they had going for them:

> So many were girls, girls, . . . who were no less aggressive and militant, no less drawn to "armed action" than the boys. There is something terrifyingly pure about their violence and the thirst for self-transformation. They renounce their roots to take as their models the revolutionaries whose conviction is enacted most ruthlessly. . . . Their rage is combustible . . . they sign on freely and fearlessly to terrorize against the war, competent to rob at gunpoint, equipped in every way to maim and kill with explosives, undeterred by fear or doubt or inner contradiction—girls in hiding, dangerous girls, attackers, implacably extremist, completely unsociable. He read the names of the girls in the papers who were wanted by the authorities for crimes allegedly stemming from antiwar activities, . . . Bernadine, Patricia, Judith, Cathlyn, Susan, Linda. . . ." (254–55)

The new terrorist turns a corner from the radical past in which a woman's commitment was expressed through adherence to ideology and to willingness to die for a cause. Radical women of an earlier generation whose commitment was not rooted in self-overcoming are passé. The torch they carried cannot be passed to a new generation of women. In E. L. Doctorow's *The Book of Daniel*, a novel based on the conviction and execution of Julius and Ethel Rosenberg for passing nuclear secrets to the Russians, fictional counterparts—"Paul and Rochelle Isaacson"—leave five-year-old Susan and eight-year-old Daniel orphaned. While Daniel grows into an adult enraged that his mother preferred political risk to mothering him, Susan remains determined to memorialize her parents' martyrdom and approaches Sternlicht, a New Left leader, to donate her trust fund in order to continue her mother's work. She discovers that the leader believes Marxist-Leninist ideology is as outmoded as "mak[ing] people read Shakespeare" (154).

What counts for the New Left's leaders in the novel are techniques of self-promotion modeled on advertising and performance art. Sternlight articulates the belief that TV "commercials are learning units. . . . Pour[ing] blood all over the induction records—that's the lesson. And the Yippies throwing money away at the stock exchange" (155). Sternlicht has no interest in martyrs: "I told her if there's bread for the Movement I don't care if it's in the name of Ronald Reagan. I told her for thirty-five thousand dollars . . . I would kiss the ass of every pig in the city of noo yawk" (169). Susan writes to Daniel: "THEY'RE STILL FUCKING US. She didn't mean Paul and Rochelle. That's what I would have meant. What she meant was first everyone else and now the Left. The Isaacsons are nothing to the New Left. And if they can't make it with them who else is there. YOU GET THE PICTURE. GOODBYE, DANIEL" (169).

Choosing death by suicide, Susan leaves the path to the future clear for Marge Piercy's Vida, named for life and the invigoration of the new vision of protest. *Vida* depicts a woman who considers herself a Marxist-Leninist but has no use for the "scientists" of history: "All that hairsplitting—that was what the poor Old Lefties had sat around doing. . . . [Now we] must speak to everyone through the poetry of the act, through the theater of the streets, through the media, the music, irrationally and rationally and subliminally. History was a sense of urgency, a rush in the blood" (126). The "rush" transforms her to a superwoman. After Kent State, where students protesting the war are killed, Vida organizes a demonstration: "She felt like Wonder Woman streaking through the city. Fast, fast she went down the block, too fast for any man to give her trouble. Running lightly in her sneakers. Into the subway, she vaulted over the turnstile and bolted into a train. That was Movement style, perfectly executed. . . . An example to other women" (250).

Women terrorists are players in a political change in which the moment of self-transformation and repudiation of one's own inhibitions and limitations is all. What fascinates the terrorists of contemporary fiction is the sensation and experience of theatrical violence in which one has the starring role. On a demonstration, Vida "led a countercharge . . . the police had not been prepared for their sudden attack. . . . She felt like laughing; she was grinning as she ran with her comrades. She wished she could see herself on film. She loved herself" (149–50).

Costuming makes it possible to experience the moment of transition from lady to terrorist as an end in itself. The terrorist dresses as a "lady" to render secret her rage and to extend the drama of self-transformation. Reversing the sequence established by Clark Kent, the average man who slips on his superhero outfit to defend "truth, justice, and the American way" as

Superman, Vida sees herself as a superheroine who dons demure, ordinary costumes for the purpose of blowing "America" up.

On her way to bomb the executive offices of Mobil Oil, Vida dresses for success: "a beige linen dress . . . demure and proper . . . gold . . . earrings. She piled her hair into an expert French Twist. . . . Passable sandals with a little heel, almost matching the bag." And to top it off, "eye shadow" because "married ladies with Black maids wore eye shadow" (257). Vida gives new meaning to the phrase "killer outfit" by intertwining the activities of dressing up and blowing up and using role-playing to intensify the passage from one act to the other.

Radical women keep the secret of killer rage under wraps. Exposing and concealing violence extends it to other women who may play supporting roles in the terrorist's drama of self-image. When Merry in Philip Roth's Pulitzer Prize–winning novel, *American Pastoral,* confesses to her therapist that she has blown up a post office and inadvertently killed someone, the therapist keeps her confession secret, literally hides her, and helps spirit her away. Merry's mentor, a Columbia University professor, teaches transgression, inspires others to perform disruption, and serves as a sympathetic audience who can look at the victims: "to laugh at them all, pillars of a society that, much to her delight, was going rapidly under—to laugh and to relish, as some people, historically, always seem to do, how far the rampant disorder had spread, enjoying enormously the assailability, the frailty, the enfeeblement of supposedly robust things" (423).

What causes the American girl whose literary status is to be what Philip Rahv called "the heiress of all the ages" to reject that posh inheritance? Novelists as different as Joyce Carol Oates and Philip Roth have seen a provocateur in the American family. For Oates, the heiress in the American Century is Kirsten Halleck who inherits the spirit of John Brown and Thoreau's tribute to the man he calls the "Angel of Light:" Thoreau wrote: "I do not wish to kill or be killed but I can foresee circumstances in which both of these things would be by me unavoidable." Kirsten Halleck remembers "old Osawatomie," who "had not hesitated to kill in obedience to a higher law. *I have pledged my life.* Justice. The exacting of justice. *I will give my life,* he said. A quiet stern fearless man. *No Quarter* his battlecry" (Oates 114).

Is the curse envious hatred for the power and superiority of others? Oates projects the American family as a modern House of Atreus. In mythology, the curse on the House of Atreus originated with Tantalus, who so hated the gods who had been kind to him that he served them a feast made of his son Pelops to degrade them with their own cannibalism. His violations of family love and crimes against generosity and virtue afflicted his descendants with child sacrifice or matricide. In Oates's *Angel of Light*, Maurice Halleck, a descendent of John Brown, has produced an Orestes and Electra in his children Kirsten and Owen. An embodiment of American moralism, Maurice is a wealthy Washington power-broker known for incorruptible virtue, a modern idealist who attracts predators and parasites. His best friend, Nick Martens, is covertly besmirching his reputation with charges of bribe-taking. The poor boy at prep school who manipulated Maurice out of a choice dorm, Nick has graduated to appropriating Maurice's wife, the beautiful Isabel. An influential Washington hostess adept in destroying reputations, Isabel uses lies, ridicule, and rumors to skewer whomever she can. Her husband, outraged by her viciousness, condemns her for her cruelty, cynicism, contempt for the truth, and for despising her victims and listeners. Isabel believes him mad, "a man with an allegiance to something she could not grasp and perhaps did not care to grasp; it was too abstract to be of interest to her" (273).

Moralists and predators find themselves in parasitic or symbiotic relations in which the inability of the former to conceive of wrongdoing meshes with the desire of the latter to do it. Both Nick and Isabel believe Maurice's moral sensitivity is proof of his madness and wait for him to crack. When he dies, the question arises: Did they kill him or drive him to suicide?

What springs from *Angel of Light* is a vision of modern evil dramatized as the politics of envy and destruction, the immorality of hating ethical fineness. Heiress to Brown's moral severity, Kirsten defines the path to deliverance through murder, persuading her gentler brother to join her in a plot to kill their mother and her lover. Personal and political revolt join in her urging on him membership in the "Silver Doves," a terrorist group suggestive of the Shining Path. Owen kills his mother and sets a bomb in her bathroom to cover the crime but then collapses into infantile helplessness.

Overwhelmed by a desire to rest after setting the bomb on a timer, he lies on his mother's bed, curls into a fetal position with his thumb in his mouth, sleeps, and is killed in the ensuing explosion and fire. In contrast, Kirsten easily lures Nick with the promise of an erotic afternoon. Charmed by the prospect of sleeping with Isabel's daughter as well as Isabel, he arrives to find himself welcomed by Kirsten's knife. Leaving behind a pamphlet from the Silver Doves, she escapes.

Terrorist women chart a path through violence to deliverance from an exploitative world focused on money and sex. In *Reflections on Violence*, Georges Sorel explored the necessity for a "warlike excitement" that carried a religious fervor. He associated political violence with moral self-righteousness. This grim vision holds that the world is damned and to deal with it one must find the "will to deliverance," a determination to change everything at once, in an act of total repudiation. For Sorel, the myth was a secular version of the Christian path to redemption through the crucifixion. Oceanic religious emotion joined politics to "a vision of life" with the "character of infinity because it puts aside all discussion of definite reforms and confronts men with a catastrophe." It fueled the rebellious spirit at a time when, Sorel complained, "capitalism was stupefied with humanitarianism" and workers had been "tamed" into trade unionism. Moralistic murder plays this role in the munificent world of townhouses, exquisite parties, and lushly landscaped prep schools in *Angel of Light* in which the repudiation of rational gain sustains the will to bomb one's own home.

Religious sentiment fuels the journey to violence sustaining it through mythic visions of sacrifice in a progression of binding intergenerational rage. In other fictions, destruction is bound up with a repudiation of established communications and connections and a determination to rewrite the story of American progress as a disaster-thriller.

In Philip Roth's *American Pastoral,* terrorism by a girl raised to be a Jewish princess explodes the ethnic, immigrant romance with American plenty. Raised on the mean streets of Newark, Seymour "Swede" Levov is a first-generation success who has wrapped his daughter in the velvet life of "the American pastoral," the idyllic world of a farm in New Jersey estate country. Swede cannot understand why his once charming child has come of age as a hideous virago, a teenage stutterer who grows grossly fat on greasy junk food, refuses to wash her hair or brush her teeth, and fumes angrily at the power structure epitomized by her parents as well as the administration waging the Vietnam War. At sixteen, daughter Merry is anything but sweet and not at all merry. She blows up the local post office, killing a kindly local doctor who had the bad luck to be mailing a letter at the moment the bomb went off. Going underground, she disappears from her family and continues her career as a movement bombmaker, killing a total of four people.

The sheer irrationality of the terrorist act, its distance from the evil it purports to want to reform, is a recurring theme in the fiction of terrorism. E. L. Doctorow connects it to the unleashing of excesses of emotional turmoil associated with the mastery of Edgar Allan Poe:

> Poe was the arch subversive. Historians of early America fail to mention the archetypal traitor, the master subversive Poe, who wore a hole into the parchment and let the darkness pour through. . . . A small powerful odor arose from the Constitution; there was a wisp of smoke which exploded and quickly turned mustard yellow in color. When Poe blew this away through the resulting aperture in the parchment the darkness of the depths rose, and rises still from that small hole all these years incessantly pouring its dark hellish gases like soot, like smog, like the poisonous effulgence of combustion engines over Thrift and Virtue and Reason and Natural Law and the Rights of Man. . . . It's Poe who ruined us, that scream from the smiling face of America. (193–94)

Instrumentalism and rationalist ideals are exploded, in this view, by irrational violence. In recent fiction the contrast between rational self-interest and destructive egotism is embedded in intergenerational family conflicts and a daughter's rage at her father's values.

The rage of the revolutionary as daughter is directed in *American Pastoral* against the progressive ideals of a father and culture who fulfill ideals of material success and liberal tolerance. The perfection of his own father's immigrant's dream, Swede Levov cannot understand why all his efforts on his daughter's behalf have come to nothing. What Merry exploded was the world of rational choices epitomized by those strivers, capable of any sacrifice, to "make something of themselves," whom Roth sees as the soul of Jewish

Newark. There "Swede" Levov was everyone's high school hero. Nicknamed for his tall, blond good looks, he was admired for his prowess at the American sports of football, baseball and basketball, his physical strength as a Marine, and his marriage to a contender for the title of Miss America, an Irish immigrant's daughter who was Miss New Jersey of 1949. A "liberal sweetheart of a father," Swede emerged from the war into a society he believed determined to adopt rationality and tolerance as antidotes to the fascism and Nazism it had conquered. Roth presents Swede as "our Kennedy":

> His great looks, his larger-than-lifeness, his glory, our sense of his having been exempted from all self-doubt by his heroic role—that all these manly properties had precipitated a political murder make me think of . . . another privileged son of fortune, another man of glamour exuding American meaning, assassinated while still in his mid forties just five years before the Swede's daughter violently protested the Kennedy-Johnson war and blew up her father's life. . . . The plague America infiltrating the Swede's castle and there infecting everyone. . . . The daughter who transports him out of the longed-for American pastoral and into everything that is its antithesis and its enemy, into the fury, the violence, and the desperation of the counterpastoral—into the indigenous American berserk. (83–86)

The "counterpastoral," the "American berserk" is the embrace of irrational and self-destructive violence in both family and social life. Roth conflates Merry's rebellious refusal to bathe and repulsive manners with her bombing of the post office. Turning herself into an object of disgust outrages her beauty-queen mother; political destructiveness defies the measured liberalism of her father. The equation of social, political, and self-destructive action is embedded in the novel in focal, violent images of the time. Irrational self-destruction is the mark of the political world in which the self-immolation of antiwar Buddhist monks or rampaging citizens burning down their own streets in Newark in a race riot stream into the home on the television news. Multiple images from the larger political world flesh out the forces of unreason as personal action. By the end of the novel, Merry is a woman in her thirties, filthy, reeking, and starving herself to death in the back streets of Newark. Merry controls the destruction of her own body as if it were an attack on the body politic.

The destruction of the American household is a literal fact in the news, where Swede finds accounts of the collapse of the elegant Greenwich Village townhouse that exploded by accident when the Weather Underground used it to fabricate bombs. The West Eleventh Street townhouse of Cathy Wilkerson had opened for the bomb business when her father went on vacation in the Caribbean. The actual Wilkerson had invited Kathy Boudin and several other Weathermen into the basement to build pipe bombs for use in guerrilla actions when something went wrong, igniting a mother lode of dynamite. Wilkerson, Boudin, and a few others escaped, but a charred body was left behind in the rubble.

In *American Pastoral* the parents of the "Wilkerson" character plead with her on television to come forward to name who was with her so that the body can be identified, and to reassure them that she is "safe." The absurdity of their hope is paralleled by Swede's hope that his own daughter will "become herself again" (102–103). Both reflect a refusal to accept daughters for who they are and to realize that what they hate is safety. When Swede discovers Merry was not under the influence of others and remains without remorse, he loses his consoling illusions about her. What is left of his world turns to ashes (261–62).

Swede attempted to construct a life of reason, affection, and plenty and to be what even his derisive brother calls "a liberal sweetheart of a father. The philosopher-king of ordinary life [for whom] . . . everything [is] permissible, forgivable" does not survive immersion in a larger America Roth sees as "berserk" (281). The daughter of a contender for the title of Miss America, Merry is the Miss America of the berserk. The inability of family solidarity to hold the forces of disorder at bay is projected in a dinner party meant to bring different segments of the culture into social play.

Hosted by Swede, the dinner party assembles immigrants, ethnics, and the entrenched WASP aristocracy around the table of American plenty, presumably to affirm that despite Merry's individualistic violence, the large celebration of diversity and American idealism continues. Instead the party serves as a wake for the American home and family. That night Swede realizes that his wife has betrayed him in his own home with the WASP architect who is eating at his table. She will soon divorce him. The immigrant's faith in self-improvement is skewered when Swede's father, trying to sober up the architect's drunken wife with food and a nourishing message of self-improvement, is stuck near the eye with a fork by her. The other guests, intellectuals and professionals, Swede discovers, are mentors of Merry who, from a safe distance, enjoy the excitement of violence. The party typifies a wider culture of disorder in which no one but Swede feels that commitments or connections outside oneself matter.

The family sources of disruption are projected in those explosions of feeling and acts of violence that take place in the unraveling of marriages and relations with children. But the bedroom and the contents of an out-fit-stocked armoire also serve in staging political theater. The daily life of the woman revolutionary is often idealized as the freewheeling sexuality of an urban cowgirl dressed to kill. Piercy's *Vida* celebrates the life of a woman radical covering the time of turmoil from the sixties through the seventies, rendering the progression of styles along the way. Precise in rendering the details and accoutrements of sixties and seventies life—the Mexican wedding dresses from Fred Leighton's old shop in the village, the hairdos of Angela Davis, the photograph by fashion photographer Richard Avedon of that icon Kathy Boudin dressed for "the field"—Piercy recreates the daily costumes and textures of life at the activist front.

Ethnicity connects the political and personal in visions of WASP power and immigrant marginality as a drama of domestic violence in a WASP–Jewish household. Conflict is literally in the heritage of Vida Whippletree Asch, who is the daughter of a WASP father who beats her Jewish mother. Domestic violence, however, is best represented in the novel not as wife battering but in its representation of its impact on the daughter who chooses denial of personal suffering and terrorism to relieve fears of her own powerlessness. This is a choice for terrorism as a sexual style, a dysfunctional choice in a culture whose mainstream has incorporated virtually all nonviolent forms of protest. Protests against the Vietnam War provide the starting point, but the war itself recedes in importance as the lifestyle of violence becomes all that matters.

Having gone underground after a series of pipe-bombings, Vida has spent the seventies on the lam. Although she rarely sees him, she is still married to

Leigh, who refused to go violent in the sixties and has become a prominent voice on the left as a TV journalist. While he and other nonviolent radicals have achieved "establishment" status, she disdains the mainstream. Her days revolve around avoiding arrest, subsisting on quasi-criminal "jobs" such as kidnapping for hire, and demanding money from former radicals who have gone on to careers as social workers, health care workers, or as agents of legal forms of community action. She has contempt for those who had once dabbled in violence but have since decided to turn themselves in for the chance to reclaim their lives after release from prison. Vida sees her life as daring, designed around risk-taking and the rush of the new.

Sex is another frontier for the woman who sees herself as an urban terrorist. Erotic violence and secrecy interact in Vida's life in what she calls "the Network." Egotism looms large in her belief that the more dangerous and violent she is, the more erotically exciting she appears. The need to keep moving to avoid getting caught is intensified by her belief that she is wanted in every sense.

Self-absorption and skill at exploiting others fill Vida's fantasies of remaining the destructive object of everyone's desire. She is bisexual. She remembers her lesbian lovers primarily for their devotion to her and for their usefulness; she believes that lesbians teach men how to be lovers. Younger men are useful for underscoring her continuing desirability. Her affair with a twenty-something man who is a deserter, begun while both are hiding out, is cemented by planning a kidnapping for hire and smuggling a wife and her child out of the reach of her abusive, policeman husband. Vida believes her violence keeps her sexually attractive to her own husband because it makes her "real," while he has sold out for success. She fantasizes a regular threesome with her lesbian lover and her deserter, spiced, now and then, by the addition of a fourth—her husband. By multiplying sexual contacts and juggling them, she remains detached from any one of them and feels able to control them all.

Keeping secrets, concealing, and hiding are her passions in both terrorism and sexuality. Disguise, secret meetings, and covert violence have the force of a clandestine tryst. In the post-Vietnam era, she stages demonstrations against nuclear facilities. Her activism consists of dropping condoms filled with black paint on nuclear power plants from a Cessna. Sex and "war" have intersected. Her terrorism divides between crime (kidnapping for hire) or comedic political theater (paint-filled condoms) performed for coverage on the six o'clock news.

Covert destructiveness is the best weapon in the war between the sexes. Vida perfects the clandestine meeting as a form of terrorism by adultery. Her secrecy is itself a destructive weapon. Lying about a harmless visit to a doctor's office, Vida permits her deserter-lover to believe she has gone to have sex with her husband Leigh. Concealing from Leigh that she will not meet him as planned in a hotel, she misleads her lover too so that both meet in the hotel room in which each had expected to find Vida. Vida has made sure the police expect her there too. Both men are arrested. By multiplying her attachments, Vida plays them off each against the other while ruining both. Sex provides the metaphor for destructive egotism in action.

The sex war and class war intertwine in the hostility of radical men to women. While common in nonfiction accounts of radical movements, Piercy's fictional portrait of male indifference or hostility to women's issues is vividly realized. Strikingly, Vida responds to their rejection of women's issues by joining them in their misogyny. Her violence is devoted primarily to enhancing her own sense of personal and sexual power, not to any ideological commitment to any feminist cause. When men in the movement talk to each other when women's issues are mentioned Vida identifies with the men (131). Although her first husband raped her, Vida is furious with her sister Nattie's complaining that she was raped by a black man and for Nattie's involvement with women's groups that address domestic violence. She advises her sister to say nothing because the rapist was probably oppressed and if she presses charges, people will accuse her of racism. Identification with the rapist rather than the victim underscores Vida's refusal to acknowledge any connection between the vulnerability of women and male violence as well as her need to see herself as an aggressor.

The personal is always political for the woman whose politics are honed by a self-affirming destructive egotism. Her politics serves as armature against her own aging and abandonment. When her husband Leigh tells her he plans to divorce her to marry a twenty-six-year-old who is pregnant with his child, Vida is able to see his rejection of her as a political defection, part of the "weak" commitment that made him refuse to go violent. She sets him up for arrest. She has so mastered the life of escape terrorism that she can use the establishment to avenge herself. Like Brecht's supremely hard Mother Courage who survives the harshest warfare with her wagon full of staples everyone wants to buy, Vida goes on, her backpack filled with essentials: her "lady's" costume, her getaway clothes, her illusions of stardom as everyone's most wanted.

The woman terrorist as urban outlaw looms large in the post-Vietnam imagination. Sex war and class war are played out on mean streets and in rough schoolyards where women and girls can be overpowered by the odds stacked against them. Their stereotyping as sex objects structures the violence leveled against them and their response. Rage as a redemptive force emerges in novels of young women whose poverty and exploitation persuade them that power is male but who band together to create a counterforce the "establishment" regards as a terrorist cell. Such fiction dramatizes the terrorism of rebellious women by projecting their resistance as criminal, sexually unnatural, and out of control.

Foxfire by Joyce Carol Oates combines the foxy and fiery in its title to express the combustibility of female sexuality and rage against the patriarchy as it is experienced in the daily life of poor girls who are ridiculed by math teachers, groped by storekeepers who offer them special deals, and hooted at or menaced by boys. A group of high school girls organizes to retaliate against a broad spectrum of slights and abuses against them in school. The victimization of women is magnified by the newspapers they read: "It was a time of violence against girls and women . . . a nineteen year old nursing student . . . was raped and strangled . . . and her body left in a drainage ditch outside town, . . . a pregnant woman . . . was stabbed to death in her house . . . and her unborn baby killed [by] her own husband . . ." (100). Why not try being the outlaw instead of the victim?

Revolt is inspired not by ideology but by the troubled quality of daily interactions of impoverished high school girls with family, school, boys, and men. The girl gang emerges as a counterweight against misfortune. The Foxfire gang is presented as a complex counterculture. Legs Sadowsky creates, formulates, and directs the group's dramatic retaliations, seeing herself as an outlaw-savior. The gang even has its "religious" icons. Her "holy relic" is a handkerchief a relative had dipped in Dillinger's blood after he was shot outside the Biograph Theater (36). What political vision she has was inspired by a defrocked, leftist priest who awakens in her a vision of community she implements in her band of high-school girls determined to resist injustice. Less ideological than redemptive, their solidarity is expressed in violent actions that relieve their sense of helplessness and depression. Together they resist and develop narratives of female power that one of them is designated to record as an official history.

Foxfire brings violence on behalf of girls into everyday encounters and provides the possibility of using the "gang" to provide an alternative community based on female power. The escalating criminal violence of Foxfire is fueled by its early successes. Its verbal assault against a lecherous, patronizing math teacher is followed by a physical assault on an abusive storekeeper, a car theft, and a series of sex-centered crimes that reverse gender roles as the girls become predators toward men. *Foxfire* uses its prettiest girls as decoy-prostitutes to lure and mug the johns they attract. Acting together, they can overpower men. The experiences of abuse that have driven each of the girls to the group underscore the passage toward empowerment.

Identification with the abuse of women leads them to increasing acts of violence. Early efforts at sexual rescue later rise to violent action and arson. When Legs sees a "dwarf woman" with a dog collar around her neck, chained to a post in the yard of an isolated house and barroom, she discovers an extreme example of abuse that merits an extreme response. She returns to the house to discover the woman is being sold by her brother to whichever man wants her. The dwarf is chained to a bed for the use of his customers: "One by one the animal-men enter the room, one by one bare-assed their genitals swollen, penises stiffened into rods, mounting the dwarf woman, the woman that's-a-body, one by one pumping their life into her . . ." (202). When Legs remembers the old priest indicting capitalism for treating people as commodities, she decides to act. "She takes up a five-gallon container of kerosene, carries it to the house," sprinkles the contents around the house, and sets it afire (203). The narrative of violence is constructed as a rescue with Legs as savior, establishing a proportionality between the provocation to violence and her response.

That the gang reflects a uniquely personal politics no one else understands is underscored by both its crimes and the response of the newspapers to its exploits. Crime and safety, the life of risk and domestic peace, are played off against each other in a series of escalating crimes in which Legs moves toward a destructive egotism beyond the limitations of her life as a woman. Blackmail teaches her she can play a man for profit. To apply for a well-paying job, Legs literally dresses up as a man. During the interview, the married manager makes a pass. Legs realizes that the blackmail she can extract from him to keep his homosexuality quiet will be worth more than the job and acts accordingly. Having succeeded at that, she goes further and kidnaps a man who is a local business leader, using two of the gang's prettiest girls as lures. She demands a million-dollar ransom. While held captive, the business leader is accidentally shot in the chest. The headlines call the kidnapping a "communist plot"; one announces LOCAL GIRL GANG TIED TO INTERNATIONAL RED TERRORISTS" (320).

The headlines see Foxfire's violence as a disruptive ideology, but they get the ideology wrong. The gang's acts highlight the role of Legs as an embodiment of female agency freed from formulaic belief, alluring as both man and woman, operating at the edge where costumes, robbery, extortion, and kidnapping for ransom imply the use of identity games and crime to develop new self-concepts. It is a personal politics of destructive egotism. Legs escapes the police who pursue her, leaving the girls wondering where she is. Is it she who is blurry in the background in a news photo of Fidel Castro addressing an adoring crowd in Havana?

Legs and Castro are flip sides of the Foxfire fantasy of male and female styles of violent, revolutionary action. Legs can play both male and female roles as an agent of change, suggesting that the identity violence of the woman is different. Legs uses male desire against men, exploiting sexuality as a revolutionary style by tying it to violence and control and by playing whatever part works. The destructive egotism bound up in her crimes is sanitized in the novel by legitimating narratives that invoke the violence against women as the reason for Foxfire's acts, as if their crimes were a form of retributive justice or at least in the service of a just cause. The gang is against patriarchy, but also against dogma, organization, and structured social orders. Just as her mentor was a defrocked priest, rejected by the Roman Catholic Church, so Legs does not seem a follower of any ideology so much as a champion of the politics of the personal. Castro's cult of the personal finds a female counterpart in Legs. Her self-image as a savior of women replays the hope that society might be a female safe-house established by cunning and force.

Reworking American traditions of moralistic terrorism and armed with religious conviction, the contemporary fiction of violence by women provides an interesting riff on the need for redemption through catastrophe. Joyce Carol Oates developed this prospect in a novel dealing with the heirs of that stern John Brown who, like the Calvinists before him, tried to establish justice by force. His spirit is passed to a female descendent and revived by his heiress in Oates's novel *Angel of Light* as a blend of moralistic murder for personal and political reasons. Oates's heroine is a figure out of high tragedy—she wants to murder her mother and her mother's lover in retribution for her father's death—and is also involved with a terrorist group. Moralistic murder and terrorism are twin obsessions that reinforce each other. The use of the family home as a bombsite in *Angel of Light* provides a powerful metaphor for the connection between political and personal violence as well as a vision of the explosive tensions within the American family. The heavy moral rhetoric in which a daughter plans her mother's murder, and the killing of her mother's lover as rectification for her mother's infidelity, underscore the perversion of Brown's Calvinist moral scheme, exploiting his communicative violence and use of terror as a form of speech.

The connection between morality and violence is embedded in consideration of terrorism by women because assumptions that women are inevitable victims provide an implicit cause and justification for their rebellion. Brown's moralistic terror transfers to America a version of what Sorel described in *Reflections on Violence* as the effect of "the Calvinist spirit" on morals, law, or literature. For Sorel, that impact is "its conception of the path to deliverance." The experience of the nineteenth century, he wrote, "shows quite clearly that . . . in this warlike excitement which accompanies this *will-to-deliverance* the courageous man finds a satisfaction which is sufficient to keep up his ardour" (15). Sorel believed that revolutionary pessimism was better than the progressivism that worked for incremental social change because it was capable of inspiring a heroism like that of the early Calvinists.

Sorel's *will-to-deliverance* argument holds that the world is damned, and to deal with it one must find the determination to change everything at once, in an act of total repudiation. In his analysis of anarchoterrorism in the nineteenth century, James Billington notes that the sites for construction of bombs in anti-czarist Russia took on a "ritual centrality" once reserved for the printing press (407). The bomb and the gun were venerated as religious icons, and the terrorists who used them were likened to the "nonviolent early Christians" (408).

Sanctified violence occurs with high seriousness in an emerging fiction by émigrés and descendants of émigrés from countries in which actual terrorism and guerrilla warfare are vivid experiences in living memory. Women terrorists in post-Vietnam fiction include those who present powerful composite portraits of religious, sexual, family, and political violence. Their perspective on terrorism is developed through dual portraits that convey the moral doubleness of their experience—of terrorism as freedom-fighting or as a form of egotistical self-affirmation; of religious expressions of a dynamic of evil or of noble sacrifice. Christian martyrdom or black magic can confound each other. Animistic religion involving blood sacrifice, spells, and a vision of the tyrant as devil or as savior or faith in the Blessed Virgin as a destroyer of adversaries reflect a disturbing doubleness of moral perspective. All reflect a response to visions of the tyrant as an embodiment of macho power. In novels about Cuba, the Dominican Republic or the lost land of Native Americans, Fidel Castro emerges as a magnet for rage—as either the tyrant who must be outmaneuvered or the liberator who refuses to help or intervene. He is represented as having an omnipotent machismo that he will not use or has misused and becomes a magnet for female frustration.

What unifies very different expressions of violent fantasy or action is the awareness that women activists must overcome not only their own helplessness but the idealization of maleness and the belief that power, dominance, and the struggle for rectification are qualities of men alone. Cubans and Cuban Americans know revolutionary violence as it saturates family experience. The American children and grandchildren of a generation of radicals or émigrés fleeing revolution bring terrorism home as a heritage and an ongoing family story. Fidel Castro emerges as both villain and savior in a novel that offers complex perspectives on social upheaval and destabilization.

In Cristina Garcia's exquisitely crafted novel, *Dreaming in Cuban,* three generations of women are affected by Castro's victory against Batista, his triumph at the Bay of Pigs, and the longevity that permits him to play a pivotal role in the imaginations of a grandmother, mother, and granddaughter. Engagement in revolutionary violence is given a different twist by each generation. The immense lyricism and power of Garcia's writing compel recognition of the ways in which sexuality, animistic religion, violence, and politics interact with family relationships over three generations of women.

Grandmother Celia represents an older generation of woman hooked on male ideas of revolution. She ardently supports Castro, having joined his struggle as a young mother and ignored the atrocities committed by him and in his name. Even as an old woman, she continues to fantasize about Castro's power and sexuality. Her capacity for oceanic emotion aroused by ardor and revolution is underscored by her work at her beachfront home where, in the service of Castro, "El Lider," she scans the sea for invaders. Her two daughters follow different but equally passionate paths. Her daughter Lourdes was violently raped as a young, pregnant wife by Castro's soldiers whose brutality caused her to miscarry her child. The violent machismo, and terrorism of Castro's tyranny spur her escape to Brooklyn, fuel her hatred of communism and her fantasies of killing Castro.

Felicia, Lourdes's sister, is deranged by her virtual abandonment by Celia for the revolution. Celia suggests that revolutionary activity rather than "wallowing in her own discomforts" will cure her. But Felicia is engaged in a revolution against precisely the macho ideal Celia relishes. Her resistance to male control is intense and personal: she sets fire to her first husband's face, seeing him as a tyrant of the home; she attributes the death of her beloved second husband to Castro's "murderers"; and she kills her third husband by pushing him off a roller coaster where he is trying to make love to her.

Sex, terrorism, and animistic religion intertwine for both generations of women. Animal sacrifice or bloody ritual saturates dramas of sin, purgation, punishment, and redemption. Celia believes in priests of Santería as well as Castro. Affected by her mother's indifference, Felicia finds meaning by becoming one—a santera—herself. Demonization of the enemy is underscored by Felicia's adaptation of terrorism to a blood-ritual.

Believing that Castro personally ordered her second husband's murder because he was too honest for his corrupt regime, Felicia is convinced that Graciela, a regular client at her beauty salon, is a spy who turned her husband in. Felicia lures her to the salon with the promise of a free permanent wave. "She mixes lye with her own menstrual blood into a caustic brown paste, then thickly coats Graciela's head. Over it, she fastens a clear plastic bag, with six evenly spaced hairpins, and waits. Felicia imagines the mixture melting through Graciela's frail scalp, penetrating the roots and bones of her skull until it eats her vicious brain like acid" (151). Her menstrual blood marks the mixture of witchcraft, bloodshed, and poison she finds at work in Castro's Cuba. The madness of the act repeats in exaggerated form the bloodletting and irrationality of both revolutionary and counterrevolutionary terrorism.

Garcia's Cuban émigrés see Castro as the source of American instability, the demon behind violent American activism. They argue over "whether Angela Davis, who's on trial in California for murder, kidnapping and conspiracy, is one of El Lider's agents or a direct emissary from Moscow" (61). Others celebrate the murder in Miami of a journalist who advocated establishing ties with Castro's Cuba. Lourdes's dreams are invaded by memory, fear, and a heritage of belief in Santería but Lourdes turns her bakery into the locus of nonviolent, legal activism against Castro, infusing law and order with a transcendent value.

A third Cuban American generation discovers nostalgia for revolutionary fervor. Pilar, Lourdes's very American daughter, is an artist who has been raised in Brooklyn. She outrages her mother by praising Cuba and making anti-American comments. To humiliate her mother, she paints a mocking picture for the opening of her new Yankee Doodle Bakery: a "punk" statue of Liberty with a safety pin through her nose, a "barbed wire halo," and "I'M A MESS," inscribed below (141). Her use of punk-art forms in a political attack expresses her Americanness, her kinship to political theater, and her distance from her mother's experience of rape and fantasies of murder, her aunt's violence, or her grandmother's virtual abandonment of her daughters to support revolutionary action.

Pilar's Miss Liberty could represent Santería lite. It is a fetish-laden object that uses punk body piercing and imagery to coopt Santería's style for a culture that embraces political satire. The visualization of political protest in mock-violent images brings the role of physical pain to an American youth culture habituated to irony and cartoons.

Propelled by dreamlike celebrations of her grandmother, Pilar travels to Cuba only to discover that she cannot paint what she likes there and that her grandmother Celia defends censorship and Castro's crackdowns. Pilar finds she feels more at home in Brooklyn. She deceives Celia and, by doing so, helps her cousin escape from Cuba, supporting counterrevolution. She discovers that her mother, object of her scorn, was her champion all along. When her punk Miss Liberty was unveiled in her mother's bakery, someone thought it was blasphemous and charged it with a pocketknife. Her mother, though stunned herself by the painting, refuses to take it down. When a customer tries to seize the painting, to protect it from harm she "swings her new handbag and clubs the guy cold inches from the painting. Then, as if in slow motion, she tumbles forward, a thrashing avalanche of patriotism and motherhood, crushing three spectators and a table of apple tartlets" (144). Defending the "punk" Miss Liberty, Lourdes makes her own statement of love for her daughter, free expression, and female power.

Women terrorists can be sisters in faith in a war saturated with religious images of women. Religious imagery may be used to sanctify the work of revolutionary terrorists who see themselves as purging evil. Historical circumstance is invoked to justify their efforts as freedom fighters. In Julia Alvarez's riveting novel, *In the Time of the Butterflies,* many opponents of Trujillo in the Dominican Republic are waiting for Castro as the savior who will attack the island and overthrow him. But Castro, once idealized for his power, turns out to be just another frustrating man.

The Marabal sisters decided to make their own revolution and accumulated firearms, organized and planned an attack. When the plot was discovered by SIM, Trujillo's secret police, those who were captured were imprisoned or murdered. Alvarez bases her novel on the exploits of the "Butterflies," the three historical Marabal sisters who helped organize the resistance and were murdered on the way home from visiting their husbands and relatives who were jailed for their involvement in the effort.

Identification with the Blessed Virgin and religious sentiment drive the sisters' willingness to risk all. The sisters praise the Virgencita and seem devotees of an elemental and active form of Catholicism in which the Holy Mother is depicted armed and on horseback as a militant Virgin, a figuration also found in European paintings of a militant Saint Mary. Alvarez's Marabal sisters explain: "And so we were born in the spirit of the vengeful Lord, no longer His lambs. Our new name was Acción Clero-Cultural. Please note, action as the first word!" (164). They define their mission as to "organize a powerful national underground. . . . After all, Fidel would never have won over in Cuba if the *campesinos* there hadn't fed him, hidden him, lied for him, joined him" (164). Castro's failure to come to their aid inspires a message more mystical than his own: they will tell the *campesinos* that opposing them will prevent reaching heaven because brothers and sisters in Christ should not kill *each other*. Trying to recall instruction in how to achieve their goals, one woman "can remember nothing practical. . . . Only the insistence on rights and the driving away of the Yanqui imperialists" (77). Alvarez, whose father participated in efforts to overthrow Trujillo and emigrated to the United States to avoid capture, blends imaginative detail with facts in a rich historical novel spanning the period from 1938 to 1992.

Activists and martyrs, the Marabal sisters inspire religious worship and pilgrimage. An old woman who claims to be possessed by them creates a shrine decorated with their pictures and that of the "devil" Trujillo, raising the question of whether only good spirits rule the shrine. That the "evil spirit" contained in a picture of Trujillo joins them on the shrine is a reminder that he is inseparable from their martyrdom. A legacy of the "Butterflies" is precisely that excess of religious fervor that involves imagining revolution as a form of purgation of evil. It ties terrorist violence to religious sentiment, enables inspirational organizing and recruiting, and fuels the practical accumulation of weaponry, providing the momentum and the means for a struggle against tremendous odds. The culmination of the sisters' heroism in martyrdom reinforces the logic of crucifixion and redemption. The descendants of the Marabals are "cursed" with the legacy of violence and suffering that enables others to idealize the pathway to deliverance through violence.

Women terrorists find that they are always women first, identified through female attributes of fear and passivity they can overcome only through risk-taking and violence. From the Marabals's self-identification with the "Virgencita" to Vida's passion for being Wonder Woman, the need to invoke mythic female power persists. One way to deal with this is to embrace femaleness as itself an overwhelming force. The greatest female powers and sources of terror are Mother Nature and Mother Earth. Can primal, aggressive forces rise from nature whose rivers have been "trapped" and "dammed" to supply electric power? Will Mother Nature send both drugs and an army of the dead to addict, haunt, and overwhelm those who oppress Native Americans with reason and technology?

In Leslie Marmon Silko's *Almanac of the Dead,* coca leaves have magical powers to wreak revenge on those who are not their Peruvian caretakers: "In the South, there were thousands who worshipped Mama Coca. Mama Coca had taken away the pain . . . and now Mama Coca was going to help them take back the lands that were theirs. That was why the white men feared the coca bushes and poisoned and firebombed them. Coca leaves gave the Indians too much power, dangerous power; not just the power money buys, but spiritual power to destroy all but the strong. All things weak, all things European, would shrivel, then blow away. Nothing would stop their passing; all their apprentices and toadies, whatever their ancestry, would disappear too" (502–3).

Cocaine smuggling and anti-imperialism coalesce and color conventional revolutionary politics in mystical reinventions of nature as a force that defeats all institutionalized control. The benevolence of "Mama Coca," the rush of cocaine, and flow of money, are milk to terrorism that flourishes beyond formulaic left politics. Just as Marxist ideology was irrelevant to Vida because of her craving for activism as a lifestyle and her preference for protests designed for the televised news, so too it is rendered irrelevant by a nature worship that opposes all forms of theory as well as electronic communication. Fine points of policy are irrelevant in a revolutionary ethos whose article of faith is the triumph of ghost spirits who overpower all obstacles presented by First World technological culture, cause one's enemies to commit suicide or murder each other, and substitute an antirationalist world view.

The "ideology" of the spirit movement is written by its most accurate historian, a psychic healer who is in touch with the tribal dead. Angelita, a Mayan engaged in cocaine dealing and organizing Mexican Indians for revolution, is dismayed by the ignorance of Marxists. She had counted on Castro to supply arms to the Indians of Mexico, but she is shocked that an agent from Castro is working with Indians in the mountains; "some internal committee in Havana wanted him to investigate the Indians. They could not be certain any longer which groups of Indians were true Marxists, and which tribes were puppets for the U.S. military, or worse, tribes which were corrupted by nationalism and tribal superstition" (504). Castro's contempt for superstition is only a mark of the inability of Marxism to create the solution. Marxism's failure to understand the power of Mother Earth and the strength of the ghost spirits causes Angelita La Escapía to exclaim: "Poor Engels and Marx! [She] had to smile at the two old white men who had waited, year after year, for the successful revolution until their time ran out" (749).

Women are the mothers of terror in the fantasy of complete revolution by spiritual and mystical means. It is women who must forge the alliance of all of the tribal peoples of North, Central, and South America to take back their continents. All that restricts Mother Earth is villainous. In this revolution of Earth and spirit, ecoterrorists help with bombs that can blow up dams to "free" the rivers. The currents of rivers and forces of nature are metaphors for the primal aggressive forces that can be unleashed as terrorist weapons. Added to these are the invasion of beliefs and dreams by mystical forces.

The cultural war between believers and secularists finds expression in a fantastic terrorism of the spirit whose goal is to restore a nature religion that will replace "new age Christianity," which is judged inadequate "in the face of the immensely powerful and splendid spirit beings who inhabited the vastness of the Americas" A Hopi Indian who knows how to infiltrate the dreams of all of the oppressed brings prisoners and bikers to the cause, and uses his facility with the spirit world as a recruiting tool (620). The "ghost dance" to reunite people with departed spirits is another weapon because the ghosts of tribal ancestors "can return to invade the dreams of mothers and compel them to drive their children off cliffs" and to infect the dominant culture with self-destruction (722). Invaders of dreams will presumably inspire all enemies to kill their offspring and then themselves. How can the machines that do the enemy's bidding be made to wreck themselves?

At an international holistic healers convention, tribal peoples are joined by loners with a knowledge of technology and a passion for chaos: "Awa Gee was interested in the purity of destruction. Awa Gee was interested in the perfection of complete disorder and disintegration" (683). A computer and electronics wizard, Awa Gee has broken into the codes of switching systems, impressed with the destruction electrical failures can wreak on air traffic control systems and industrial America. Hoping to harness electricity to destroy technology and to use computerized information systems to spew disinformation is hoping rationalized technological culture can be made to implode.

Politics as personal experience is expressed in the equation between poverty and the direct experiences of women who are struggling for survival as single mothers and face a future in a female underclass. The fight for Mother Earth will be waged, according to Silko's novel, by her human embodiments: "black women, Hispanic women, white women, homeless with starving children" (747–48). That oppressed women are one with spirit-warriors is a complex metaphor for the mingled depression and helplessness that accompany grandiose dreams of violent retribution. Like the Native American myth of Sister and her dead baby who bring disease to humankind to avenge injustice discussed in chapter 1, Silko's impoverished women and ghost warriors express a vision of the helpless and the dead as actually a living virulence that can destroy the body politic.

Highly rationalized technological culture is the enemy in *Almanac of the Dead*, demonized as the weapon wielded by men against the female powers of the Earth. The association of patriarchal power with reason, heartlessness, and the destruction of organic life is reversed in other recent literature that presents female biology as a trap and pregnancy as its unbreakable lock. How can that power be overthrown?

The revolution that matters in fiction that emerges from microchipped America offers women a path out of the biological determinism that dictates the terms of the female condition. While *Almanac of the Dead* represents terrorism enacted by an alliance with Mother Earth to defeat technology, other works have celebrated an opposite path toward empowerment. This fiction describes women terrorists as seeking a way out of the limits of the body and visceral emotion through embracing technology as a force for self-transcendence. The destructive egotism of such activists is evident in their mastery of the politics of the image in the time of the photo-op.

The terrorist as seductive star and filmmaker embodies the spirit of the age in Thomas Pynchon's vision of a California girl whose passion for power transcends any other cause and who masters communications in a culture addicted to "tubal intoxification." Both leftist radicals and conservatives feel betrayed in that America in which no ideology, no conviction, and no politics seem to matter any more. Pynchon's *Vineland* begins in 1984, a time when the nation is obsessed with what he calls Rex 84—the reelection of Ronald Reagan, the president who is a master-communicator and Pynchon's King of the Tube. In this McLuhanist novel, which spans the period from the sixties to the mid-eighties, the major tool for both reaction and revolution is electronics technology. In the sixties, both protests and conservative advocacies are staged for the tube; the medium is the only message that counts. But in the eighties the activist wants to do more than supply violent images for the tube. She wants to *be* a media image. Her willed construction of her own image explodes Baudrillardian conceptions of woman as only a fixed object.

The making of a woman terrorist is a cinematic production, a media birth for a mediagenic future. As the heroine of the sixties revolution, she is the woman with the camera. Frenesi is a radical filmmaker who, in the sixties, sees the camera as a gun and filming injustice as an attack on it. As head of a film collective, Frenesi joins the protest at the College of the Surf in an endless Summer of Love orchestrated by the People's Republic of Rock and Roll. The purpose is to protest privatization of the college's real estate by capitalist condo-builders. Their intellectual leader is a radical young math professor whose name, Weed Atman (Marijuana Soul), suggests his perpetual high. His flower-power politics suggest his affinity with nature. Frenesi is his confidante. A red-diaper baby, Frenesi only seems to be following the radical path laid out for her by her parents who stood firm against McCarthyism. Named Frenesi after a fifties pop song, she is a product of pop culture, a rebel without a cause other than her own destructive egotism.

Frenesi betrays Weed and the green power he suggests. She sets up his murder, becomes an informant against the cause, and turns against political conviction of any kind. Instead, like the anarchoterrorists Billington described, Frenesi is fascinated by the gun as a mechanical representation of pure power, of what she wants to be. Introduced to the gun by an FBI prosecutor, Brock, whose loveplay involves the allure of the gun and its sexy, killing release, she begins her transformation in her affair with him. Excited, she agrees when he suggests she arrange the murder of good-natured Weed. She sets up the scene and films the murder, preserving on film Weed's pained recognition that he is dying and she is responsible. Atman's death ushers in more violence, provoking a brutal police action. Frenesi discovers that beyond "penis/gun envy" is the pure joy of complete control: staging murder and filming it.

Frenesi epitomizes the media culture's infatuation with graphic, recorded violence, role-playing, and treachery. She is the spirit of revolt as a California girl devoted to the "thriller" that would view terrorism as a form of reality TV. The controlling mechanisms of recorded violence are the camera eye, the film, digital recording, and the will to stage and shoot the drama. She wants to be fluid, category-defying, and as gravity-defying as an image on a screen. Bisexual, she is determined not to be bored or ground down by the conventional female trap of motherhood. She sees the celluloid life of film or the pixel life of computer graphics as a release from mortality.

Terrorism against the human condition is expressed in a radical inversion of the meaning of birth and death. Frenesi sees pregnancy and birth as her encounter with death. Bearing a child, Frenesi thinks, is a "descent to cold regions of hatred for the tiny life, raw, parasitic, using her body through the wearying months and now still looking to control her. . . . (286) 'This is just how they want you, an animal, a bitch with swollen udders, lying in the dirt, blank-faced, surrendered, reduced to this meat, these smells. . . . ' Taken down, . . . from all the silver and light she'd known and been, brought back to the world like silver recalled grain by grain from the Invisible to form images of what then went on to grow old, . . . get broken or contaminated. She had been privileged to live outside of Time, to enter and leave at will, looting and manipulating, weightless, invisible. Now Time had claimed her again, put her under house arrest, taken her passport away. Only an animal with a full set of pain receptors after all" (286–87). In revolt against biology, she looks like a woman but dreams of the freedom of being a computerized image.

Frenesi prefers silicon life to humanity with its fleshy, carbon-based realities of childbearing and nurturing. Like Pynchon's V., who is imagined in V. as an autoerotic machine with perfect plastic skin, Frenesi is a disruptive adventuress in the violent but semi-animate world captured on film. In actuality, she becomes involved with three men who represent her options: Weed Atman, the intellectual she helps kill; Zoyd, an amiable doper whom she abandons, leaving him her daughter to raise; and Brock, whose talent for control and betrayal she desires and exceeds.

Frenesi uses Brock as her erotic videogame of power; his life as prosecutor is the power game she can play "just for the score. . . . His erect penis had become the joystick with which, hurtling into the future, she would try to steer . . . [into] underground time . . . that could take her nowhere outside its own tight and falsely deathless perimeter" (292–93). For her, computer-generated "life" offers the illusion of immortality.

Frenesi's pursuit of "immortality" ironically foreshadows a conception of politics and the family recast by media and information technology: "While the Tube was proclaiming youth revolution against parents of all kinds, and most viewers were accepting this story, Brock saw . . . the need only to stay children forever, safe inside some extended national Family" (269). But the family is tubal, the umbilicus of cable and electronic connections, each a conduit of the larger culture of information in which surveillance and consumption intertwine. This is the computerized world in which every time one uses a bank or credit card, one's needs can be gratified, even as one's whereabouts can be clocked and recorded. Families like the Brady Bunch feed media images of human interaction while the secret of togetherness is the electronic network, the cables that bind the nation.

Frenesi's terrorism symbolizes the transformation toward destructive egotism. Her choices reverse resistance as the usual relationship between terrorist and the dominant culture. She is a co-conspirator with the dominant culture that relies on media and information technology. Media culture has so softened political discourse as to neutralize differences and reconcile them in images of self-absorption as old-time warriors of the left and right find themselves obsolesced by eighties youth for whom political violence is only entertainment. Frenesi's daughter and her boyfriend, Isaiah Two Four, who was named by his flower-power parents for the biblical passage exhorting the transformation of swords into ploughshares, are a couple with plans. Isaiah Two Four wants to develop violence theme parks for family fun featuring "Third World Thrills, a jungle obstacle course where you got to . . . blast away at surprise pop-up targets shaped like indigenous guerrilla elements" (19). Terrorism as a theme park makes it all a matter of personal thrills.

The moralistic terrorism that aims for achieving retributive justice by violence is obsolesced by a vision of life as videogame and ride. Entertainment technology, interactive videogames, interfaces between graphics and reality, and the theme park ride all suggest how the power of the individual woman might include all that she can switch on. Technology and politics, religion and history can negate each other in fantasies in which the film of injustice can be reversed. In *Vineland*, "Karmic Readjustment Clinics" are built in which events of the past can be run backwards and edited as if they were films. The moment when Frenesi smuggles in the gun and Rex shoots Weed can presumably be reversed. But the content of what has happened no longer matters; what counts is watching the show. The unjustly killed, the Weed Atmans, are "Thanatoids" who are neither dead nor alive but simply couch potatoes who view their own lives, watching what happens and making no effort to demand redress. Are the images women watch only those of predators and not victims, only successfully violent woman? They are the Frenesis, the Lara Crofts, the sexy killers everyone, it seems, wants to watch. Are women terrorists in fiction reality's sisters?

Of aspiring contemporary American political assassins in the real world, only two have been women, but each could stand with her fictional sisters in fusing a rejection of conventional roles with a covert war against rage at her life as a woman. Neither has anything resembling a commitment to conventional political ideology or public policy, but neither should be dismissed as operating out of personal pathology alone. Harold Lasswell, for example, distinguished the ideologically motivated from those who had what he called "a political personality." He describes them as driven by a personal pathology that causes them to rationalize their own rebellion in terms of larger social goals, when in actuality they pursue power to gain fame and repair their low self-esteem. He sees them as entirely separate from those driven to violent acts by a commitment to ideology (40). He defines politics in terms of formulaic ideology.

But it is difficult to separate the personal rage of women political activists from the fact that women in revolutionary groups have often been second-class members denied participation in formulating policy. Discriminatory, condescending, and humiliating attitudes may prove as entrenched and disturbing in revolutionary groups as they are in the mainstream. Not surprisingly women may become involved in acts of violence that communicate their own situation. Accounts of their terrorism have tended to describe their actions as evidence of personal pathologies that have nothing to do with social issues except in the distortions of individual psyches. The intellectual underpinnings of radical political thought are filled with arguments for revolutionary changes that nevertheless preserve the subordination of women and by that fact alone place women radicals in a vexed position. Fictional terrorists are granted voices that, taken together, speak with great variety about the formation of self-concepts through violent action. What do accounts of the motives of actual terrorists describe?

Actual terrorists document the inability to be heard as a driving force in violent action and the craving to utilize or even dominate a charismatic man who will, in some measure, express their views. The violence of such women is often depicted by them as a last resort.

Before attempting to assassinate Gerald Ford with a gun, Lynette Fromme had tried and failed to develop a group of radicals who would make terrorist threats followed by assassinations of those corporate executives and their wives she held responsible for managing the companies that had polluted the Earth. She felt her organization would serve as an "International People's Court of Retribution" (Clarke 148). Arrested for the attempt on Ford, she said, "Well you know when people around you treat you like a child and pay no attention to the things you say, you have to do something" (Clarke 143). The drive to be taken seriously and to have her argument for the environment heard was a major part of her motivation. She wanted to commit a high-profile crime to gain a high-profile trial she could use to publicize her views. She planned to call Charles Manson as a character witness in her defense. She saw him as amplifying her voice and believed the two of them could win followers for her antipollution agenda.

Fromme felt ignored and diminished—her nickname was the hardly terrifying "Squeaky." Assassinating the president would, she believed, bring her a wide audience, and convey the horror of industrial pollution. It would also enable her to provide Charles Manson a forum and gain a measure of respect from and power over him as his impresario. The effort to repair a past of painful slights and insults was part of her motive, but it would be difficult to separate and quantify the mixture of rage, self-sacrifice, desire to appropriate Manson's charismatic voice on her own behalf, and her convictions about pollution. A heady combination of factors was involved in her attempt on President Ford against whom, she admitted, she had no real complaint.

Sara Jane Moore, after whom Sara Jane Olson had named herself when she stopped using her own name (Kathleen Soliah) and went underground, had somewhat different motives. Sara Jane Moore seemed still another version of the lady as terrorist. Moore had made five marriages, each to a more successful man, and had determinedly earned CPA credentials when she left her wealthy physician-husband and became enmeshed in radical politics. James W. Clarke, writing in *American Assassins,* describes the facts of her background that I believe support my view of her relationship to the lady-terrorist paradigm. Moved by Kathleen Soliah's eloquence on behalf of the Symbionese Liberation Army [SLA] and the need for revolution, Moore volunteered as the accountant for the People in Need [PIN] program that the SLA had demanded from Randolph Hearst in exchange for his daughter. The program was set up by Hearst when his daughter's kidnappers demanded that he distribute two million dollars to the poor. Sara's combination of ladylike demeanor and radical politics endeared her to the SLA members who thought she would be their spokesperson in their dealings with Hearst. It also made her sought after by the FBI who wanted to use her as an informant and assumed this comfortably off, middle-aged woman was no threat.

What Sara did reflected above all her commitment to the life of risk as an antidote to the boredom of respectable marriage, motherhood, and career. Sara was pleased to help both the SLA and the FBI and had no profound ideological commitment to either. A woman who had not taken kindly to motherhood and had sent her children by previous marriages to live with her parents or ex-husbands or in boarding schools, Sara had found a new world in which her destructive egotism could flourish. She was working both sides of the ideological fence, living on the edge, and loving the political intrigue. Helping both the FBI and SLA, she gave information to both sides. As a double agent betraying everyone, she embodied the amoral rush of chameleon-like change.

After the FBI arrested Patty Hearst in the apartment of Steve Soliah and Wendy Yoshimura, Sara was treated with increasing suspicion by both the FBI and the movement. She resolved to prove her solidarity with the left by finishing the job begun by Lynette Fromme and shooting President Ford. Before her assassination attempt, Sara Jane Moore had been confronted by both the police and the FBI and accused of disloyalty. Despite her possession of a gun, the FBI concluded that she was incapable of shooting anyone. Just as Lynette Fromme had been dismissed, so Sara Jane Moore was not regarded as a threat. The FBI said she was not "of sufficient protective importance to warrant surveillance during the President's visit"

(Clarke 165). Nevertheless, she shot at President Ford outside the St. Francis Hotel. "It was a kind of ultimate protest against the system. I did not want to kill somebody, but there comes a point when the only way you can make a statement is to pick up a gun," she explained (*Los Angeles Times,* September 25, 1975, I1). Pleading guilty to attempting to assassinate the President, she was given a life sentence. Like Lynette, she felt intense anger toward "the system" and those who had underestimated her, but she had no real list of grievances against President Ford.

The common thread that runs through accounts of both fictional and real women terrorists is how repellent the life of stability, decorum, and affection summed up by the word "lady" is. It comes to symbolize boredom, humiliation, and all the behavioral strictures the patriarchy and ordinary life imposes on women. It seems, however, tolerable if conceived of as a cover for rebellion. When she went underground, Sara Jane Olson seems to have spent more than twenty years happily living the upscale life of the wife of a successful physician and a devoted mother.

Sara Jane Olson's years of good behavior were not rewarded. After a plea agreement offering five years and four months in prison for her admission of guilt for the attempted murder of two policemen by planting a bomb under their car in 1975, Olson's sentence was extended to fourteen years by the Board of Prison Terms. Olson subsequently received an additional six years for participation in the robbery of the Crocker National Bank in Carmichael, California, that resulted in the death of a forty-two-year-old woman who was there depositing funds for her church. "I never entered that bank with the intent of harming anyone," Ms. Olson said. "I am truly sorry, and I will be sorry until the day I die" (*New York Times,* November 8, 2002, A18). Contributing to Sara Jane Olson's decision to accept the plea agreement was the fact that the heiress Patricia Hearst Shaw would have been subpoenaed to testify against her. Hearst Shaw had already provided a detailed description of what happened during the robbery in her book *Every Secret Thing* long after she herself had been released from jail and had returned to the life of wealth into which she was born.

The seesaw between the life of risk and the life of security seems a necessary oscillation. The requirement to suppress rebellious instincts kept

Moore alternating between maintaining appearances of marriage and motherhood while subverting them through abandoning her children and divorcing her husbands. The SLA's demand for commitment and orthodoxy proved equally difficult to fulfill. Although Fromme and Moore display some aspects of Lasswell's "political personality" and contempt for political dogma, far more is involved than their simply acting out of personal grievance or compensating for low self-esteem. The ability to maintain alternating styles of normalcy and revolt reflect a destructive egotism that needs to be fully in charge, using concealment as an instrument of control and taking no others into account.

Conventional female roles involving commitment seem a straitjacket that can scarcely be endured. Rage at the "system" or the "patriarchy" or obvious social injustice is nourished by rage at all forms of constriction. In response, the terrorists in fiction both exploit and suffer from a world that responds to them primarily as women whose concerns are easily trivialized. The experience of personal turmoil informs but does not limit a communicative public voice for empowerment through violence. They refuse to play only the lady or the terrorist and become adept at manipulating both roles to increase the options available to them. Sometimes the craving for change impales the terrorist in a tragedy of her own devising. News accounts rarely provide the depth and texture of feeling or context of high tragedy provided by fiction, but some do suggest similarities.

The passage from sheltered idealism to self-sacrifice on the altar of social good frames the story of Katherine Ann Power. In the early months of 1970, Katherine Ann Power was an eminently respectable and bright young woman who had won both a Betty Crocker homemaker award and a fellowship to Brandeis. She was poised for the best kind of upward mobility at the beginning of new, feminist times. Power grew up in Denver and was the oldest child in an Irish Catholic family of seven children. Her parents provided a Catholic education and encouraged a respect for authority. However, the Chicago riots in 1968, the Vietnam War, the invasion of Cambodia, and the killing of students by the National Guard at Kent State had all challenged her sense of justice and moral order. At Brandeis she first joined nonviolent protest groups but also met more radical students and became involved with a group of violent parolees who had been admitted to Brandeis as part of a prisoners' rehabilitation program. They were involved in running guns and ammunition and robbing to support their cause. Drawn to them and their violent radicalism, she took part on September 23, 1970, in the robbery of a Brighton, Massachusetts bank. A Boston policeman, Walter Schroeder, who was the father of nine children, attempted to stop the robbery and was shot through the back and killed.

Although Power was not directly responsible for the death of Schroeder, she drove the getaway car in the bank robbery and went underground as police pursued her as a cop killer. She eluded capture by appearing so completely non-threatening and wholesome that she escaped notice. Cultivating a blandness of appearance, she was able to disappear among women at bus stations or airline terminals even when police searching for her were present. Over time, her fellow radicals were arrested. She found herself increasingly shunned by the radical groups from which she had hoped for support. Avoided by radical men who considered her too feminist, she was seen by feminist radicals as uninterested in women's issues and manipulated by the male-dominated left. In her isolation, she dealt with suicidal depression.

In 1978 she gave birth to a son. She settled in Lebanon, Oregon and opened a restaurant with a business partner, developed a long-term relationship with a man and raised her son until he was thirteen. At that point she sold her share of the business, donated the proceeds to Oxfam, and left her husband who had agreed to adopt her son. In 1993 she turned herself in, she said, to atone for the death of Walter Schroeder twenty-three years earlier.

While she was surely justified in wanting to atone for her participation in the robbery that led to Schroeder's death, Power's decision eerily reenacted the willingness to destroy her own stability that accompanied her attraction to violence in the first place. Turning herself in destroyed her family in pointed ways. By donating the proceeds from the sale of her business to Oxfam, she chose not to support her son. She left him and her husband. Although she had turned herself in and cooperated fully with law enforcement, she was treated badly. She had been told and believed the state of Massachusetts would transfer her to Oregon to serve her sentence so her son could visit her while she was in prison. Instead, she was sent to the Massachusetts Correctional Institution at Framingham and served six years of an eight- to twenty-five-year sentence before her release. While she was in jail, her son began drinking, dropped out of school, and became a father at nineteen. Her relationship with her husband ended completely. Nevertheless, she declared, "I am not sorry I surrendered. It satisfied some human obligations I had to the Schroeder family."

The constant in Power's life was a rejection of stability. Although the violence of her past involved a repudiation of her parents, her abandonment of her own husband and son only recapitulated her repudiation of the primacy of family ties. Her debt to the Schroeder family, like her commitment to the violated underclass that fueled her political violence, enabled her to distance herself from family entrapment with claims of altruism. In a sense, she used her sacrifice of her family, suffering, and depression to equalize the loss she had helped inflict on the Schroeder family.

Much of the terrorist action in fiction enacts psychosocial dramas that have neither the organizing structures nor justifying ideas of sophisticated, established ideology nor the comforts of the like-minded in the terrorist cell or group. Violent action in its origins and aftermath tends to replicate the vexed position of women in relation to both family and revolutionary group. However promising at the outset, the solidarity of the group is always destroyed by external forces or by its own internal differences. In mid-nineteenth century Italy, Buonarotti, who was powerfully impressed by the political understanding and dedication of women while in exile in Switzerland, found eager converts to social revolution in the young women he and his friends taught for a living. Yet, as James Billington pointed out, such women were never incorporated into his organization because of "the congenital insolence of men (who treat them as 'pieces of domestic furniture') and the inability of women to get along with each other under stress" (Billington 484). The kinds of tensions described in contemporary fiction correlate with such difficulties while providing complex narratives of meaning and purpose.

The women terrorists in fiction often invoke the power of iconic female figures to lift them beyond the ideological narrowness they see as irrelevant to their hopes in a world in which ideology and male revolutionaries have failed them. Silko's Mother Earth and Mama Coca, Alvarez's Virgencita, Piercy's Wonder Woman, Roth's American Princess turned terrorist—all come alive as alternative visions of female agency. Writers such as Alvarez and Garcia who draw on the experiences of postwar exposure to actual dictatorship, tyranny, or the denial of basic freedoms in the Dominican Republic or Cuba, bring to the imaginative representation of revolutionary activism the ability to depict both the tensions between women and the configurations that enable women to invoke militant visions of the Blessed Virgin and Santería to sacralize political activism in a world ruled by men but lacking male "saviors."

Women terrorists in contemporary American writing convey the darker forces that track our traditions of individual sovereignty. Their destructive egotism transforms the political arena into a theater of power in which they can play starring roles. They are icons of cultural revolution with a gun or pipe bomb whose power, unleashed only in the moment of violent rebellion, connects them with the vital part of themselves and attacks the behavioral strictures institutionalized in female roles and in the family. In his documentary history of violence in the United States, Richard Hofstadter reviewed outbreaks of violence throughout American history, and concluded that our violence, lacking a coherent political thrust, "has been too various, diffuse and spontaneous to be forged into a single, sustained inveterate hatred shared by an entire social class" (3). The violence of women, long ruled out as a historical phenomena of importance, has, I believe, enormous importance in bringing a mythic form to anarchic, individualistic unruliness. As a savage passage, their violence, to borrow Emerson's phrase, shoves "Jesus and Judas" equally aside and undermines moral categories in the focus on a destructive egotism in which the world matters only as "this *other me*."

The particular relationship between the destructive egotism of fictional women terrorists and the social world under attack highlights the operations of destructive egotism as a moral and psychological force. It shadows explorations of individualism and power that once flourished in American writing. In "Mr. America," a brilliant meditation on Emerson, Harold Bloom writes of Emerson's disdain for conventional moral distinctions in favor of a call to power that Bloom terms "a call to selfhood." Part of what Bloom calls Emerson's "cheerfully amoral dialectics of power" is Emerson's perceptive recognition that enacted power always involves destructiveness, an observation based on nature's potential for violence and the recognition that human power was morally doubledged: "Vivacity, leadership, must be had, and we are not allowed to be nice in choosing. We must fetch the pump with dirty water if clean cannot be had. Inspiration at any cost, by virtue or by vice, by friend or by fiend, by prayer or by wine" ("Power" 60). Power exists in action, marking the pace of change. This language might do for the fiction of women terrorists who claim alliances with both the destructive power of Mother Nature and the coercive power of media technology.

Emerson's cheerful nihilism is realized in the fiction of women terrorists, which arrives like postcards bearing cryptic messages from the dark side. Sexuality is the conventional arena in which women express their wildness. The terrorist women in fiction offer a communicative violence based on acts of self-affirmation, self-display, and repudiation of conventions of the left and right. Such repudiations can be seen as acts of unmasking designed to show the hypocrisy of promises of freedom or equality. Merry's repudiation of the perfect father and beauty-queen mother, Vida's rejection of all forms of stability, the rejection of Marxist ideology and exasperation with revolution on the male model embodied in much of this fiction by Fidel Castro—all underscore the failure of both conventional lives or conventional activism. These narratives celebrate instability and transformative change, antipathy toward all that is promised by both the conventions of middle-class life and by the countertradition of male radicalism.

Art performs that unmasking function in uncovering hypocritical speech. In her meditation *On Violence,* Hannah Arendt wrote: "If we inquire historically into the causes likely to transform *engagés* into *enragés,* it is not injustice that ranks first, but hypocrisy. . . . Words can be relied on only if one is sure that their function is to reveal and not to conceal. It is the semblance of rationality, much more than the interests behind it, that provokes rage" (65–66). By seizing control of language, images, symbols, and narratives, the fiction of terrorist women finds new strategies for dealing with hypocrisy, particularly the hypocrisy surrounding woman's place.

Traditional approaches have stressed the importance of unmasking the lies surrounding the idealization of woman. Hypocrisy was one of the first great subjects of nonviolent American feminists. Margaret Fuller's *Woman in the Nineteenth Century* struck at the deceptions of male talk about women, identifying male praise as the sound of contempt. "Hypocrisy," she wrote, was "the meanest of crimes" (27). Woman were not declared outright inferiors but were named superior in matters of emotion. This very superiority was part of what rendered them unsuitable from the taxing stresses of government and the professions. Fuller pointed out that weakness was an attribute credited only to middle-class white women, since the "Indian squaw carries the burdens of the camp," and black women performed hard labor even when pregnant (34). Although Fuller saw straight talk as the counterforce to male, hypocritical speech, she aimed for the sublime enhancement of the political dialogue by adding the truths women knew. The fiction of women terrorists reverses that process.

In vivid imagery and deceptive speech, terrorist fictions use oscillations between masking and unmasking to convey female truths. This fiction appropriates hypocritical speech as its own. The costume and narrative of the "lady" is used as the tool of deception for the terrorist. Claims of idealism and justice are employed to support criminal violence. Violent action is the communicative form substituting for speech. Destructive egotism is given a positive spin. Moral hypocrisy is dealt with by appropriation of its power and by sheer amorality. Even as violent women expose hypocrisy in the promise of fulfillment through normalcy, they appropriate the look of normalcy as a weapon.

Margaret Fuller was to speak in religious terms of independence as reclaiming the female self for God. The terrorist woman in contemporary literature sometimes reclaims omnipotence for herself. Her Americanness is expressed in her appropriation of Emersonian faith in the indwelling nature of divine power and in her exploitation of an older morality that charts the path to deliverance as leading to God. The violent woman's vision of the world as hostile and determined to keep women down can be compared to Georges Sorel's assertion that pessimism is a strategy for action. In his *Reflections on Violence,* Sorel advocated a revolutionary pessimism he saw as better than progressive and rational efforts to bring about incremental change. The workers of the world, according to Sorel, should adopt a myth of armed pessimism that justified destroying everything in its path much as the Calvinists did in the belief that the world is damned and to save it one had to make a violent and total repudiation. To fuel this will required religious fervor. For Sorel, the myth had to be secular, a General Strike that "was neither an economic strike (simply for material benefits)" nor one designed to fulfill a particular ambition. The General Strike was a mythic strike, a strike "to stir the soul . . . a vision of life" based on negation of all that was.

The women terrorists of contemporary fiction have no faith in any general strike, but make of themselves a mythic strike force. Images of immortality reflect the destructive egotism of appropriating a perfection exemplified by Vida's identification with Wonder Woman, or Frenesi's longing to be an eternally young beauty in cyberspace. In other tales spiritual divinity is claimed by invocations ranging from the militant holy Virgin, or Mother Earth, or rituals of Santería, or Silko's avenging spirits. Claims of mastery of natural forces can be involved in imagining Mama Coca's power over the use of drug traffic to support terrorism. Mama Coca inverts expectations of maternal nourishment, substituting the poisonous flow of cocaine for mother's milk. All these pop, religious, or mythical iconic female forms convey a blend of destructive egotism and personalized, unprogrammatic politics on a scale both grand and grandiose. Violence by women seizes images and narratives of spiritual divinity and inverts them to demonic form and purpose. Narratives associated with subjective cognition and individualism support a twisty logic of destructive egotism and radical personalization. They define a dark world in terms of violent, sacred destroyers.

The elated violence in much of this fiction defines a personalization of politics that reflects not so much a recoil from social concerns as a knowing refusal to perceive a difference between private and public issues. The prevalence of destructive egotism sets it apart from the therapeutic model Frantz Fanon established for terrorist violence in which individualism is sacrificed to the bond forged when each man performs "an irrevocable action" to cement himself to the group (85). Fanon's belief, that "the practice of violence binds men together as a whole since each individual forms a violent link in the great chain, a part of the great organism of violence which has surged upward," is absent in the lives of women (93). Their recourse is to break their own chains and resist being trapped.

Women terrorists in fiction find social comfort in neither cell nor family but in self-images as quick-change artists whose costumes and speech can brilliantly parody normalcy without getting stuck in it. They invoke a variety of mythic female icons who represent an alternative ancestry. Mastering the twists and turns of hypocritical speech and empowered by violent action, women terrorists in fiction annihilate the cultural meanings and roles language assigns women. In their uninhibited rejection of every fixed role and their ability to play all parts, they reflect the development of destructive egotism as a political style.

CHAPTER 5

VIOLENCE LITE

Entertaining Aggression

SPECTACLES THAT DEFINE THE MOMENT CAPTURE THE PASSION FOR CELEBRITY through violence. Violence lite is mediagenic, born of the camera's love for lingering on the bizarre or dramatic, of the power of filmed action to be replayed again and again until its images become icons of transgressive style. The practice breaks the wall between reality and fantasy as the events that are thought to embody the essence of a time are self-consciously replayed. Nothing illustrates this more vividly than accounts of the differences between Woodstock '66 and Woodstock '99. According to news reports, "Unlike the audience at the original Woodstock 30 years ago, today's generation of festivalgoers and performers is not intent on overturning the system. It is intent on being on television" (Strauss, "New Spirit," B8).

The festival was lit up by the exploitation of once political symbols as instruments of individualistic violence. The *New York Times* of July 26 reported that "'peace candles' were used to set fire to an overturned car" (Zielbauer, "Fans Rampage," B1). The concert ended with security forces fleeing from a crowd creating bonfires out of giant speakers, burning trucks, overturning trailers, smashing ATMs, and piling up images of chaos. Why did they do it? Was it to protest the high price of food and water? Those concessions were spared despite resentment of price gouging. One news account said, "It was a revolutionary act signifying nothing.

Through it all, the crowd chanted 'U.S.A! U.S.A! Canada! Canada!' and 'Woodstock!'" (Strauss, "New Spirit" B8).

But more than that was involved. One explanation was provided by "a body piercer" from New Hampshire who "walked away from the flaming trucks in a gas mask he had brought to the festival" and claimed the riot was a form of self-definition. As he put it, "our generation isn't about peace and love anymore; they're all about destruction and hostility'" (Strauss, "On the Night," B5). Widely attributed to cynicism about the possibilities for change, the violence clearly meant more. Woodstock '99 meant to revisit the sixties' ethos of peace, love, and communality, but the audience had become competitive with the performers and the crowd's aggression became the show. As bands urged the audience to express themselves by breaking things, television cameras "documenting the event . . . zoomed over the crowd, eliciting cheers wherever they went" (Strauss, "New Spirit," B8). The audience at Woodstock '99 became actors and then spectators of their own performance. "Media savvy teenagers painted themselves green"; posted everywhere were "signs that warned audience members that by attending they were giving consent for their 'likeness, name and voice' to be exploited 'in any and all forms of media' and 'without compensation throughout the world and in perpetuity'" (Strauss, "On the Night," B8). Many had signed legal forms at the festival's beginning, transferring rights to their own image in anticipation of becoming new icons.

Fred Durst, the lead singer of Limp Bizkit, announced to the crowd at Woodstock '99 just before the blowup: "They want us to ask you to mellow out. They said too many people are getting hurt. Don't let nobody get hurt, but I don't think you should mellow out.' When Limp Bizkit played 'Break Stuff,' which rants against 'the he says–she says' and promises to 'break your . . . face tonight,' the crowd exploded" (Smith 38). R. J. Smith, applauding the blowup, described it as "the quintessential rap-rock moment, when everyday pressures and the old he says–she says ignites in an updraft of rage" (Smith 38). At Woodstock '99 there were eight reported rapes in all; but in the final "updraft of rage," women were part of the burning and trashing (Zielbauer, "Woodstock," B1, B5).

One way to control the grossout of hostile sexuality is to appropriate it. Although much of the violence of women is directed against men and not women, virtually all of it displays profound ambivalence about assigned female roles. Appropriating misogyny and sexual hostility, women provide glitzy and surprising images of revolt. Controlling and mitigating the damage of a world conceived of as punitive by directing it against oneself is both the urge of the pathological cutter and the essence of punk style, now transformed into hip style by the prevalence of body-piercing. The body-piercer at Woodstock '99 had practiced self-mutilation for show: his studded face and body, like the burning stage and bonfires of speakers, were meant to be seen, filmed, and photographed, to be visible signs of inner rage.

The egotism of celebrity culture and the suitability of violence for visual media have combined to transform our symbols of change. At the beginning of the twentieth century, it was the rapidity of the steamship that made Marinetti declare in his 1909 *Futurist Manifesto,* "Time and space died yesterday. We already live in the absolute because we have created eternal omnipresent speed" (22). In 1923, Hart Crane used a high-speed train to symbolize that dizziness. In his poem, *The Bridge,* the Twentieth Century Limited is the train that whirls all before it, leaving the populace standing in its dust as dumbfounded as hobos who can no longer hitch a ride. At the close of the twentieth century, the instrument of transformation is the camera slowly panning the audience, redeeming a face from the crowd, creating an individual's triumph over her own anonymity. Change as performance comes to the fore when it is the audience that determines what breaks ground and compels the camera to seek among its members for the shock of something different for the news.

Staging passages of self-transformation for the camera eye uses violence as performance art. It breaks distinctions between inner and outer reality by permitting the individual to enact both her sense of anonymity as a spectator and her revolt against nothingness by upstaging the outrageousness of the performer. Just as the raging beat and lyrics hurled by the bands and the actions of the audience blurred the distinction between art and reality at Woodstock '99, so the guys on the platform and the audience compete for attention as performers when the show is the trashing of the show.

Destructiveness is the dysfunctional form of building celebrity, of breaking the wall between rock star and riot star as each stakes claim to performance art. Punk attitude and metal rap use violence and porn as slick surfaces that reflect a dark alliance with aggression in a universe in which nothing but hostility can be counted on. The one who seizes the camera eye is she who steps out of nowhere to be the woman who stages misogyny as glitzy porn.

The rage orgies in which rap, wrestling, and porn entwined to make the World Wrestling Federation's "Raw Is War" a top-rated show on cable television may justify *Spin Magazine*'s definition of trashing as part of a new youth movement. "Generation *echt,*" as R. J. Smith claims, is about over-the-top violence generally seen as male (36). Female misogyny, postfeminist hostility, and the violence of women are usually left entirely out of the rave reviews its advocates write. But what is new in the phenomenon is precisely the role of women in obscene, raw misogyny.

Women are players in the mass performance art that seems a comedy of participatory nihilism in the new alliance between metal rap, porn, wrestling, and visual media. Eminem's crush lyrics (four Grammy nominations) and Kid Rock concerts have brought "pornoviolence" to a wide audience. Smith's description of a Kid Rock concert represents it as a rerun of Woodstock '99: "As the music roars on, the fans raise the plywood sheets over their heads. Limber teenage boys leap up on top of them, . . . Teenage girls climb up, too, and pull their tops off as the boys whoop. Every few minutes, a girl loses her footing and falls, sometimes headfirst, into a whirlpool of grasping hands. This has happened before. . . . There is nothing spontaneous to any of it. It already happened, of course, at Woodstock. This was a reenactment of a crime, played for laughs the second time around" (38). Life imitates art with a difference as the girls seize control of the misogynistic moment and, by doing so, change it.

Women are starring in the hostility orgies once confined to men. Men want what Smith calls "the fusion of metal, rock and wrestling," which particularly appeals to young white men who "grew up immersed in hip-hop" and rap and have appropriated its rage for a free-floating anger not defined by racism or conditions in the ghetto as it was for African American bands

(Smith 38). That rage "can fix on any target. . . . And the easiest targets get flayed the worst: women of course . . ." (38). Although the derision of women blasts louder from these spectacles than the Bloodhound Gang's CD, *Hooray for Boobies,* Smith cites for its cover of photos of animals' and women's breasts, the WWF and MTV offer aggression orgies crafted for a youth market of both sexes.

Eroticized violence is fueled by the woman who is an ally in attitude, appropriating the "Fuck you!" stance of punk, rap, and heavy metal. She joins the war against the good girl by claiming to be a "ho." At the wrestling matches you can, Smith says, "hoot at warrior women in black leather halter tops and at the miniskirted 'bad girl' act of Stephanie McMahon. Wrestling has become just another jiggly entertainment, soft-core porn wed to fighting and better story lines. Message is 'Behave badly. Speak freely'" (40). He describes an evening at the Kiel Center, where "packs of little kids chant 'slut' and other sexual crudities at the top of their lungs, and the female M.C. wiggles through the abuse" (40).

Self-promotion by the trashing of the self is not in itself a new form of female attention-getting. What has changed is its ironic use as a tool for controlling the camera eye. Smith thinks that "Portraying yourself as a 'ho' or a porn star, or just taking your top off and surfing the mosh pit, gives you momentary top billing" (41). It works. The over-the-top Lil' Kim "makes the case that the woman who controls a man's attention also controls the man" (Smith 41). Lil' Kim, however, also sings. The women who emerge from the crowd with "Ho" signs are into participatory misogyny as the only performance that counts.

The "pornoviolence" show puts male dominance into competition with sexy women for the camera eye. "The Godfather" is the wrestler as pimp, a mock version of the controlling man. Smith describes his act this way: the Godfather shows up "with 4 white 'hos' who dance around the ring" (41). His show is interactive; the audience is part of it. At one performance, Smith writes, a young woman who is a law student creates a happening when she: "parades down the stairs, carrying a sign spelling 'HO' in glitter. The fans think this might just be part of the act—she might be one of the Godfather's women—when in fact it's something better, the moment when a fan becomes part of the show" (41). When she falls down the concrete stairway, men only scream at her to take off her top; no one seems to care whether she is hurt. Smith never questions why a law student would want to carry a "Ho" sign. But the student has made sexual aggression her own. She has seized the upper hand not only by exploiting the whore identity but by putting glitter on the "HO" in HOSTILITY.

Violence as mass entertainment structures the grossout as a form of control for postfeminist women. It markets punk style and bondage chic to defeat stereotypes by appropriating them for a counterculture in which women use negative stereotypes and hurl them back at their accusers. High-end versions of the tendency affect fashions in which the bruised, battered woman or the recreational masochist can be appropriated as chic styles. Tom Ford, having taken over the house of Yves Saint Laurent for the Gucci empire, tapped the trend. His first show presented bandage dresses selling for thousands of dollars. Strips of beaded, velvet, satin, or chiffon "bandages" both bound and revealed the breasts and body as if the revenge of the beaten down could be decorating the bruise.

Psychological explanations for the perpetuation of male violence are generally drawn from learning theory. Repetitive exposure to violent behavior throughout childhood is seen as the means of transmitting brutality from one generation of men to the next. The ritualized, repetitive groping and verbal abuse of women in wrestling, metal rap, and porn spectacles eerily parody the worst male behavior toward women but also establish misogyny as a method women can adopt too. A mixture of sport and show, ritualized or stylized misogyny invites and rewards with the camera eye the participatory antics of women in the audience.

Women in such spectacles constitute an avant garde that uses a grim vision of sexual violence against women, once associated with fear, pain, and self-erasure, as a form of ironic self-expression and self-invention. Youth culture is the site for the development of styles of transgression that can be represented as performance art in which women are projected as cartoon images. Fiction provides deep, satirical, or ironical portraits that reveal the depth of changing styles of rebellion-by-appropriation and the conscious processes of self-implication and self-fashioning at work. Fictional genres open up the core of ideas, emotions, and manipulations of narratives involved in entertainment violence.

Entertainment violence in fiction involves distortions of scale, genres, and characterizations to produce sendups of conventional forms. It brings genre fiction to sophisticated, ironic heights. It takes familiar female situations and restructures and rewrites them with an edge. It appropriates conventions of popular genres for new effects and new meanings. The conventions of the romance, the horror story, science fiction, and even a serious fiction of manners are all exploited to seize control of the stereotypes of women as victims and to reinvent them as aggressors.

Violence lite has to confront violence in its most traumatic forms to raise the possibility of transforming its meaning and force. Entertainment violence devised by women writers plays with the conventional assumptions and stereotypes found in pop genres. Romance fiction depends on both male and female stereotypes: the bodice-ripping hero who overcomes the heroine's virtuous reluctance by sheer male sexual power. A sendup of the romance genre twists the bodice-ripping hero into the rapist whose traumatic violence can be twisted by female coolness into an ironic joke. The newest black comedy springs from representations of a hostile social world in which virtually all men are potential rapists, all relationships are steeped in aggression, and the woman involved is impressed by none of it.

Violence lite in literature uses the more intense and destructive concept of rape for the reverse purpose of undermining the trauma it inflicts on the victim. It uses distancing devices to distort conceptions of scale and relies on a mastery of craft to reduce or end the impact of a male attack. Like the gang rape "documentary" staged and touted by Grace Quek described in chapter 2, can fiction seize control of the experience of violation to reverse the identity of victim and attacker?

In spare, continuous irony that seems the perfection of a style of female stand-up comedy, Lisa Blaushild rewrites the tale of a brutal attack as a clumsy first date. Blaushild's 1993 short story "Love Letter to My Rapist" is a wildly ironic attack on a woman's violator in the form of a love letter written to him. She seizes control of the rape story by rescripting it as a mock-romantic confessional narrative written on stationery scented with

Chanel perfume and calling her attacker a "dreamy hunk." Her humor hits hard at the stereotype of the lovesick romance heroine while nailing her attacker: "Like I described to the boys at the stationhouse, you're an interesting cross between Robert Mitchum and Ted Bundy" (172).

Bright manipulations of language and tone enable women writers to reinvent the relationship between victim and attacker by striking at assumptions of female delicacy and romantic longing and stripping the attacker of his power to bury her in the pain of the attack and destroy her independent mind. Ironic parody of the romance form restores both distance and a dominant perspective.

In her poem "Rape," Jayne Cortez seizes control of a male attack with a few deft formal touches. Command of a precise and compressed poetics reverses victimization through grammar and metaphor. For example, a careful use of "for" instead of "to" places the female speaker in a position of control and choice:

> What was Inez supposed to do for
> the man who declared war on her body
> the man who carved a combat zone between her
> breasts. . . .
> She stood with a rifle in her hand
> doing what a defense department will do in times of
> war (58).

The military metaphors enlarge the speaker's violence against an attacker and legitimate it by the analogy to a retaliatory strike in war. The war between the sexes is made concrete in a poetry that sees woman as a strike force.

Who the speaker is as important as what she says in a poetry that reinvents the bodice-ripper genre. The seductress is more than seductive in "Salome" by the poet Ai, who chooses her as the poet's persona and voice. Salome responds to a man's exploitation of both a mother and daughter with a sendup of the delicacy of Japanese women arranging flowers:

> I scissor the stem of the red carnation
> and set it in a bowl of water.

It floats the way your head would,
If I cut it off (6).

The aestheticized violence of the simile of floating carnation and severed head grounds in ordinary life the conjunction of beauty and violence
associated with the Salome whose dance commands the price of the severed head of John the Baptist. The retaliatory context of the beheading
simile in the poem carries the logic of violence by beautiful women home
to the triad of mother, daughter and culprit, all under the aegis of the legendary power of Salome.

What if women simply didn't take the strength of men seriously? Irony,
military metaphor, and a legendary heroine are joined by boredom as techniques for obliterating the force of any male with a will to overpower. The
bodice-ripper romance finds its nemesis in Margaret Atwood's funny story,
"Rape Fantasies," in which even the girls in the office cafeteria are bored
with "rape." One complains: "The way they're going on about it in the
magazines, you'd think it was just invented, and not only that but it's
something terrific, like a vaccine for cancer. They put it in capital letters on
the front cover, and inside they have these questionnaires like the ones they
used to have about whether you were a good-enough wife or an endo-
morph . . . with the scoring upside down on page 73" (2299). The merchandising of violence against women as well as female masochism
undermine male aggression.

"Do you have rape fantasies?" asks the magazine. Instead of playing
cards during lunch as they usually do, the women in the cafeteria answer
the question. No rapist's strength survives fantasies that reverse the power
situations in the attack. Here are some of Atwood's scenarios in paraphrase:
in one, a would be rapist is unable to get his zipper open and begins to cry
because nothing he does goes well and, besides, he has pimples. The
woman who is his intended victim refers him to a dermatologist and reas-
sures him. In another, the man has a "terrible cold" and the woman hands
him a Kleenex, offers him cold medicine, and they watch the Late Show
together. "I mean, they aren't all sex maniacs, the rest of the time they must
lead a normal life," she explains (2304). Another fantasizes that she is a

Kung Fu expert and blinds her assailant, only to feel guilty afterwards. When another woman tells another would-be rapist she has leukemia, he says he does too. They weep, move in together, and spend their last months of life as soulmates. None of these women fears violent assault or sees male power as in any way threatening. Domestication is a female force so powerful in the story it can defeat any antagonist. Their rejection of male power and bored distance from victim status provide the edgy humor of the story, but also raise questions.

Has media exploitation of rape narratives normalized them? Atwood's ironic humor attacks male violence against women but also mocks its trivialization as an issue. The women in the story never confront the extent of male aggression or fully accept their own. Dreaming of the impact of love and devaluing male aggression, the women condense actualities of sexual difference in a vision of female power so great it enables them to imagine transforming their would-be attackers into perfect companions.

Domestication of male sexuality is Atwood's sendup of both the bodice-ripper and the trivialization of violation in women's magazines. Her focus on the audience of women as a source of narrative fantasies provides a measure within the story of what women want in or take from reading them. The audience enables and even dictates those distortions of the victim into a compassionate exemplar of power. Female bonding in the cafeteria ironically underscores the problematic authority of women.

Think men can really be monsters? One of the most popular genres is the tale of occult horror in which men are literally not human. The hero with oversized canines and thirst for blood preys on women and makes the lovebite the prick of death and a cursed afterlife. The vampire novel has always been a sendup of male-female relations and the dark, gothic horror of superhuman power "pure" women respond to by self-sacrifice. But even that home of horror, the vampire novel, once the inviolable seat of Count Dracula, is being transformed by genre-bending modes into a new stranglehold, if not embrace, of the occult.

As popularized by Anne Rice's *Interview with the Vampire* (1976) and more widely applauded in a number of films over the past decade, new vampire narratives acknowledge the dual role of women as eager objects of the vampire's desire and vampires themselves. But they go further. In a new collection of vampire stories by women, *Night Bites: Tales of Blood and Lust,* Victoria Brownworth and Judith Redding interestingly describes a lesbian vampire genre extending back to J. Sheridan LeFanu's *Carmilla* (1872), in which a woman vampire lures other women through offers of friendship. Brownworth and Redding see a continuation of such perspectives in contemporary fiction. They see contemporary versions of the female vampire as inherently political and updated for the era of "AIDS, drug and gang war, and global destruction" (xiv). In the process, old conventions of victimization and self-sacrifice are destroyed and the vampire emerges as a feminist.

The genre-bending in new lesbian vampire stories offers the vampiress as neither villain nor victim but pure celebrity. The vampiress may always be the "other," as Brownworth and Redding insist, but such "otherness" can be presented only as an aspect of her unique celebrity. That the major relationships within the narratives are between women diminishes the influence and power of men and recasts the vampire's violence as evidence of female power.

A woman singer and a vampire bring new meaning to blood relations in "Women's Music" by Ruthann Robson. The story is narrated by a rock singer in love with Sammy, a pale woman with a blood and heroin habit. Sammy's lovemaking is distinguished by bites to the neck and a need for blood that leaves the singer weak with love. Together they form a successful band and supply sex-and-blood-driven allure in their playing that excites the audience. Their bond is performative and public and brings them fame on the club circuit. The singer and her Sammy are celebrity "others" to audiences who are "women with their lovers, women looking for lovers, and women trying to forget lovers" (186). As the rock star recognizes, "all of the women in the audience, in at least a little secret part of themselves, wish they could be me. The women with shy voices and little ambition, the women who watched their brothers play guitar as they took up the clarinet, the women who croon from the depths of their diaphragms and play air guitar as they clean their apartments. The women of my audience" (186). There are no victims in the story but only allies who live out their audience's fantasies of daring and success.

Becoming a vampire is the fulfillment of the singer's love of Sammy, whose groupie she seems to be. When, after trial bites and exploratory nips, Sammy actually bites her singer into vampirehood, their celebrity and happiness seem to be made eternal. The blood drain that in *Nosferatu* means an unholy fate worse than death is represented as the fulfillment of a symbiotic bond between two women who are loyal lovers; being among the undead is a sanctification of love by eternal life. Metaphors of blood loss and gain are associated in the story with the renewals of the menstrual cycle, with the ebb and flow of love and time, or with the rhythms of all three as "female music." That every woman in the audience wants to *be* the singer suggests an idealization of the vampire as celebrity-player of "women's music" and its monthly rhythms through the cycles of nature for eternity. Transgressive blood lust, music, and eternal life presumably take the sting out of a time of AIDS, fear of death by blood transfer, and recognition that fame may be only momentary. By such steps, the occult horror, vampire genre is revised as a female love story stressing eternality.

The *künstlerroman*—the novel of an artist's coming of age—is a highbrow genre not often devoted to the emergence of women artists. Willa Cather's notable exception, *Song of the Lark,* describes the commitment of a woman singer in terms of the experiences she must forgo for a life in opera. Conventions of the woman-as-artist novel often involve the sacrifice of family and love on the altar of craft. Violence lite democratizes the genre and abandons the inherent irreconcilability between the life of experience and the life of art. In recent tales of women writers or aspiring artists, living itself is a form of performance art. In *Slaves of New York* and *A Cannibal in Manhattan,* Tama Janowitz incorporated the aesthetic sensitivity and creative ambitions of women characters into urban lives as prostitutes or on the edge.

Role-playing, identity violence, self-implication, and art blend in fictional portraits of the woman artist as a working girl. This "democratization" process takes the form of breaking the wall between imagination and fact when the writer claims she actually was a sex worker. The fictional and real merge as the writer whose subject is writers who are prostitutes implicates herself in the content of her stories and uses a kind of identity-twisting to sendup conventions of the licit and illicit, the imaginary and real. Her well-crafted fiction of contemporary women stands on its own, but in her interviews Mary Gaitskill has perfected the confession as a form of literary commentary on her work and placed her fiction and her life in direct relation to each other.

Mary Gaitskill has made a point of talking about having been a sex worker. Susan Walsh, in her *Village Voice* interview with Gaitskill called "Notes on Trick," describes her as a stripper and sex worker dedicated to the creation of a "stripper persona" (15). Wanda Urbanska praised Gaitskill in the *Los Angeles Times* as "the rare author who has lived whereof she speaks" (November 28, 1989 E 5,10).

The prostitute-writer in Gaitskill's fiction is working her way toward art by experimenting with self-fabrication and role-playing in the bed and brothel. Prostitution, not writing, emerges as a form of communication twisting that uses imaginative play as a form of fashioning character and building identity. Gaitskill's writer-prostitutes reflect related but compartmentalized possibilities. They are variously daring bohemians with contempt for sexual inhibitions who are acquiring worldly knowledge, or they are failed writers who can't sell their work and sell their bodies instead. These positive or negative identities interact with the scripts each lives by in her encounters with various johns.

In two related stories, Gaitskill offers choices that dictate success or failure for the woman writer whose natural habitat is the brothel. In "Trying to Be," Stephanie is an aspiring writer who "kept her secret forays into prostitution neatly boxed and stored away from her real life" (106). Gaitskill adds: "She had an image of herself, sprawled half on and half off a bed at Christine's, her upside-down head patiently looking back at her from the mirror as some galoot humped her. This vision blended discordantly with the idea of herself at her desk at the magazine and she was unable to separate them" (127). When her regular client, Bernard, idealizes her as a daring sophisticate and accuses her of only "playing prostitute," she replies, "'Actually, I'm not playing. This is for real. I'm not going to give you your money back'" (113).

Stephanie's and Bernard's competing visions of the writer-prostitute highlight the power play between male and female. Bernard needs to see Stephanie as special and asks her out on a date to bolster his self-image as a lover who is more than a john paying for sex. Stephanie initially maintains the upper hand in the situation by insisting she is a whore who must be paid and denying everything else she is. However, Gaitskill complicates the story by opening up the extent to which prostitution reflects Stephanie's effort at self-fashioning. She is turned on by Bernard's idea that "she wasn't a directionless girl adrift in a monstrous city, wandering from one confusing social situation to the next, having stupid affairs. She was a bohemian, experimenting" (114).

In "Something Nice," a related story, a writer-prostitute name Lisette meets Fred in the brothel where she works, and after repeated visits, he asks to see her as a date. Nevertheless, she refuses to see him outside the brothel, and months later, after she has stopped working there, he sees her by chance in a restaurant, overhears her conversation with another woman, and is disconcerted by the aggressive vehemence of her opinion about a lesbian friend. The overheard remarks prove to him that she really is an adventurous bohemian, and they scare him off.

Prostitution is a control mechanism that scripts the woman's power as enforced by extracting money from the man she keeps in the clear position of a john. In "Something Nice," Lisette maintains control by rejecting Fred as anything but a customer. In "Trying to Be," a similar situation turns out differently. Stephanie is so intrigued by her client Bernard's view of her as an exciting and creative bohemian and flattered by his desire to get to know her that she does agree to see him outside the brothel, although he leaves her money each time. But as they continue to trade confidences and get to know each other, his interest in her fades and her guilt and sympathy for his wife increase until their boredom with each other one flat night persuades her the relationship is over. She cries when, after he has left, she realizes he will not return because he has not left her any money. His failure to pay is less important as the mark of his disappearance from her life than as a sign of her failure as a prostitute. Being a prostitute is as much "trying to be" as being a writer.

The reverse resolutions of the two stories illustrate not only the possibilities of the prostitute-john relationship, but also the prescription for control the characters within the stories write for themselves. One is scripted as harsh realism, the other as "romance." In both stories the man asks for more assurance than the brothel relationship allows. In "Trying to Be," Stephanie is needy and unable to accept the compartmentalized sex required by the prostitute role. She agrees to an unstructured affair and loses. In "Something Nice," Lisette maintains control of the situation by replying with a harsh realism that controls her desire to think better of herself, and imposes a rigid structure. In both stories it is the woman who controls the script and can structure it for either success or failure. As architect of the narrative, the prostitute-writer who fails in the prostitute role destroys the story she is making of her life. The identity she is scripting for herself as a success must be one of controlling narratives. Both stories orchestrate personal identity, male-female relationships, and power in terms of the conscious, structural choices artists make.

Role-playing and communication twisting figure large in the conception of the woman artist as driven by the need to see art as dominating the process of identity formation. Maria, a photographer in Paul Auster's novel, *Leviathan,* sees her camera as determining truth, as establishing hierarchies. She photographs a friend who is a prostitute. She then takes her friend's place at work, where she photographs herself. The concealed camera also serves as an instrument of control over the john. The equation between a photo shoot and a gunshot hovers through her belief that the camera brings her a superior power no man can equal and that she controls sexual activity by capturing it on film. In that scenario, filming herself as a prostitute involves capturing her own identity and using the john as a disposable prop. Her camera-gun backfires. She is badly beaten and put out of business by a john who discovers the camera and believes she will use the photographs for blackmail.

The photo-shoot epitomizes the use of art as a complete control mechanism on reality. In *Leviathan,* Maria as the creator and framer of the scene becomes a player and observer of her own act, confusing the relationships between originator, subject, and object of art and ignoring its potential meanings for the john whom she sees as an extra in that process but who mistakes himself for the leading man, the central object of her quest. Her condensation of the roles of player and observer through her self-absorption blurs the relational aspects of identity formation and destroys clear differences between abuser and abused, since it is the john who feels so exploited that he beats her.

Prostitution as fictional device is a tool for reconciling dependent and aggressive impulses in a way that blurs the issue of violent exploitation. Game-playing, role-playing, and black comedy emerge as means of turning violence against itself, reversing the places of exploiter and exploited.

The mystery/thriller action film is a genre that reflects role-and-game playing with manners and mores in a world conceived of as a theater of treachery, cruelty, and planet-threatening danger. Even the James Bond films, which have sustained the same formula over time, reflect changes in male female relationships in the violent lifestyles of the rich, ruthless, gorgeous, and hip. Women as players in the aggression game are the culmination of an emerging series of powerful and attractive film heroines who have, until recently, largely played supporting roles.

Nineteen sixty-two saw the release of *Dr. No,* the first of the James Bond films. Starring Sean Connery and Ursula Andress, the film focused on Bond's attempts to foil Dr. No's elaborate extortion plot, which involved diverting rocket launches from Cape Canaveral. The film introduced Andress as "Honey Rider," the first in the series of wildly named (by the fourth film, Pussy Galore appeared) women who were sexually assertive and even lethal to others but who either fell for Bond, or were outwitted or defeated by him.

Honey Rider established the genealogy of the Bond film women: they have typically been raised in isolation by strong fathers (often scientists) or controlling father-substitutes; they are independent and fearless but are eventually threatened by a villain. The self-confident daughter of a scientist killed by Dr. No, and educated only by her father, Honey Rider was left alone at his death. She was attacked by a man who overpowered her and forced sex on her. She retaliated by placing a black widow spider ("A female. They are the worst!") under his mosquito netting. "He took a week to die," she tells a disconcerted Bond. "Was I wrong to do that?" she asks him innocently. Predictably she becomes meltingly dependent on Bond and adores him.

As the series progressed, Bond and his women were played with a degree of irony that kept pace with the times, but the women—ranging from the Soviet spies to the powerfully athletic Grace Jones—remained in sup-porting roles however adept they were at killing.

Recent representations of killer beauties go further into sexual violence games. Enactments of exploitative sex may involve those once-distinct com-panions, the sadist and the masochist, each of whom no longer seems to re-main in his or her appointed role. Entertainment violence unmasks each as the projection of the other's needs. The sadist and masochist are each en-grossed in a need to dictate the script of the fantasy of identity violence.

Popular films document how male erotic fantasies may focus on beauti-ful women who are probable killers, have a talent for duplicity, and have emerged as "contenders" whose familiarity with violence, coupled with great legs and cleavage, fit them for tougher forms of sexuality and help jus-tify male anger. Desire and hostility provide a mixture that gives the sexu-ality of the films a particularly sharp edge. Ellen Barkin and Al Pacino in *Sea of Love* are a signature couple, presaging the fascination of the cop with a beautiful suspected killer that flowered in *Basic Instinct.* Carrie-Anne Moss in black leather and Keanu Reeves in black raincoat bring sex as fighting for the same cause to the cyberpunk landscape of *Matrix.* Catherine Zeta-Jones in *Entrapment,* Brigitte Nielsen in *Beverly Hills Cop II* and a series of action films, and Grace Jones have become poster girls for the fearless violence of strikingly athletic women that verges on porn. Their familiarity with vio-lence makes them appear the equals of their leading men but also renders them appropriate objects to hunt and kill.

The popular genre of the crime thriller in which the detective eventu-ally gets his man is complicated by violent women who reverse the power relationship between law and outlaw by seeing them as flip sides of the same coin. The man drawn to killer women is no wimp; but nevertheless, he seems masochistic in his need to be near them. Those paired compan-ions, the sadist and the masochist, once male and female stereotypes, find themselves condensed into new power figures who keep changing places. As the balance of power shifts from male to female, their relationship seems an eroticized exchange of intimidation.

Basic Instinct typified for a popular audience love as eroticized power. The relentless detective, once the embodiment of law and order, is reinvented in the film as the edgy Michael Douglas who has himself committed out of control violence in a questionable past shooting. He is drawn to a beautiful, violence-infatuated Sharon Stone as Catherine Tranell, a writer of thrillers whose recent novel describes the murder of a retired rock-and-roll star whose girlfriend ties his hands during sex and stabs him to death with an icepick. Stone's character is a mesmerizing figure who carefully "plots" her life to generate a violent sexuality, enjoying playing both fantasist and suspect.

Stone's Catherine draws Douglas's detective to her by implicating him in the living narrative of murder games and sex play she makes of her life. She sees his recent and accidental killing of two tourists as part of an unacknowledged penchant for serial killing and debauchery. "How much coke did you do the day you shot the tourists?" she asks. She knows everything about him, from the circumstances surrounding his wife's death to his efforts to give up drugs, drinking, and smoking. He cannot distinguish between her imagined murder plots and the facts of the actual murder he is investigating.

The "he says, she says" of the relationship is projected as a seesaw between the facts of her life and the distorting mirror of her fictions: "I'm a writer. I use people for what I write," Catherine comments. She's a suspect in a murder that mirrors the killing in her recent novel. She picked the detective up to research her new book about a detective who falls for the wrong woman and gets killed by her, implicating her real life in another unfinished fiction. Their relationship charts the detective's craving for the rush of violence and disintegration. He begins to drink again, behaves sadistically with a longtime lover, and discovers that the bisexual Catherine has been involved with two women who attempted to kill him. When her new book is finished and the character she based on Douglas is dead, she wants to drop him. He still cannot let go.

Entertainment violence revisits as theatrical farce what was once the stuff of real tragedy. Can a real machine-gun toting, bank robbing terrorist, a victim of kidnapping and traumatic brainwashing, come back years later as a star and promoter of violent kidnapping for fun? Patricia Hearst and John Waters are co-conspirators in *Cecil B. Demented,* a film described as a kidnapping caper that revisits Hearst's abduction by the Symbionese Liberation

Army and features Hearst in a supporting role. Melanie Griffith stars as a kidnapped movie goddess turned terrorist in a farce in which violence is all about entertainment. What is under attack is the film industry.

Promoting the film together, Waters and Hearst are described in the interview as "two birds of a feather" plotting the script. Waters collects memorabilia of criminals now available to all on internet auctions. He was questioned on the Bill Maher show, *Politically Incorrect,* on August 7, 2000, about his predilection. He remarked that people somehow just sent him things owned by the likes of serial killer John Wayne Gacey. He shrugged it off, saying that it was OK to display them because he put murder memorabilia mostly in the guest room. Patty Hearst, who has appeared as an actress in earlier films directed by Waters, is a key exhibit in his collection; *Cecil B. Demented* is built around her.

The film is a sendup of her kidnapping and life as a revolutionary and bank robber. In the *Newsweek* interview, Hearst jokes, "'I should sue for copyright infringement'" (Miller 62). Breaking the wall between reality and entertainment, the two collaborate on fusing real and entertainment violence. Waters explains: "'I wanted to do a movie [in which] people were as radical as they were in the 60's about politics but about movies.'" A Hollywood star, played by Melanie Griffith, is kidnapped by terrorists who want to destroy "Multiplex America" (Miller 62). The imagination of the nation as a movie theater projects Patty Hearst's transformation from wrapped-in-velvet heiress into Tanya the Terrorist, a gun-toting bank robber. In Waters's chatter that seems only a form of performance art that included her prior abduction, severe mistreatment, and brainwashing—all of which led to her becoming a revolutionary sentenced to two years in jail for her role in the robbery. Mark Miller describes Hearst calling *Cecil B. Demented* a "homage to her famous experience with the Symbionese Liberation Army which kidnapped her in 1974" (62).

How can Hearst see as a "homage" to a "famous" experience a comedy based on an abduction she herself had described in her book *Every Secret Thing* in harrowing terms and that actually netted her jail time. The pursuit of the SLA led to the death of many of its leaders in a shootout and ended in a retaliatory attempt to blow up a police car. Sara Jane Moore, an

SLA hanger-on described in chapter 4, even made an assassination attempt on President Ford to impress the SLA. The turmoil produced by the SLA was felt through the early months of 2003 when it was ended by the conviction of Sara Jane Olson for setting a bomb under a police car and participating in a bank robbery in which someone was killed; and by the surrender of James Kilgore, the last remaining SLA member at large, who had been living in South Africa for more than twenty years. The trivialization of the deaths, violence, and havoc wreaked by the SLA is essential to the plan of *Cecil B. Demented* as a parody. Nevertheless, Waters believes: "There's good bad taste and bad bad taste. She [Patty Hearst] doesn't do anything that happened to her. She's not playing a kidnap victim. It would have been bad bad taste to have her play Melanie's part—and she wouldn't have" (Miller 62). Hearst knows better and lays claim to the starring role, saying: "I don't know that I wouldn't have done it" (Miller 62).

An edgy contemporary fiction of manners reveals changes in social attitudes that trivialize all forms of violence and inhibition. In tales of contemporary mores, identity violence is effected precisely through role-playing that breaks taboos and makes entertainment out of appalling behavior. The conventions of the novel of manners are turned upside down by the transfer of the action from the drawing room or suburban living room to the beds, back rooms, and lofts of hip urban spaces where violation is an unfolding show.

Role-playing in a grungy theater of cruelty raises the question of who gets to star. Role-playing consumes even sadomasochism as a style of interaction. As women characters resist compartmentalization, playing both victim and perpetrator, the clear distinctions between one and the other break down. In an ironic sendup of current mores, Mary Gaitskill's impressive collection, *Bad Behavior,* uses black humor to look at the rapidity with which sadist and masochist can change places. The most interesting accounts reveal not only the interactions between "lovers" but also the intrapsychic baggage each brings to the encounter.

Gaitskill provides brilliantly detailed portraits for a gallery of modern dysfunction. In skirmishes between the sexes, each of the "lovers" in a pair may project desire, disappointment, and aggression on the other. The mixture drives their relationships from one pole to the other, with the "masochist" and "sadist" oscillating between roles and busily changing place in a struggle for control. Communication twisting, role-playing, and rage sustain a narrative dance in which quickly changing positions provide an angry energy that passes for passion.

A woman who claims to be a masochist, and a man who sees himself the sadist whose hope is to beat, bite, and bruise her are paired in Mary Gaitskill's story, "A Romantic Weekend." The woman is thrilled that "a psychic had told her that a relationship with him could cripple her emotionally for the rest of her life. . . . she felt like an object unraveling in every direction" (32). Her lover has fantasies of drawing blood and using her as his slave. She buys him flowers. Are they made for each other?

This parodic sendup of romance takes a detour to the question: who is the sadist and who is the masochist? Each has projected needs upon the other and each will be outraged. He complains: "with other women . . . he had experienced a relaxing sense of emptiness within them that had made it easy for him to get inside them and, once there, smear himself all over their innermost territory until it was no longer theirs but his. . . . This exasperating girl, on the other hand, contained a tangible somethingness that she not only refused to expunge, but that seemed to willfully expand itself so that he banged into it with every attempt to invade. . . . Why had she told him she was a masochist?" (41–42). For her part: "Her desire to abase herself had been completely frustrated. She had pulled him to the rug certain that if only they could fuck, he would enter her with overwhelming force and take complete control of her. Instead she had barely felt him. . . . How, she thought miserably, could she have mistaken this hostile moron for the dark, brooding hero who would crush her like an insect and then talk about life and art?" (47). The twisty bond of mutual frustration begins a whirlwind anti-romance.

Identity violence fueled by contempt and anger enables conventional male and female positions to be reversed. Identity violence is a function of who controls the role assignments, who scripts the overall drama of the relationship. In the story, the woman's aggression is inflamed by sexual contempt for the man's failure to live up to her script. His frustration with her resistance to his domination sparks an interest in her that signals *his* masochism. Her verbal cleverness weaves a sadistic net that pulls him into entering her fantasies. When he says he wants to piss on her and have her drink his urine, she quickly replies, "Do you like people to piss on you?" (47). Her aggression is coercive and shrewd, permitting him to delude himself that she is a failure as a masochist, even as he submits any claim to sadism by yielding to her control. "You're really not a masochist, you know," he says: "You might have fantasies, but I don't think you have any concept of a real slave mentality. You have too much ego to be part of another person" (51). Cleverly, she replies: "With me it's more a matter of love. It's like the highest form of love" (52).

The highest form of sadism is writing the script that controls someone else and uses the promise of submission and masochism as a form of coercion. When she equates masochism with love, "he thought this was really cute . . . it was feminine in a radio-song kind of way. . . . He was beginning to see her as a locked garden that he could sneak into and sit in for days, tearing the heads off the flowers" (52). She, on the other hand, "was scrutinizing him carefully from behind an opaque façade as he entered her pasteboard scene of flora and fauna. Could he function as a character in this landscape?" (52). Whoever scripts the role-playing games controls the other's identity.

Identity violence stages a theater of cruelty driven by the need to multiply the positions and tonal colorations one can adopt along a spectrum of sadomasochistic violence. What maintains the dark comedy of manners in this contemporary anti-romance is the author's skill at splitting and condensing emotion so that violence is always seen and defined from the perspective of the person who designs and shapes it.

In the comedy of bad manners, narrative perspective rules and permits the person in charge to craft identity violence with the distance of a voyeur and the self-implication of a player. A sexually hip urban singles scene establishes the social climate in which nothing is taboo for stand-up comedy or dinner conversation. In Gaitskill's "The Dentist," a magazine writer covers "a performance piece by a masochist who tortured himself onstage in various complex and aesthetically pleasing devices of his own making, while he made jokes and talked about his childhood. . . . When he drove a nail through his penis, one man passed out" (153–54). The writer is inspired. Theatricality governs her fantasies of sadomasochistic role playing as performance art. When she visits a dentist to have her painful wisdom tooth removed, she is smitten and tells her friends she wants him, "to pierce my genitals with needles" (168).

Her friends are part of the theater of identity violence and role playing and are interested in the costuming and staging of her fantasies:

> "Was he wearing his white coat while he pierced you?"
> "No . . ."
> "That's the trouble with your fantasies," said Alex.
> "You haven't got the right clothes." (168)

The details and props that secure role-playing shape narratives of identity violence. In a variation on the theme of control, games of role-playing weave narratives that counterpoint expected behavior and identity formation. For example, Gaitskill's stories often reverse the position of the stereotypical female masochist into a super-sadist whose coercive disdain and covert aggression humiliate the man who aims to achieve power over her. Communication twisting and intrapsychic processes combine to affect the man's behavior and the woman's own self-image by imposing roles, behaviors, and scripts to gratify her own need for control. The separation of roles and the mechanism of splitting into all good or all bad are used to protect the heroine's ego by actively keeping apart contradictory experiences. Contradictory emotions may be activated but they always alternate and do not blend. In current fiction, this absolute dictation of roles centering on conflict serves to control the conflict by treating the other person as only an extension of one's own needs. The person is not the "other" but as controllable as one's own limb.

Omnipotence and devaluation of the separateness and autonomy of the other make it possible to perceive the sudden reversal of the disappointing sadist, the "hostile moron" of "A Romantic Weekend," or the dentist who won't cooperate into someone who can play the assigned role. The man's behavior is scripted by the woman and is as much under her control or coercion as if he were part of her own body. Role-playing enables women characters to enjoy oscillations of power, to make a game of passing from masochist to sadist and surpassing entrapment in either position.

In the theater of destructive egotism, competitive and mutually exclusive concepts of oneself as both all-powerful and subservient are another manifestation of the mechanism of splitting or compartmentalization as a narrative device. When the self-contradictory roles played by the violent heroine become untenable, the delicate exchange of power cannot be maintained. The man must be dependent on her authorization of his role for identity violence to be sustained. For example, in Gaitskill's "The Blanket," Valerie completely dominates a much younger man who is her lover by suggesting to him that they role play and "act out fantasies." He is happy to do what she wants because the fantasies are fun: "She would be a slutty teenager who's secretly hoping for love, and he would be the smug prick who exploits her. . . . Feverishly, they'd nose around in each situational nuance before giving in to dumb physicality" (90). The affair works beautifully under Valerie's control until reality invades it when she realizes she has unleashed more than she wants: "Michael pretended to be a sleazy boss dropping in on an unsuspecting housewife just after her naïve husband has left for work. The boss was a terrible malefactor, but in the haven of fantasy, he was safely confined to her script. There was great drama as the poor housewife struggled to resist him, but to no avail: Valerie opened her eyes just in time to be a little startled by the look of almost demented malice on Michael's young face as he ejaculated across her mouth and nose" (93). On a mellow drive in the country, she tells him she was once actually raped. She is surprised that, although she has stressed that it was a real and devastating rape, her announcement turns him on. She realizes he cannot distinguish her anguish from her role-playing and that, as he turns off the highway into a dark, wooded area, he is preparing to rape her. How can she force him back in line?

Identity violence involves self-definition through omnipotence, through being able to write the script for a man's fantasies as well as one's own. How much aggression a man can express is controlled by the man's fear of rejection if he should step out of the emotions and behavior the woman has prescribed. For example, Valerie's casting Michael in the role of sadist has masked her own sadistic urges. She regains control of him by coercing his overt and open subjection to her "rules." If he breaks them, the game is over.

The Oedipal drama is inverted in more extreme portraits of female power in terms of the ability of a seemingly omnipotent older woman to control younger men and boys. A darker fiction projects the power of women through sexual dominance. The omnipotence of mother to young child is taken to the edge in transgressive, criminal seduction by older women of boys. Such fiction reveals darker ways of maintaining control by pursuing ever younger objects of desire. For example, In "The Kid," by Daytona Beach, a thirty-five-year old woman who has no sexual feelings for the assortment of men she meets, develops an obsessive passion for the sixteen-year-old son of her friend and rediscovers she can feel lust only as a sexual predator of boys.

The arousal of self-hatred for her own sick exploitation of the dismayed, obedient boy and the twisting of her self-image from being a seducer to a rapist only intensify her feeling and determination to continue. After the *frisson* of violating taboos of friendship and decency diminishes, the heroine quietly accepts her impulses. When the sixteen-year-old's family moves away, the appeal of his youth and vulnerability lead her to pursue other boys and to equate freedom and self-fulfillment with life as a happy sexual predator. The story is designed to shock by placing an older woman in the familiar position of the male child molester and by representing molestation as a female sexual style. Ebullient in describing the most disturbing of predatory obsessions, the story opens up the deeper forces at work in pop forms—the trash talk show, the Court TV coverage of women in their thirties pregnant from teenage boys, the perverse world of the Jerry Springer show.

Even as a media culture of aberration thrives, violence lite provides a complex theatricality that enacts what is at stake in violations of hope and trust. The condensation of sexual, aggressive, and dependent drives is sometimes expressed in accounts of relationships between women. Love between women seems to offer the prospect of getting out of stereotypical male-female roles and off the sadomasochistic seesaw. In Mary Gaitskill's "Processing," two bisexual women begin an affair with each promising not to role-play but to be herself. Neither of them can do that and hope for authenticity soon crashes: "I felt an impersonal half cruelty that was more titillating than real cruelty. But she wanted to be cruel too, or rather to pretend that she was. . . . She was a nasty teenaged boy, she was a silly kid, she was . . . a deep woman all the way down to her private organs. She slapped me and she pulled my hair—but she demanded that I beat her . . . And when I did she whispered 'thank you,' her face transfigured with sorrow . . ." (216–17). Self-conscious and sophisticated, the women project violent role-playing as a hip "game about aggression that made aggression harmless" (221).

Sexual violence games are not exactly harmless but they may express a less self-aware form of primal drives, a working out of primal fantasy. If love of a woman doesn't provide a female role model out of the morass of violence play, attraction to a father figure can be enacted as a kind of masochistic involvement that mingles sexual, dependent, and aggressive impulses in a comedy based on the exchange of power.

Electra fantasies are writ large in games of sexual violation in which sexual interest coexists with a taboo against engaging in actual genital contact, much less intercourse, with a father substitute. In Gaitskill's "Secretary," a plain girl who graduates from a typing school gets her first job from a lawyer who has her bend over her desk and spanks her when she makes mistakes. Excited, she masturbates afterwards. One day, after spanking her, he goes further, telling her to pull down her stockings and ejaculating on her body. She leaves, refuses to return to work, and seems abjectly humiliated. The lawyer pays her a generous severance award and asks that she remain silent about what happened.

The lawyer's distant, correct, and polite demeanor except when he is spanking her arouses the secretary's masochistic interest; his ejaculation provokes her fear and flight but also turns the story into a joke on penis envy. His use of his penis ultimately undercuts his own power; it gives *her* the power to destroy him by telling the tale. Her power increases when she learns he is running for mayor and reporters want to question her. She knows the joy of the predator when she receives the reporter's call, learns her former boss is running for mayor, and realizes she can destroy him by selling her story to a tabloid or draining him dry through extortion.

In the theater of identity violence, black comedies are about inversions of power. Role-playing and table-turning are all designed to project the violence of women as unexpected and ultimately triumphant. Characters are self-conscious in stylizing roles that both express and keep under control their aggressive and self-destructive impulses, refusing to accord them any emotional significance. Entertainment violence takes masochism and payback lightly.

How violence games by women appeal is underscored by a new film with a script by Erin Cressida Wilson based on Gaitskill's story. The film is called *Secretary* and advertised as "the story of a demanding boss and the woman who loves his demands" starring James Spader and Maggie Gyllenhaal.

Under the tag "SPANKORAMA" in the *New York Observer,* Andrew Sarris applauded the heroine, played by the "marvelously gifted and scrumptious Maggie Gyllenhaal" as "a sad sack ex-mental patient with a history of cutting and then patching up various sectors of her flesh whenever she feels the onset of self-hatred—and judging from the scars on her body, this is a frequent occurrence" (23). She finds a boss who spanks her and then withholds spankings when she seems to like them too much. "I find these outrageously romantic maneuvers funny and endearing," enthused Sarris. "Ms. Gyllenhaal will never get an Oscar from the Academy's still prudish voters for this trail-blazing and courageous performance, but she could be well on her way to a much-deserved stardom" (23). He is apparently not the only man who adores the deceptively supine heroine. The ads carry blurbs like "A Feel-Good Romantic Comedy"—David Ansen, *Newsweek,* and "Sly and sexy"—Owen Gleiberman, *Entertainment Weekly.*

The contrasts between the film, crafted to titillate a mass audience open to the perverse, and the edgy, black comedy of Gaitskill's story are important. The film takes care to strip the heroine of outward aggression and positions her in the apparent masochism of enjoying the spanking. Moreover, she is driven to cut herself. The film shows her as a self-harming, otherwise passive plaything and damsel-in-distress in need of rescue from her own impulses. The condensation of sexual and aggressive drives Gaitskill's story encodes in the ironical turnabout in which the "victim" secretary enjoys knowing she can ruin her former boss is omitted, so as to turn the story into a lighthearted romance. In the film, the lawyer and his secretary happily unite. The change underscores a flirtation with female violence but a need to project it purely in terms of self-harm.

The psychology of cutting, however, complicates a flat explanation that it is only about self-harm. It expresses an effort to seize control of the troubles life supplies, to allay destruction from outside by inflicting pain on oneself in controlled portions. The impulses to control by dealing with what happens by seizing control of surrounding rage and directing it against oneself becomes an explicit subject in Gaitskill's "Because They Wanted To," in which self-mutilation is seen as a female tool. A customer in a tattoo salon who is having cosmetic tattooing of her lips for a permanent lipliner begins to describe a girl who cut herself even as her own "lips were swollen and bleeding from the needle" while she explains that "they do it to distract themselves from the terrible pain they feel inside" (54). Gaitskill plays on the customer's ironic use of "cutting" for a purely cosmetic effect, a controlled construction of how she wants to look, and her attribution of inner pain to others. Through the metaphor of choosing cosmetic cutting, Gaitskill conveys how self-inflicted pain can serve as an instrument of control in a world of hurt.

At the end of the story "Secretary," Gaitskill's heroine discloses the aggression and urge to dominate concealed in her willingness to be spanked. She relishes the prospect of either extorting money from the lawyer or ruining him. Gaitskill's sophisticated entertainments uncover that impulse to dominance concealed in the apparently supine female masochist. The film based on "Secretary" is simplistic in its use of both cutting and spanking in ways that underscore the disparities between what a pop audience wants in a film and what fiction can achieve. The film based on the story reverses Gaitskill's meaning by divorcing the attraction to cutting from the desire for control. Gaitskill's fictional heroines use cutting or masochism as seductive ploys or instruments for controlling their situation.

By treating the secretary's masochism as unalloyed, the film preserves her appeal for her sadistic boss who marries her and perhaps for a male audience for the "spankorama." Gaitskill's darkly ironic tale turns into a Lubitsch-style comedy filmed for a kinkier time in which the heroine seduces with self-harm and masochism rather than frothy charm or high-jinks. Drawn to the "spankorama" along with the secretary's boss is a male audience that may include film reviewers who, not unlike the men in Gaitskill's fables, enjoy illusions of male control. The secretary in the film serves as a visual cliché comparable to the French maid in a sex farce. Literature does more. Skillful, ironic sendups of the romance genre may exploit clichéd female roles in which women seem only objects of male desire, lust, and aggression for new purposes.

Women in literary forms of entertainment violence often use expectations of their passivity to take charge of the narrative of identity formation within the driving action of narrative and plot. In doing so, they break out of that passive position as objects defined by men to which they are consigned by French representation theory. Their narrative violence constitutes an assault on the theoretical abstraction of the Lacanian model that associates the "presence" of women only with Lacan's presymbolic "Real." By definition, that relegates them to the feminine position, denying them agency, linguistic artfulness, and active self-invention through the structures of the symbolic code. The failure of representation theory to reconcile agency with the narratives of women is reflected in the tortured assertions that the speaking subject, by definition, emerges when "the Real of dynamic living process is replaced by a 'dead,' immobilized image" [in the Lacanian mirror phase] (Žižek, *Plague of Fantasies* 94). In that moment of identity formation, entry into the symbolic code as women who are active agents appears ruled out.

Art historian Hal Foster illustrates a larger exhaustion of postmodern representation theory in his comments on Andy Warhol's fascination with the literal "dead immobilized image" of mutilated corpses in his series of car crash paintings. Foster comments: "This shift in conception—from reality as an effect of representation to the real as thing of trauma—may be definitive in contemporary art" (*Return of the Real* 146). Reality here is presented in terms of the bloody corpse; the "real" or "presence" is equated with the traumatized dead body. It is neither a "dynamic process" nor a symbolic "effect of representation" but a reminder of death's silent finality. Is the corpse what remains after the symbolic code?

Violence lite is an art form by women rich in the energies of experience and the dynamism of life in its endless reassertions. It exploits traditional expectations of and comfort with visions of woman as passive object—even, for example, a spanked sex object—to reverse the ground of agency and set in motion all that seems immobilized. The drama is shifted from women as the passive objects of aggression to women as inventive users of coercive, verbal power. Women are not created by the "male gaze" so much as masters of an abundance of visual and verbal roles that can be creatively combined in new narratives of self-invention and self-interest. The narrative violence of women in fiction is richly articulate and active in self-invention. It is the revenge of agency on all that pins it into stasis and abstraction. It embraces physical reality as active experience. It constitutes the real as an overt transgression of the unreality of the symbolic code, a way of practicing agency in turnabouts, revelations, and as an inventive force for change.

Experience returns as the creative agency of women representation theory has denied. Yet the prospect of the return of reality or "presence" as inventive, self-inventive, and verbally fertile speech inspires opposition explicitly directed against women. How Žižek engages issues of gender, creativity, and representation by women writers can be illustrated by his comments in "There is No Sexual Relationship." Žižek attempts to show that only male artists can achieve representations of the "Real" and only by forgoing their proximity to the symbolic code that guides representation. To do so, they must appropriate the "feminine" and the "Real" by choosing to undergo the "trauma" of the "Real." Žižek's discussion of the male artist's dissolution of self in "the Real" suggests the male artist can achieve absolute presence through undergoing the "trauma" of submission and loss of identity he equates with the "feminine." In doing so, the artist loses the ability to construct any narrative but gains a mystical role as a conduit of some abstract force of the "sublime," the "spirit," or the like.

Žižek equates the creative "frenzy" of the "[Wagnerian] artist who sees himself as a medium through which impersonal spirit expresses itself" with the feminine Real: "What is crucial is the explicit sexual connotation of this highest form of freedom: feminization (adoption of a passive attitude toward the transcendent absolute) serves as the inherent support of masculine assertion. . . . [and] the eternal feminine . . . is the ultimate meta-physical support of the worldly aggressive attitude" ("There is No Sexual Relationship" 184). In effect, the Lacanian "Phallus," principle of "joy" and the symbolic code, emerges as the conduit of a sublime creativity for the male artist who yields his own identity to appropriate the "transcendent spirit [absolute]" (184–85).

The achievement of artistic representations, exemplified for Žižek by Wagnerian opera, depends on the male artist conceiving of himself as the best conduit for the eternal feminine. Like Baudrillard who conceives of men as the "best" women (see chapter 1), women themselves remain only a nothingness, a "black hole," and apparently not conduits for anything but the fantasies of men. As Žižek notes in "Otto Weininger, or 'Woman Doesn't Exist,'" it is out of the "constitutive negativity of woman" that men create the fantasy of the "eternal feminine" (140). Women might fulfill male fantasies through masquerade, but beneath that masquerade there is no authentic or inner self, but only the "unsignifiable void" (128).

For Žižek the paradigms of romance or any art based on relationships between the sexes, which he describes in "Courtly Love, or Woman as Thing" and "There is No Sexual Relationship" all involve a primarily male performance. All, he claims in "Otto Weininger, or 'Woman doesn't Exist,'" involve a search for ways a man can "empty out himself," can experience the Phallus as a principle of inventive pleasure so that "man's love for a woman . . . . is a thoroughly *narcissistic* phenomenon: in his love of a woman, man loves only himself, his own ideal image" (131). In the process, he adds, women are always victims because male love involves a "necessary . . . empirical destruction of the woman" (132). Conveniently, Žižek also believes: "Woman is not free: ultimately, the urge to be raped by man in one or another way always prevails in her . . ." (133). Woman remains Lacan's "universal ideal emptied of all substance." Adding to Lacan's famous provocation, "Woman does not exist!" Žižek adds Weininger's "woman is nothing but man's expression and projection of his own sexuality," able to achieve at best "a premonition of her constitutive enslavement, which leads her to strive for salvation through self-annihilation" (133). She is helped along by men whose love, Žižek suggests, is by definition, "murder" (132).

Seizure by women writers of narratives of misogyny or masochism for purposes of their own aggression can be seen as an attack on the violence done to women by such representation theory as well as a blow to its logical absurdities. Such seizures are raw engagements with sexual anger, narrative attacks using the twists and turns of relations between men and women to forge new narratives of self-invention and identity. Experience returns through violence and lodges a physical assault on the reified category of the "feminine," rebuking those like Žižek and Baudrillard who remain committed to seeing representation as an alternative to "presence" rather than its complement and defining creative force as only a phallic pipeline to the sublime.

Žižek's vision of the male artist is rendered irrelevant by the emphasis on patterns of interaction between men and women, on women and their own self-concepts, and on women and social order found in the violent entertainments of women. The patterns of violence that emerge reflect a persistence of core issues but a great fluidity in the narratives used to describe them. All of them employ sophisticated narratives and self-representations to manipulate not only the scenario of violence but also its meanings and reception by the surrounding society. Doing so enables a vision of narrative violence as relational. It is not a masquerade of surfaces with no inner content, but instead an active expression of the will of women characters.

What distinguishes entertainment violence is precisely that insistence on the primacy of will in controlling all. In narrative violence, the heroine's choice and viewpoint dominate the script. Whether in sendups of the bodice-ripper romance, the occult horror tale, or the fiction of manners, women characters feel fully in charge. Volition, choice, and omnipotence shape stories in which even S/M scenarios seduce the male "sadist" into a drama not of his own making but scripted by the woman, most often as a joke on him.

Women are in the avant garde of reversals that are reshaping traditional entertainment genres into violence lite. The rock-wrestling spectacle, the romance, the horror-vampire story, and the tale of manners are all reshaped by changes in self-conception and attitudes about love, family, friendship, and culture. Fear of a loss of familiar stabilities of place and practice surrounded the fascination in the pre-Hellenic world with the legend of Medea. That articulation of a craving for the strange and new, colored by fear of the breakdown of state, family, and sexual roles, played out on the scale of cosmic magic. Now the encounter with a world that appears dangerous, hostile, and unfamiliar is played out on urban streets or in bedrooms where women weave narratives of competitive aggression that speak to our own sense of the new and dangerous. But in pop culture it can also achieve a cosmic scale.

The advent of women in heroic roles in action movies brings the self-mastery, militarism, and courage of women to a genre in which they once served primarily as eye candy. The *Alien* series starring Sigourney Weaver as Lt. Ellen Ripley, which began in 1979 with the release of *Alien* and culminated in 1997 with *Alien Resurrection,* eerily tracked the currents of the decades: the rise and evolution of feminism, and current anxieties over a spectrum of gender issues ranging from the repudiation of domesticity to the backlash evident in the growing attack on abortion rights.

Transformations in values and attitudes toward feminism are clear in the changing focus of the films over the eighteen years they span. The four *Alien* films heralded the first movie triumph of a woman as action hero. In *Alien* (1979), Lt. Ellen Ripley was one of only two women on the commercial spaceship, Nostromo, and the only survivor of its encounter with a hideous alien species of monstrous predators. Initial versions of the script followed the norm for action movies and made the sole survivor a man. The role was rewritten as a starring role for a woman to increase the commercial potential of the film during the heyday of the feminist movement. Although *Alien* was commercially successful, Sigourney Weaver's performances over time gave the role a complex dimension that opened up both the promise and fear of being both a woman and universal soldier.

Committed to the exercise of power and military virtues, Ripley was nevertheless linked with children, childbearing, and maternal protectiveness in remarkable and interesting ways. In the second *Aliens,* released in 1986, a fascinating suggestion of the complexity of female issues began. Warring against the hideous aliens, Ripley balanced a little girl in one hand and an automatic weapon in the other. Saving the former meant using the latter.

Woman as mother held the automatic rifle as essential to care; woman as warrior did battle with the hideous, female alien she could refer to as "bitch." The futuristic weapon balanced by the child provided the moral equilibrium for the woman warrior, the "mother" who tries to save the world from her evil "alien" counterpart—the monster whose twin thirsts are for killing and implanting her "eggs" in human bodies of either sex.

Femaleness, pregnancy, and violence keep interacting in the relationship between Ripley and the aliens she fights. Action heroes find their victories bring pleasure and celebrity, but Ellen Ripley's success brings haunting dilemmas associated with birth, violence, and rape. Gender issues dominate and darken *Alien 3*. Ripley has crash-landed on a prison planet with a group of former murderers, rapists, and violent thieves who have "found God." She sits next to a man who tells her, "You don't want to know me. I am a rapist and murderer of women." Her cool reply: "I must make you nervous." Irony is not enough. The total maleness of the prison-planet represents the universality of patriarchal control. An alien monster has stowed away on Ripley's vessel, survived the crash, and begun to kill on the prison planet. Without weapons, Ripley plots a way to kill it with the help of the prisoners until she realizes she is a kind of rape victim, impregnated by an alien during her long, drugged sleep in space.

The patriarchy designed the phallocentric prison-world in its own image and wants to use female reproduction in its service. It demands Ripley give birth to the monster. The men who run things want to sell the alien as a weapon of mass destruction. To defeat them and to avoid giving birth she backdives into a hellish cauldron of molten lead and flames, her arms stretched out to form a cross, just as the monster breaks through her body, only to fall into the flames. She "crucifies" herself along with her alien "infant." The film's resolution presents her heroism as female self-sacrifice, unites her "motherhood" with futuristic visions of child murder, and enacts the killing of the violent and rapacious monster within as both a sacrificial act and murderous "abortion."

The commitment of a ruthless patriarchy to forcible birth looms over the final film, *Alien Resurrection* (1997). It eerily recapitulates the abortion controversy by dramatizing the threat posed by men who force women to bear children against their will. Ripley is sought by the patriarchy, now named "the company," a powerful male oligarchy determined to sell the alien queen she once carried to the highest bidders. Such men now control life itself through their mastery of cloning, and their power now renders even her death and murder of her alien infant meaningless. Ripley is resurrected two hundred years after the time of *Alien 3* by their cloning techniques, using genetic material obtained from her sleep module during her "pregnancy." They bring her back to life as she was when pregnant with the alien. Their determination to enforce the birth of a live alien queen who can endlessly lay more eggs has outlived Ripley's suicide to prevent it. The men in charge subject her cloned, drugged, pregnant body to a caesarian delivery of the alien predator she murdered.

Heroic and noble in her sacrifice in *Alien 3,* Ripley is a female mutant in *Alien Resurrection.* Metaphors of birth and rebirth, human and mutant, call into question what is human and female. Ripley is not, in the science fiction of the film, resurrected as only the woman warrior she was; she is a mutant whose DNA was modified by pregnancy with the alien queen and who merely looks exactly like Sigourney Weaver. She has blood that is acid, like the alien's, has superhuman strength, is more predatory than before, and is beyond sentiment. Her sexual identity, evident even in *Alien 3* in a quick, cool affair, is virtually restricted to her acting as mother to an alien queen. She is shown nonsexually caressing or being held by female "robots" or by the female alien queen, her daughter, and a mutated alien, presumably her "granddaughter."

Emerson celebrated power as occurring in the "moment of transition" from savage to civilized. Metaphors of a reverse transition abound in *Alien Resurrection* in visions of the transition from human to alien, civilized to savage. Ripley finds monstrosities from the cloning experiments that visibly display the intermingling of human with alien: there are Ripleys with the head of the double-mouthed lizard, hideous mixtures of human and alien limbs, skin, and scales. One "clone" is visibly half Ripley with a mixture of alien and human arms and legs who begs to be killed. Ripley kills all her sister clones in an eerie reenactment of her suicide to kill the monster in herself. As she kills all the monstrous embryos that are suspended in liquid, one of the men shouts, "What's the big deal? A fucking waste of ammo! Must be a chick thing!"

But there is no longer any "chick" thing around since "human" nature as far as women are concerned no longer exists. Only a robot, played by Wynona Ryder, behaves like an old-time sentimental woman because she was programmed to care. Ripley demands, "You're programmed to be an asshole? You're the asshole model they're putting out?" Ripley is cradled by her daughter, the alien queen, and she cradles *her* alien offspring but unhesitatingly causes its death.

A mutant created by cloning Ripley is a new hybrid with a womanlike appearance and alien viciousness. She is part of a new female line free of conditioning for sentiment and fit for "child" murder. As a "woman," Ripley believed in self-sacrifice dying to save humanity. That vulnerability is passé. The discontinued model of robot-woman built "to care," represents the detritus of a past idealization of womankind while Ripley represents the disturbances of the present and future, the woman-mutant who is sufficiently predatory to survive in a world run by ruthless men. In the fantastic birth, cloning, murder, and mutation images of *Alien Resurrection,* Ripley emerges as something new and different—a figure for *fin de siècle* America who conquered her vulnerability by being reborn as a shrewd, unsentimental, survivor.

The new use of entertainment violence is structured for changing how we think about the injuries of change. It is double-edged. From the perspective of women, it documents efforts to overcome victimization. Through scripting, communication twisting, delicacies of ironic form or genre twisting, control of the narrative of power is wrested from men. At the same time, the vision of relationships rooted in competitive aggression arouses nightmarish fears that without protective, maternal love and compassion, the mold of human nature breaks.

Stabilities of home and hearth crack under the weight of aggression, turning the family into a casualty of war. The Mafia was once the most interesting intact family in American film in which women played traditional roles. David Chase produced the most celebrated show in *fin de siècle* America in HBO's *The Sopranos,* which dispensed with the loyal old Italian mother of Mafia myth. Tony Soprano, a New Jersey *capo,* suffers from panic attacks and is driven to see a woman psychiatrist to recover from the effects of his chronically rejecting and dissatisfied mother, Livia. Wily and manipulative, Livia is genius at derogation, undermining her men and manipulating their fears and their actions. The mob matriarch as Medea, she orders a hit on her own son.

A dutiful son who, bearing cookies, visits his mother regularly, Tony is shocked to discover that his psychiatrist was right to name his mother as the person who had ordered him killed. Livia is a woman so practiced in concealment and brutality that only another woman, an expert in the dark side of "family" feelings, can spot her evil. When Tony is confronted by the FBI with a tape of his mother ordering the hit, he resolves in fury to kill her. But, feigning illness and surrounded by hospital orderlies, Livia escapes the pillow Tony has brought to smother her. Wheeled past him on a swiftly rolling gurney, she evades him with the smoothness of Medea fleeing Jason's wrath in her flying chariot.

Chase's portrait is partly an exercise in hostility. He did away with the loyal old Italian mother of Mafia legend. That is Mama as she was "meant" to be: a woman who adored the grandkids, cooked, and supplied an endless feast of food and unconditional love, never taking notice of the family business. Chase's anti-Madonna is a wily old woman who is the real power in the mob, manipulating the Godfather and amassing a bodycount of her own. Not since writer-director Lina Wertmuller cast an obese woman who delights in depriving, exploiting, and humiliating men as the *kommandant* of a Nazi concentration camp in *Seven Beauties* has there been such a large projection of ruthless female power and the mixture of male fear and impotent rage it can arouse.

Although they are most frequently the objects of hostility, women in entertainment violence have attempted to appropriate and control violence in part by denying the power of men to inflict harm. Can women beat misogyny by joining it? Rape, once considered the pure product of male rage and contempt, has been literally reversed into a spectacle of a woman's complete control. From *Sex: The Annabel Chong Story* (see chapter 2), which documents Grace Quek's effort to establish and hold a world's record for the "biggest gang bang," by staging and filming her "gang rape" by 251 men, to Margaret Atwood's light story "Rape Fantasies," women have represented male violence as under their control. In tales of sado-masochistic role-playing, in the example of the law student at Kiehl Center who rose from the crowd with a sign saying "HO" in glitter, they use sexual violence and insult as forms of their own bravado.

Is the way to control the grossout of hostile sexuality or sexploitation to appropriate it? In fiction the communications generated by eroticized violence have greater subtlety and variation. Taken together, they form a new black comedy of self-invention. Fictional violence can exploit the bizarre, the occult, and the taboo. It travesties traditional genres ranging from the occult to the romantic to the modern tale of manners to forge an edgy irony. Witty, verbally supple, and pointed in its use of sexuality to subvert conventional assumptions, violence lite reveals varieties of aggressive experience. Spinning profane acts into twisty triumphs of narrative wit and irony, it affirms the power of controlling narratives.

The violent women in new sendups of old genres seize control of negative stereotypes of women as passive victims to affirm agency as forceful narrative action. The ultimate heroine is the verbal trickster who outwits male power by exploding the genres that supported it and weaving new narratives of female control. That trickster's humor may be dark and bitterly ironic, but in violence lite, she always gets the last laugh.

CHAPTER 6

HEARTBREAKING PATTERNS

THE VIOLENT WOMEN OF FICTION, FILM, AND MEDIA ARE A STRIKE FORCE in a public world dominated by the power of the screen to make the wildest events seem real. This mediated violence offers narratives that bring home William James's "knife-edged" moment when truth and action can intersect in crises of behavior, meaning, motive, and action ("Feeling" 196). Those biological, structural, and psychological factors that are usually cited as clear sources of violence in the lives of men are disproved in the mediagenic violence of women. Video culture mediates between the real and the staged; its multiple perspectives fracture the wall between inner and outer life. Icons of disruptive change, violent women weave patterns of meaning and motivation that display a radical personalization of social currents of unrest registered in deformations of vision, relationships, and behavior. The view of the world as entirely hostile, the pipe-bombed building, the death of the child, the husband, the lover, the stable self—all add up to a raid on ideals of citizenship, love, and pleasure.

Media culture confounds violence with beauty, placing the unruly heroine on the menu as available eye candy. Serious fiction and poetry open up the depths and struggles at work in motivating and shaping her perceptions and actions. The narrative richness of contemporary fiction and poetry underscores how imaginative writing, symbolic associations, and fantasy can illuminate the more subtle currents, conflicts, and pressures at work in the culture.

The violence of women is richly communicative, employing in nearly every portrayal a remarkable command of language and interpretation to convey the passage from vulnerability to violence. From the preceding chapters, four types of violence emerge: performance violence, identity violence, retaliatory violence, and violence shaped by destructive egotism.

Although performance, identity, retaliatory, and destructively egotistical violence all overlap and may all be present to some extent in every representation of violence, each predominates in shaping particular expressions of the violence of women. Performance violence is related to the effort to cope with the demands of fulfilling traditional roles and self-damaging feelings of failure. Performance violence brings extraordinary verbal skill to bear on a damaged and damaging vision of motherhood. Identity violence, expressed most vividly in entertainment violence, uses theatrical role playing, irony, and black humor to shock, to undermine authority by questioning differences between control and self-control, playful roles and power relations. Retaliatory violence is most clearly dramatized in intimacy between lovers, in friendship and families. It reverses the interactions between men and women in which women are conventionally victims and involves imposing an alternative value system on apparent deformations of relationships and behavior. Destructive egotism is evident in individualistic political violence that involves a rejection of conventional radical models. Instead, destructive egotism springs from a pessimism about society in its broadest sense and lodges its own, nontraditional expressions of revolt and advocacy of female power.

PERFORMANCE VIOLENCE

Conflicts over the performance of once clearly defined female roles are most vividly illustrated in the literature of child murder discussed in chapter 3. Women impaled on contradictory ideals of freedom and self-sacrifice enact, through the horror of child murder, agonies of their heritage, self-image, and prospects. Competitive rage receives an unusual elaboration in such fiction as women live out a struggle with internalized ideals. They struggle between self and self-sacrifice, between their own protectiveness and dependency, between a complementary dualism with their child and a striving to be free of the child who seems a parasite on their self-esteem.

The complexity of narratives and language woven for such struggles makes relationships between internal and external life fluid and ever changing. In grandiose fantasies of mythic maternal power or in affirmations of perfect altruism, the mother exploits a language of concealment masking the affect and thoughts surrounding child murder. Describing the child through deformations of logic or oceanic sentiment, the mother emerges as a voyager on a fluctuating frontier where her narratives wage border warfare between child murder and its meaning. The mother may weaken realistic and reasonable bonds by seeing her child as either an all-good or an all-evil extension of herself. Her language for child murder may verge on grandiose lyricism, ingenious arabesques of innocence woven from claims of altruism or accident, fantasies of taking the child back into the womb, open rage at the youth and beauty of the child, or her own suicidal longing. As the heroine oscillates between demonized and idealized self-images, or as her vision of the child fluctuates from seeing the child as her other self, her complement, her competitor, or as her ball and chain, the crime itself is cast in different light. The death must be scripted to obscure its horror. The mother is engaged in a struggle for her own idealized self-image; she is in the grip of an all-or-nothing vision that is bigger than a child's life. At stake is the issue of control: if she cannot perfect the child's life as testimony to her skill, she will manage the child's death, relieving her performance anxiety through eliminating the child.

A competition between self and self-sacrifice is most evident in the relationship between generations of women. Intergenerational relationships reveal both the effort and the failure of an older generation of women to transmit traditional values and a younger generation's refusal to receive them. Intergenerational trouble forces a collision between traditional cultural ideals of motherhood and a media-driven culture of youth, pleasure, and freedom. The horror of child murder is so great that fiction in which it occurs requires and reveals an extraordinary narrative skill in weaving justifications—the murder is altruistic, *the mother's* sacrifice *for* the child's benefit, or really a suicide, or someone else's crime. The spin surrounding the murder reflects both the mother's awareness of how terrible the crime is and the dilemma on which she feels impaled. She craves high marks for her performance and achievement as a mother and intellectually recognizes the social importance of that approval, but she also craves love, satisfaction, and escape. The existence of a dependent, needy child marks her failure to achieve either of these opposing goals.

Competition between the all-pleasurable, rule-breaking free part of oneself and the idealization of the bonds of motherhood and self-sacrifice propels the child onto center stage as either a drag or, in psychological terms, a projection of failure, dependency, and weakness. What is striking in this fiction is the treatment of the child as a hated aspect of oneself, not as a separate being. Killing the child is like eliminating that despised part of oneself, enacting a destructive egotism that does not acknowledge the child's independent life.

In most fiction of child murder, suicidal fantasies project a performance anxiety in which the child's unmet needs are a constant reminder of one's own dependency. In the fantasies of an eternal, unencumbered youth or an escape from the biological trap of pregnancy, women in this fiction project the images of perfection spawned by a new entertainment culture that directly conflicts with the traditional ideals of motherhood. In the attempt to cope with frustration and rage, feelings of impotence and self-hatred often cause anger to turn against the child who seems the faulty part of oneself.

Portraits of the interaction between mother and child that ends in the child's death reveal both efforts to be the perfect mother and rage that one has to want to be that. Self-absorbed turmoil permits the child to emerge in the mother's mind as an interference with the thirst for the culture's competing ideals—youth, craving for pleasure, or even hedonism sustained by freedom and good looks. The hatefulness of child murder spawns enormously fertile narratives woven by the mother trying to win the competition for *both* idealism and self-interest. The death is presented as accidental, the child's choice, for the child's own good or even as part of a denial that the infant was ever alive in the first place. These slanted scripts only reinforce the uses of child murder to symbolize a complete break in the intergenerational chain of transmitted meanings and values.

That violence has a genealogy and is passed from one generation to the next is most frequently illustrated by social learning theorists identifying the presence of an abusive father as the determining factor in shaping boys with violent fathers into men who batter their wives (Rosenberg and Mercy 25). Maternal bequests seem different. The chain of mothers and daughters in the fiction of child murder breaks down; women do not reproduce their kind. Child murder is the metaphor for that breakdown and for the inability to sustain engagement long enough to transmit values, attitudes, and beliefs. The feeling of female heritage coming to an end surrounds the death of the child with intimations of apocalypse. When mother "love" ends in murder, the world as we know it appears to end.

The sense of an absolute ending is inscribed in the frequency with which the fiction of child murder invokes suicide. It reflects a close connection between suicide and violence. Freud wrote of suicide as deriving from unconscious hostility toward a lost loved one (159). He described how the individual incorporates and identifies with the person who is lost and turns the anger she feels toward that person back on herself. According to this formulation, suicide is an inverted homicide, the outgrowth of the unconscious desire to kill someone else. But in the fiction of child murder, the reverse seems true: homicide seems a displaced or inverted suicide. It springs from the texture of feeling between mother and child and from the vision of the child as the source of an injury to the mother's self-image and self-esteem, an impaired part of her self-concept. The destructive egotism involved in this view sees the child as an unwanted part of oneself, not as a separate being.

The child seems living proof of its mother's age, entrapment, loss of innocence, and impotence. The child's unhappiness is a reminder of her own unmet needs, a living indictment of her inability to perform as a mother or protect the child. As such, the very life of the child inflames performance anxiety and drives the need to eliminate the needy child as the external mark of her maternal failure and an expression of the failed part of herself. The death of the child serves as a kind of partial suicide, an effort to rid oneself of a defective part. Poetry stressing both overt rage and self-hatred uses representations of suicide and the mother's own death to maximize the intensity of hostility toward the living child as well as herself. The mother's connection to the child is overwhelmed by a sense of impasse, sometimes expressed in images of folding the child back into the mother's body as if neither could survive as a separate being. In fantasies of murder and suicide, narratives of child murder express the vision of motherhood as itself the child's destruction of the mother's life in a stark bargain: a life for a life.

Current infotainment news has focused on sensational cases of what seem to be totally callous infanticide. Melissa Drexler delivered her baby in a stall in the ladies room of a catering hall during her high school prom. Authorities "suspected that Miss Drexler dislodged a metal container for sanitary napkins from a wall in the stall and severed the cord with the container's serrated edge." She strangled the infant, put it in plastic bag, and stuffed it in a trash can (Hanley, A1, B4). She would later claim that the baby was born dead. After dumping the baby, she checked her makeup, returned to the prom, and danced with her date. She seemed completely calm throughout, reassuring a girl in the next stall that she was fine and asking her to tell their boyfriends that she would be right out.

The response of others in her high school was interesting. Although blood was all over the bathroom she had used, it was attributed to a heavy menstrual flow and the other girls asked only for a cleaning woman to make the ladies room usable again. After Drexler was charged with murder, students seemed to treat the episode as a sports event: "Students have started placing bets on whether Drexler will show up for graduation this Saturday. Others are still arguing over whether she was the one to request the maudlin Metallica song "Unforgiven" at the prom" (Koehl 64).

Here the power of metaphors of resumption of the freedom before the error of pregnancy may be part of a larger denial, evident in other episodes of infanticide, that even a baby born kicking and screaming was ever anything but a miscarriage. The central common factor in such instances is the need to deal with rage at pregnancy by playing the alternative role of freewheeling partygoer. The performative drive of media culture and the celebration of the bizarre and dysfunctional evident on trash-talk shows and in infotainment news sustain the illusion that the party is always there to find. Oscillations between inner and outer reality often shape such accounts into competing narratives that script the murder as either nonexistent (the baby was dead anyway) or a surreal event, a competition between the mother and the world around her—parents, others at the prom or party, and eventually the police and courts—over whose script will prevail.

Although media accounts generally include predictable condemnations of crime, they offer little understanding beyond that and no serious questioning of why, in an era of legalized abortion and infertile couples eager for adoption, such crimes should occur at all, particularly among affluent and educated young women. An article in the *New York Times Magazine* (November 2, 1997) attributed infanticide to "maternal wiring" and noted a cross-cultural prevalence of the desire to "triage" children. But that explanation seems as callous as the act itself.

The circumstances surrounding many accounts often unwittingly illustrate more profound social changes in the relationships between generations of women and offer a new picture of the genealogy of violence. They cast a harsh light on deformations of authority and independence evident between young mothers and their own mothers who appear unwilling or unable to face the reality of the girl's pregnancy themselves. The young girl may not want to see herself as pregnant, but neither does her mother want to notice that she is. These infanticide narratives most vividly dramatize lethal dysfunction: a declining capacity to accept or to face realities, a need to prefer the invented story to the actual reality, a determination to render physical facts unreal. The effort to treat real pregnancy as if it were not there suggests changing patterns of motherhood not only in the mother who kills the child but in a more extended breakdown of motherhood in the capacity of older women to adapt or develop new, realistic styles of authority to help their daughters who seem to fall so easily toward infanticide and to disavow all sense of themselves as mothers. Such repudiations of motherhood are projected in science fiction in iconic images of unfeeling and violent women as the genetically altered, or mutant women who have found a doorway out of female biology.

Repudiation of motherhood is bound up with a need to remain in control of one's own life and to acknowledge nothing that interferes. This may interact with economic and historical as well as personal forces that enforce the subordination of women and restrict their ability to control their own destiny and determine their child's future. Outer and inner forces converge in the mother's thinking about the child whose death can be scripted as both the product of circumstance and the mother's determination to beat all the social or economic odds against her. Winning the competition with such forces is more important than life itself. It can be such an ideal that the mother may claim the murder was for the child's benefit (see the discussion of *Beloved* in chapter 3), a way of saving her from the power of circumstance. The mother sends a message by child murder that if society will not permit her to control the child's life, she will control the child's death. Child murder resolves her competition with "history" by refusing to yield to it.

Imaginative fiction offers symbolic representations of women who have defeated the inexorable course of historical circumstance by claiming to control its movement toward greater violence in the slaughter of innocents. Thomas Pynchon's *V.* is represented as the mother of the twentieth century, the era of modern war. As mother, she abandons a generation to mass death and destruction. In science fiction thrillers, representations of cyborgs or predatory, nonhuman mutants vividly suggest the escape from reproduction and embody dreams of a world without pregnancy or motherhood. Such metaphors attack the conditioning of women for nurture and reflect an attempt to counter what is seen as a genealogy of self-sacrifice and victimization with a genealogy of self-gratification and violence.

IDENTITY VIOLENCE

Entertainment violence weaves complex comedies out of will and subjectivity, expressing both in the development of role-playing as a hip style of self-fashioning through identity violence. Like other expressions of violence, it challenges conventions of obligation and intimacy but does so with verbal distance and play, calling into question those genres ranging from the bodice-ripping romance to the Mafia movie, to achieve an ironic inclusiveness of aggression in the menu of female styles. The mixture of wrestling, rock, and porn events and new twists on genre fiction underscore the fascination with role-playing as a form of identity violence that can co-opt or appropriate misogyny as a tool for controlling the camera eye, for turning the shock of abuse into a self-aggrandizing entertainment tool.

A 1982 report by the National Institute of Mental Health, *Television and Behavior: Ten Years of Scientific Progress and Implications for the Eighties,* studied the question of whether violent programming contributed to an increase in both aggressive behavior and a vision of the world as more malevolent and terrifying than it is. Studies of the content of television shows within the report underscored both a repeated distortion of reality toward increasing violence and a subsequent finding that viewers did conclude that the United States was actually as violent as it appeared to be on television. A critique of the report by a group of independent scholars supported the findings that the prevalence of crime shows and accounts of actual crimes influenced popular estimates of the general crime rate and increased mistrust of other people (Cook 173, 162). It said that "case studies of imitative violence indicate that events which are rare in real life have sometimes been committed soon after they were televised as part of a dramatic fictional show or a news account" (Cook 192). Neither the report nor the critique is likely to end debate over whether watching violent shows contributes to actual violence. Although there may be evidence of some causal relationships between viewing and violence, that issue is not all that is important. What should also concern us are the qualitative associations surrounding the violence of women.

Film, media, and genre fiction are sites for the development of transgressive styles. Genre fiction reads its audience as much as its audience reads it. Entertainments with glitzy fights and erotic violence may or may not actually cause transgressions, but they surely normalize them by placing them on the menu of what can be seen and enjoyed. Highly sexualized, provocative, or even pornographic renderings of violent heroines underscore the deliberate effort to make violent action titillating. If art imitates life, life can imitate art by adapting and normalizing projected ideals of aggression or treachery and the confrontational manners that accompany both and blend sexuality and violence. Nor should the violence of women be celebrated as payback for male violence. It may easily serve as a justification for male violence against women by purveying images of women who are equals or superiors in combat and therefore legitimate targets.

Current violence narratives about women run counter to the prevailing wisdom in media studies that has recognized radical qualities in commercial art forms but seen their popularity as deriving primarily from their reassurance about the stability of the way things are. Darrell Hamamoto, for example, has focused on the role of television as "ultimately supportive of the status quo . . . within the larger framework of liberal democratic ideology" because progressive aspects are presented moderately and produced "for private profit alone" (Staiger 41–42). Just because a show is produced with private capital and makes a profit does not mean it is inherently a stabilizing influence. There seems to be profit in destabilization.

Conventional wisdom also holds that domestic subject matter is apolitical. However, that view overlooks the remarkable concentration of social disruption in families and the contrast in American life between overwhelmingly stable and secure public institutions and the rage and unrest provoked by changing sexual mores. Culture wars are fought out in family courts and media debates over what constitutes marriage and the very definition of a married couple or a family. In a media-saturated world in which even the narratives of cases of child murder reflect changes from a sixties concern over women's sexuality (as in the case of Alice Crimmins discussed in chapter 3) to new questions about whether women care about life at all (as in the cases of Amy Grossberg and Melissa Drexler), the family can emerge as the malignant universe instantiated in an "ordinary" home and its new, nihilistic *jeune fille*.

Women and young people are increasingly seen as the audience for trash talk shows and for the character and relationship-driven narratives of reality TV shows like *Castaways* or *Survivor, Temptation Island* or *Bachelor.* Such shows promise to entertain with destructive games and strike at conventions of keeping faith, turning romance into a competitive test. They are sendups of the genre of domestic sitcoms that unravel the sitcom's basic concept of togetherness no matter what happens. Temptation, betrayal, successful treachery, or winning strategies are what people come to such "reality" shows to see.

Are audience responses changing? Traditionally both the demands of selling advertising and reaching women who control purchasing power in the home, as Lauren Rabinovitz pointed out, required the successful sitcom to be a "melodrama . . . which is character and relation based" (Staiger 40–41). Commentators have largely avoided finding overarching concerns or meanings in sitcoms except to indicate that the dictates of a mass audience require that the sitcom uphold the essential conservatism and traditional values of mass art. However, Staiger notes, "We have significant anecdotal evidence that programs such as *Father Knows Best*—which only once made it into a year's top ten list—contributed to the archetypal image of an era" (50).

It is precisely that archetypal image that provokes a nontraditional response in the fiction in which the domestic sitcom is mentioned. The traditional sitcom with its projection of articulate, wholesome, and competent mothers and engaged and wise fathers impels the hapless Janice in *Rabbit, Run* toward the "blue light" of alcohol. She sees herself in a competition with normalcy and skills she will never achieve; she feels like a loser in a world intoxicated with family values. In Pynchon's *Vineland, The Brady Bunch* provides the only cohesive family that virtually motherless, couch potato children are likely to know. The show still casts a glowing but ironic "tubelight" on the lives of a generation whose constant babysitter is television.

Identity violence involves deformations of family conventions as well as extreme role and genre exchanges. Even as infotainment news breaks new ground in defining the irrepressible and rebellious teenager not as the boy who borrows the car without permission, but as the girl who stashes her newborn in the girls' room trashcan. Films go further. Oliver Stone's *Natural Born Killers* (1994), like much of the genre fiction discussed in chapter 5, exploits sendups of multiple conventions. Its parody of the fifties sitcom presents an anti-world of dysfunction in rendering the home life of the not-so-innocent young girl played by Juliette Lewis. Victim of a vile father, a raucous mother, and a horrifying exposure to every taboo, she is "rescued" from her family by her equally violent lover played by Woody Harrelson. The damsel-in-distress plot becomes twisted toward a damsel-causes-distress scenario. On their honeymoon, the young lovers murder fifty people. Juliette Lewis as a "bride," forces oral sex on a man at gunpoint in a modern sendup of the humiliating, female victimization scenes that fill old-time adventure thrillers. A female predator, she signals that there is no exit from the new universe of violence in old dreams of marriage, love, and forgiveness.

What Americans will accept as entertainment has moved along with the times. The family sitcom such as *Leave it to Beaver* or *I Love Lucy* is light years away from the *Roseanne Barr, South Park, The Simpsons,* or *Married with Children.* The interactions between husbands and wives reveal distinct changes. None of the women in these recent shows has the lovable, lighthearted wackiness that endeared Lucy to Desi despite his frequent exasperation with her escapades. The interactions between men and women are more egalitarian in the new shows, but the equality is often based on mutual insults.

David F. Luckenbill identifies a type of interaction that leads to violence by husbands against their wives (Rosenberg and Mercy 25–26). At issue are exchanges in provocative remarks in arguments. He investigated seventy incidents of assault and homicide in California and described a series of "offender" and "victim" interactions leading to the man's attack. The husband complains. The wife responds with a cutting remark the man experiences as a threat to his control, sexual expertise, or self-esteem. He replies with physical force (Luckenbill 176–86). A lighter model of interactive verbal violence is evident in TV sitcoms, which capture perpetually arguing couples and use the insult as the primary form of conversation.

Married with Children began airing in 1985 and is a prime example of a couple whose major verbal form is the put down. On Thursday, January 25, 2001, Mr. Bundy complains there is no food and no dinner. His son suggests they look for food on the floor between the oven and the kitchen cabinet where he has found "fuzzy M & Ms" in the past. Mrs. Bundy comes home sporting big hair and wild prints having spent a relaxing day out shopping for clothes. She has only two half-filled shopping bags. "You see," she complains, "this is all that everything you make will buy." Mr. Bundy suggests they have sex later. She declines. Neither is supplying the food, sex, or money the other wants. Mr. Bundy's lack of money, her lack of sexual interest in him, his general incompetence with the children, and her lack of interest in a family dinner constitute their interaction in what is now an established success formula. While their routine does not rise to violence, its basis in mutual derision establishes hostility as a comic domestic style. In contrast, reruns of *The Dick Van Dyke Show* showing the gentlemanly Dick Van Dyke with his articulate, elegant wife, Mary Tyler Moore, appear to have been filmed on another planet, not in another decade.

Although the audience at home may feel superior to the Bundy family, the Bundy's verbal abuse is only a lighthearted reflection of the procession of pathologies evident in trash talk shows or crime shows emphasizing troubled intimacy and the torture of women. Mass media are comfortably countercultural in merchandising the sick and bizarre dimensions of human interaction. An HBO special starring Joe Mantegna features a man who captures and locks up his former girlfriend whom he tyrannizes until she is rescued by Mantegna. An episode of *CSI,* aired on January 12, 2001, shows a serial killer truck-driver whose close accomplice is a woman who travels his supermarket delivery route with him. She lures unsuspecting women to his refrigerated truck. The man rapes and murders them, putting their bodies in the truck with the frozen foods he delivers. Wrapped in plastic gauzy with frost in the freezer, the dead women seem wrapped in bridal veils that are raised in the macabre spectacle that climaxes the episode.

Extreme violence *against* women provides the backdrop for an increasing number of shows involving violent women. Retaliatory violence finds its justification in the context of violence against women who are treated largely as objects of assault. Such shows frequently contain other women engaged in passages from vulnerability and victimization to powerful behavior. The violence of women is legitimized by the context established by male violence. The more pervasive emerging identity violence discussed in chapter 5 is about beating the lighter forms of misogyny in pop culture at their own game. Much entertainment violence on television deals with beating back male attacks or humiliating men for efforts to humiliate women.

Beautiful woman warriors are not in themselves new. The magic bracelet and lasso of Wonder Woman projected female power that, like Superman's, was used to defend "truth, justice, and the American Way." Wonder Woman, however, had little revealed interior life or ambivalence. She has been upstaged by "warriors" with attitude. *La Femme Nikita*'s heroine hates the system that sends her out on violent adventures. *Dark Angel* enjoys abusing the men who think they can take advantage of a gorgeous eighteen-year-old. The cultural and social resonance of fantasy shows such as *Xena, Warrior Princess* bespeaks joy in beating beefy men in combat; *The Black Scorpion* is all-powerful against crime only when she turns from her day job as policewoman to nights as the "scorpion" when she fulfills her ideals only on the dark side. This series, by Roger Corman, is distinctly twenty-first-century not only in having a premiere in January 2001 on the futuristic Sci Fi Channel, but also in its mixture of pornography, violence, and crime-fighting. Sexy Michelle Lintel, as the cop who mutates at night into a superheroine, does battle with female villains who include a former *Playboy* Playmate. In episodes to come, according to *New York Magazine,* there will be evildoers named "Medusa, Vapor, and Pollutia" (January 8, 2001, 57). The show is simultaneously a joke on female violence, a turn-on for men, and a normalization of the fun of watching comic-book sirens in full Bam! Pow! action. Using the sexiness and violence of women as interchangeable forges an equivalency between the two as if a woman who transgresses in one way will also do anything in the other.

Heroines in such shows are warriors who may uphold ideas of justice and rectification of wrongs consistent with traditional values, but they are cynical about established authority and contemptuous of men. Their allure comes in part from their multiplication of female roles through seizing and inverting expectations. The women in chapter 5 who bestride the World Wrestling Federation rock events, semi-nude in leather or carrying a glitter "HO" sign, or gyrating to an audience yelling "slut, slut, slut," may control the camera eye, but they reinforce their illusions of power by appropriating misogyny as their own. Gaining celebrity through misogyny, such women heap contempt on the good-girl ethos. They also show that sexploitation by men is meaningless except as a tool for their own advantage.

Identity violence assumes destructive egotism can be used for role playing and beating men at their own game. Sadomasochism as a metaphor for the structure of male-female relationships is subverted in the literature, discussed in chapter 5, by women who seize control of the scripts both partners play, determine what happens, and subvert stereotypical male and female assignments of roles, smashing expectations that women will play subordinate roles. Identity violence reflects a destructive egotism that uses self-concepts to fabricate roles that undermine subordination and oppression by draining meaning and substance out of familiar male images of power. That destructive egotism sees the world only in terms of one's own needs and places one's own power and freedom above all else. Disconnection from humane values enables the destructive egotist to play different roles, or simulate normal or traditional roles, without any deep connection to anything but control.

RETALIATORY VIOLENCE

Violence in intimacy is anti-puritanical and morally radical. It addresses in graphic, erotic imagery the destruction of male images of power and control. Retaliatory violence involves a sendup of a moral universe in which ideas of crime and punishment are turned inside out and traditional morality is redefined through its violation. It reflects a concern with sin and criminal violence by the compulsive commission of both. Our fiction of violent intimacy illustrates the effort to seize control of conventions of victimization and rewrite them as narratives of triumph. The incest victim, the prostitute, the abandoned lover or wife or the abused daughter or sister seizes control of the story of male-female relations to rewrite it in richly diverse narratives of power.

Retaliatory violence narratives use tales of father-daughter, brother-sister incest to attack the narrative of the destruction of the girl through exploitation and reverse it to a story of the achievement of female power through the sexual manipulation of men. Puritan New England made incest victims wear the letter "I" to signal God's designation of them as lost souls marked for suffering but new narratives exploit such violations as the path to celebrity and success. Such tales shadow the media's predilection for the confessional memoirs or revelations on the trash talk show by using devices for self-implication within the narrative. The first person narrative, the confessional diary, the novel as prison memoir—all implicate the speaker who describes childhood incest, adolescent prostitution, and adult violence. Subtle and deft in its craft and command of language, Carole

Maso's *Defiance* boasts a heroine (discussed in Chapter 2) who breaks taboos and destroys associations of power with maleness by seducing and killing her lovers only after teaching them to crave cross-dressing, bondage, and humiliation.

Retaliatory violence has more complex psychological meanings than simply payback. The ways in which individual and social maladjustment can be expressed in the real world are clearly limited—suicide, violence, neurosis, crime, drug addiction, and alcoholism. In literature about violent intimacy, language games extend the list to embrace the most essential interactions between people. Inventive accounts of predatory women may romanticize, idealize, or celebrate their violence as a means of carving self-affirmations from instability and sexual aggression.

Narratives of retaliatory violence take the image of the young girl and reverse its associations with innocence to one of amoral confusion about right and wrong in a verbal universe of degradation and obscenity. The role of language in exploring rage is emphasized by Kathy Acker, whose *Blood and Guts in High School* (discussed in Chapter 2), implies the evolution of a female language of disgust by going back to the wellsprings of writing. Her heroine is a young girl whose experiences with incest and prostitution do not end in resignation. Her meditative spin on incest and prostitution invokes mythic and legendary victimized women as ancestral figures who serve as catalysts for a justifying narrative of change. Employing ancient languages, cuneiform tablets, drawings, nonsense language, eschatological obsession, baby talk, and sophisticated musings on the inscription of female enslavement over time, Acker conveys an evolutionary genealogy for narratives of modern female fury. Her young heroine, who robs, beats, attacks, and creates a verbal universe of aggression for the audience, is heiress of ages and types of writing that inscribe contempt for women in legend and obscenity. Acker establishes an inversion of values through subverting the charged meaning of the words that capture and impale. Her young girl sees herself not simply as an incest victim or prostitute but as someone who can use her body as a weapon that inflames the dependency of men and her speech as a tool for redefining relationships of power and subordination. Moreover, her prostitution is intended to redefine the body as a weapon for rebuking the commodity culture in which money is the index of worth. Sexual provocation is used as a measure of power and a manipulative tool.

The communicative richness of literary violence in intimacy expresses several things about the uses of sexuality as the primary site for the war between the sexes. Violent intimacy erupts from unmet needs and displays both a woman's thirst for male protective love and rage at its absence. Fury at the inversion of intimacy to power relations is evident in the focus on the deformations of love and the desperate measures taken to deny pain. Such desperation is registered in incest stories in the young girl's insistence on reaffirming incest as a means of unraveling the power of men and as the key to a hostile or murderous sexuality.

The substitution of sexual power for all other paradigms of authority is a major part of narratives of retaliatory violence. Intimacy expresses entrenched cultural attitudes toward commitment. The unraveling of those expectations mirrors in dark forms the passage from vulnerability to violence as it occurs over the life cycle: from childhood incest, to adolescent crime and prostitution, to murder in adulthood. What is striking are the developments in narrative language over that cycle.

Violence as an evolutionary development is embedded stylistically in Acker's sequential use of cartoons of what is happening, to employing eschatological obscenities to convey meaning, to commanding literary traditions of classical legend or philosophical avant garde writing or lyrical poetry. Acker's command of *belles lettres* is fully assimilated into the quality of consciousness that perceives and expresses a violent vision in both tragic and heroic terms. Thus her young heroine can draw on Greek mythology and French experimentalism or modernist poetry to invoke past literary structures for tragic justification. Legends and lyricism situate the violence of her heroine as an emissary from those structures of devastation that invoke the power and sanction of earlier great art. Versions of this literary process are employed by a number of writers to situate violence in romantic literary traditions that equalize and rectify both victimization and violence in visions of the universal price love extracts. The result is an aesthetic of violence that transforms classical images of the young girl as innocent and calls into question the treatment of death as an aspect of romance.

The sheer fluency of the craft and the mechanics of narrative evident in the fiction of violent women creates a communicative power that coincides with a co-opting of powerful literary tools in the depiction of a destructive egotism that is made to seem both the final term of literary invention and the point of literary history. Its very power rebukes alternative literary models that advance idealization of the young girl as Persephone before Hades captured her, the faith in a purity that survives physical and intellectual degradation, or is sanctified by traditional visions of the Blessed Virgin as the compassionate or even militant embodiment of the triumph of faith and purity over injustice and despair.

Fictions of intimacy offer a new take on the view that violence is the product of an almost ritualized form of male-female interaction in which men need to impose control on women who don't want to be controlled. Psychologist Anne Campbell believes that aggression means something different to men and women. For women, she believes, "aggression is the *failure* of control" while men see it as "the *imposing* of control over others" (Brownstein 99).

The styles of violence evident in fiction and even infotainment news suggest otherwise. Acts of violence are calculated, planned, and structured before they occur, and afterward they are scripted with skill and control. Even actual female violence is far more complex and communicative, offering nuanced narratives that capture a woman's longing for a loving and romantic man and for a mutually protective and caring bond between them. Even when the relationship ends by the death of the man from the woman's actions, the woman may continue to see and describe him in ideal terms as a lover and savior, as the caring friend and rescuer from despair he was not. Diana Trilling's novelistic portrait of Jean Harris on trial for the murder of her lover, Herman Tarnower, conveys Mrs. Harris's scripting of what happened the night she shot him as his heroic effort to keep her from killing herself over his abandonment of her for a younger woman (see chapter 2). The simple payback involved in a "crime of passion" was made complex by Mrs. Harris's need to preserve her idealized, romantic image of the man who had exploited her talents, profited from her help in writing the Scarsdale diet book that had brought him a fortune, and treated her callously during a long affair. She paid for her need to script her violence as romantic tragedy with conviction and a long sentence.

As creator of a narrative of Harris's crime, Diana Trilling brought an equally complex agenda to her judgment of her script. She compared Mrs. Harris's tastes and choices negatively with her own life as the wife of Lionel Trilling, a distinguished writer and professor, and entered into a competition with her that Mrs. Harris could only lose. Mrs. Trilling's need to control the narrative of her own relationship to her husband not only became part of Mrs. Harris's story but of her own and, years later, revealed itself in the violence of defamation. Trilling's subsequent writing continued her control of the narrative of her own husband's life but rewrote it as the story of his dependency on her. Not long before her death, she retaliated in evident bitterness for years of her protective nurturing of her husband's reputation and presented that protection as a form of concealed truth. She published an account of her marriage saturated with complaint, asserting that it was she who had made him a writer and claiming her general superiority to the man whose career she had devoted herself to advancing.

The violence of women in intimacy is less about a loss of control, than a reflection of the changing agendas of relationships based on power struggles. The violence of women expressed in intimacy seizes absolute control of the script they write for the men under attack. Moving from an idealistic, romantic scripting of their relationship to an unmasking of their own once suppressed rage, the passage suggests that from the house of troubled intimacy only one will emerge.

Covert and manipulative violence is often the technique of choice in narratives of female violence that use children as weapons against an offending husband or lover or burdensome domestic situation. Such narratives, discussed in chapter 2, include those such as the Bradshaw murder, in which a mother coerced her teenage son into killing her father, using the child as a murder weapon. In other narratives mothers use children as servants and/or surrogate mothers for younger children in order to free themselves. The children may be demonized as reminders of the hated husband or lover who abandoned them or designated as winners, idealized as the daughter whose beauty or talent may redeem her mother from anonymity.

Either way children are used to act out aggressive impulses or as surrogate hedonists who can achieve and live out the dreams of pleasure and social success their mothers were unable to fulfill for themselves.

Deadly families weave competing narratives of violence that often reflect the disparity in male and female views. Most narratives of retaliatory female violence are related from the perspective of the violent woman and involve her vision of the intergenerational relationship between women in her family. For this reason they are similar in some respects to narratives of child murder. The rage at the expectations of her mother and fear they cannot be met play into Janice's drowning of her infant daughter in *Rabbit, Run*. In Judith Rossner's novel *Perfidia*, a teenage girl has been used as a housekeeper by her beautiful, freewheeling mother. Enraged with the girl's decisive autonomy, the mother turns on her in a drunken rage and tries to kill her with a broken bottle. Her daughter responds, "[I] smashed the broken glass into her . . . beautiful breasts, under her white T-shirt. It was when the T-shirt was sopping wet with her blood that I stopped and sank all the way to floor with her. . . . Her arms were almost around me" (213). The mother in rebellion against conventional motherhood and the daughter who believes only one of them can survive are locked in a deadly bond, a cycle of retaliatory violence.

The intergenerational relationships between women can be abusive even when the mothers have lavished everything on daughters they used to fulfill their own ambitions. The mother who has inculcated a hatred for her husband in her own daughters may acquire an ally in the daughter to whom she has given all she has and entrusted with her hope of vicariously enjoying a privileged life. The real Mrs. Bradshaw and the fictional Mrs. Springer (discussed respectively in chapters 2 and 3) are sisters in finding that the daughters they wrapped in velvet have absorbed their exploitative behavior but not their devotion, can easily dispense with them, and retain the self-absorption and craving to get all there is.

Retaliatory violence enacts fantasies not only of revenge and power but of control of one's own life and life story. It expresses in the interaction between men and women or, in the dynamics of family life, the will to destabilize every established conception of domestic order.

VIOLENCE SHAPED BY DESTRUCTIVE EGOTISM

Although destructive egotism is present in all types of violence by women, it is the dominant characteristic of political violence, upending expectations of community and social betterment as possibilities. Narratives of political violence and terrorism by women upset much of the conventional wisdom about radicalism. Fictional narratives of women terrorists are invariably nontraditional in following no ideologically coherent politics. American fictional activists are typically women from middle class or wealthy backgrounds who have access to legal means of protest and rarely focus on the institutionalized oppression usually cited as sources of political violence. The conventional radical emphasis on the interests of the group over the individual is belied by the power of fictional activists to ignore traditional master narratives of revolution and class conflict in favor of telling the story of activism as a tale of self-fashioning. Because of this, fictional women terrorists bear a closer relationship to those projections of power that are located in the literary rather than political imagination of cultural revolution. In the literary imagination, changing icons of power focus political antagonisms in images that are existential or spiritual.

Past female icons associated with defining qualities of culture provide an interesting context for contemporary women. Henry Adams described irreconcilable differences between his aristocratic class and culture and modernity as a contest between that great female icon, the blessed Virgin, and a sexless machine, the dynamo. The Virgin symbolized ideals of spiritual beauty and benevolence and a holistic vision of culture unified by faith. The dynamo represented for him a future driven by amoral technology and the fragmented world represented by those polyglot hordes of immigrants at the St. Louis Exposition of 1904 that he describes with misgiving in *The Education of Henry Adams*. They serve the machine and the future it is creating. Adams's conservatism was symbolized by his belief that his class, his values, and his Blessed Virgin were doomed by the new America of amoral industrial power that would destroy coherences of language and faith in its adoption of the power morality represented by mechanical force.

Opposing that conservative iconography is the radical vision of change that emerges from the fiction of women terrorists. That vision is shaped by a destructive egotism that projects amoral historical force as female power and that sees Adams's virgin *as* the dynamo, often uniting them in a vision of enthralling seduction. Destructive egotism lays claim to both moral and social power as if each were only an attribute of will or an idealized female icon, and the world at large only the "*other me.*"

Women activists inhabit a hostile political world that is a great stage on which repudiation of its power by violence can be enacted. Although political movements are usually credited with enabling people to identify the structural or institutional sources of their oppression and providing companions in the struggle for change, the political activism of women in fiction is violent, theatrical, and as compellingly solitary as a one-woman show. Richard Hofstadter's conclusion that American violence is too individualistic to constitute a coherent revolutionary force finds support in imaginative narratives in which activism involves little comradeship and less support from radical groups dominated by men. This fiction exploits political rhetoric but shifts ground repeatedly. It challenges the establishment as if it were the domestic world, both exploiting it as a cover and using the "safe house" and the home as if they were interchangeable. It derives from the two a means of transcending the disparity between the lady and the terrorist by forging equations between them. Behind the details of specific fictional representations discussed in chapter 4 is the overriding desire for self-reconciliation and self-affirmation through violence.

What is unique in the literature of women terrorists is the prevalence of the divided self-image of woman as both civilized ideal and destroyer and the search for a mechanism that will encompass the contradictions suggested by being the "lady" and the "terrorist" at the same time. Although the overriding driving force may be for self-affirmation through violence, the self being affirmed is intensely dualistic. It is marked by a desire to appropriate religious or mythic imagery and oceanic spiritualism and to use intimations of grace to sanctify those instruments of lethal power, the bomb and the gun.

Goddess and gun are reconciled in the dream of action and in its implementation to promote sensations of wholeness. In his 1910 essay, "The

Moral Equivalent of War," William James identified the psychological appeal of destruction by pointing out that "showing war's irrationality and horror is of no effect upon [modern citizens]. The horrors make the fascination (163). He found that "War is the *strong* life; it is life *in extremis*" (169). The craving for release from provisional, subjective realities in the concentration provided by violence drives the quest for life "*in extremis*" and is an important feature of literary activism.

The literary imagination of violent activism is driven by the all or nothing of the experience and the need to elevate even the dreariness of times between violent episodes. Just as Georges Sorel advocated the total negation of a mythic general strike in *Reflections on Violence* because "the torment of the infinite produces moral value," so women terrorists in fiction operate as though maximizing disruption increases their distance from stereotypical femininity and inflates their moral capital. Women terrorists are looking for the rush of infinity, the felt experience of the sublime that makes destruction the proof of omnipotence and a value in itself. Yet what distinguishes the efforts of women terrorists in literature is the use of femaleness in the process.

The mother of contemporary American fictional terrorists is Henry James's Christina Light, the heroine of *Roderick Hudson* and *The Princess Casamassima*. Through both novels she is in search of ways to actualize her beauty as a source of power and value combined. She does so by searching for a target that can yield the moral value and sense of "infinity" she craves. Through her, James forecasts the age of instability as a condensation of aggressive and erotic drives packaged in that iconic beauty, the *femme fatale*.

The seductive stylization of violence is an intrinsic part of the representation of the lady-terrorist. From the choice of victim to selection of settings for the act, staging has importance in expressing the actualization of the killer's womanliness. Such choices express a complex, destructive egotism in which the victim completes a drama of self-affirmation by also serving as an adoring audience who may be seduced by the encounter that kills him. In *The Princess Casamassima*, James described the drama as a fusion of European and American forms of violence, an alliance between the savagery possible in the aristocrat's drawing room and in the "genes" of an heiress of frontier ruthlessness. The illegitimate daughter of an Italian and an impoverished but wildly ambitious American widow, Christina Light has a heritage of ruthlessness, a classic, disturbing beauty, and the will to promote social instability. She has caused the Prince Casamassima to forsake his own class and marry her, giving her access to his immense wealth and ancient name. Outraged that she needed marriage to him to conceal her illegitimate birth and shield her mother from the creditors who sustain their show of wealth, she resolves to kill an aristocrat—any aristocrat—while in evening dress at an opulent party. She has displaced her rage at her own position onto all of those with wealth and privilege as if they were only mirrors in which she sees reflections of her own corruption and hypocrisy. Violent acts of repudiation are meant to shatter those aristocrats who are the mirrors of her duplicity. She equates murdering any one of them with purifying her image.

Staging murder to promote powerful and confident beauty involves a loving use of dramatic detail and investing essential props and tools with special meaning in the fiction of women terrorists. Obtaining the weapon or building the bomb may be invested with particular erotic overtones as an exchange of power from male to female in which the weapon becomes a technological extension of one's own power. The princess's eroticized anarchism takes the form of fascination with acquiring a gun through the intermediaries of a notorious anarchist, James's fictional Hoffendahl whose purity of commitment sanctifies the weapons he supplies.

American history provides an interesting baseline against which the princess's purposes can be measured. James exploited two factors—one actual and the other fictional—for underscoring the historical connections between Europe and America. Lionel Trilling pointed out that Hoffendahl was modeled on an actual anarchist named Johan Most. The blend of fact and fiction in the novel enables James to exploit an anarchist history of investing the bomb and the gun with spiritual meaning and of endowing the places where bombs were constructed with what James Billington called "the ritual centrality" that seemed comparable to the role of the cathedral for the religious (407). Christina Light, is, as her name suggests, a Christ figure represented lightly. Her beauty and sense of style similarly parody the seductive power of religious sentiment and violence Johan Most exemplified. On the day President McKinley was shot, Johan Most published his tract in favor of tyrannicide, which concluded with the exhortation, "Let us save humanity with blood and iron, poison and dynamite." Fiction brought that sentiment across the Atlantic.

Johan Most was also the model for the hero of a popular novel, *The Bomb*, by Frank Harris, who called him Jacob Ling and credited him with one of the major episodes of American anarchist violence. Frank Harris used the Haymarket Affair (1886) as a dramatic vehicle for conveying Ling's purpose. During a demonstration in Chicago's Haymarket Square called by the Knights of Labor who were striking for an eight-hour workday, police had opened fire on the workers, killing and wounding a number of demonstrators. The following day the strike continued and also involved a protest against police violence. When the police moved to break up the event, someone threw a bomb at them. The bomb-thrower was not found, but eight anarchists were found guilty of murder. The convicted men became heroic symbols of injustice, Christ figures whose conviction was called into question. The survivors were pardoned six years later by the governor of Illinois after four had been executed and one had committed suicide.

Frank Harris, like James, embedded in his novel a psychological and spiritual meaning for the bomb as a symbol of both heroic, sacrificial suffering and retaliation. *The Bomb* is set in part in New York and links anarchist violence to both the human costs of an expanding economy and the grandeur of the cathedralesque arches of the Brooklyn Bridge. The great bridge rests on the nitrogen poisoning of the workers who descended beneath the riverbed to lay its foundations and died from caisson disease. *The Bomb* aimed for a mythic anarchism in its symbolic use of the bridge as a two-way street between heaven and hell, justifying the Chicago bombing as originating in Ling's exposure to both the sublime and horrific. The appeal of the bomb is personal and subjective. Ling's attraction to it slides into an attraction to death as a transcendent, sublime power: "death has this strange power over men, that when you are willing to walk within his shadow you feel yourself the equal of anything that lives." *The Princess Casamassima* goes further in presenting the seduction by death as literally an erotic force in the psychology and action of Christina Light as *femme fatale*.

The princess who would be an assassin uses death as moral and social vindication, a demonstration not of equality but of her superiority to the limitations of social categories that indict her illegitimacy, her contempt for the prince, her craving for his money, and her acute shame at having to marry the prince to acquire social viability. The mixture of great beauty and great destructiveness is directed against the compartmentalization of classes and categories. The wish to kill an aristocrat at a party while in dazzling dress reconciles her self-hatred for social climbing with her craving for the appearance of a moral grace that will provide her with the ultimate adornment: absolute purity of commitment. Christina is a prime player in a vast drama of social chaos, summed up in the theatrical scenario of imagining how she will kill. Erotic and violent display shape her dream of assassination and the instrument that will carry it out. The use of destabilizing social change is equated with the princess's remorseless self-absorption, her sense of individual sovereignty, and the destructive egotism that prizes the gun as the fulfillment and extension of her power. The gun concentrates her life.

Is it possible to make social myth out of the desire for personal power, to tie it to the solitary self and not an oppressed group? Virtually all of the women terrorists in the fiction discussed sever their individual problems— shame at past behavior, class anger, or present humiliation—from those of other women.

Myth, language, action, and fact intersect in the fiction of women for whom the repudiation of inhibition is a political act, a seizure of the power of the bomb or the gun, and an expression of revolt against delicacy and unimportance. The fiction of terrorism casts them into an enlarging story that destroys the compartmentalization of the separate social boxes of the "lady" or "terrorist" and the exigencies of ideological commitment. Mythic appropriation of symbols in the nineteenth century used women in the shocking ways James does with Christina Light or Henry Adams does in his exquisite use of the Blessed Virgin as an embodiment of a culture of moral value and compassion that was the direct opposite of the dynamo.

Modern women activists live in a culture of technology that has gone beyond ideals of power, force, and speed and that now includes information and intelligence. In recent fiction, seductive and violent images explode that opposition between human and machine. The spirit of the age is a union of contrary forms, suggesting that the "Virgin" for our time is neither fully human nor machine but a synthesis of both, a mutant between the animate and inanimate. She is imagined by Thomas Pynchon as an eternal and egotistical virago: "skin radiant with the bloom of some new plastic; both eyes glass but now containing photoelectric cells, connected by silver electrodes to optic nerves. . . . Perhaps even a complex system of pressure transducers located in a marvelous vagina of polyethylene . . . all leading to a single silver cable which fed pleasure voltages direct to the correct register of the digital machine in her skull" (*V.* 411–12).

The analogy between virgin and mechanical virago is meant to shock by attacking biological determinism and the sanctification of woman's virtue by using the profane image of an autoerotic machine. Female biology is further challenged by cyberimages of women who are weightless as pixels on a screen or predatory mutants. Similarly mythic images of spiritual transcendence defy the human condition by altering it, drawing in images from video and information technology, celebrating it as silicon-based rather than carbon-based life. The grandiosity of this destructive egotism is so great it reaches toward sublime images of transcendence of mortality. In most fiction, however, destructive egotism and self-absorption take the form of a disdain for realistic social progress and an embrace of the show, the theatrical effect. The hip icon may be Pynchon's activist turned rock musician who sings:

Just a floo-zy with-an U-Uzi
Just a girlie, with-a-gun . . .
When I could have been a mo-del,
And I should have been a nu-un. . . .

[But] Mister, you can keep yer len-ses,
And Sister, you can keep yer beads . . .
I'm ridin' in Mercedes Ben-zes,
I'm takin' care of all my needs. . . . (*Vineland* 104–105)

Terrorists in the fiction of violent women do not claim their acts will defeat entrenched power or cause it to change its ways or spend much time developing justifying social narratives. Their purpose is to paint the world as they see it, to impose the illusion that they can color it as they wish in order to destabilize the status quo. They focus on the rush of planning and implementing violent protests or the lifestyle of escape and evasion. The outrageousness of even some nonviolent acts is in itself a revelation of what they are fighting for in aesthetic gestures. For example, by dropping condoms filled with black paint on a nuclear facility from a Cessna, Marge Piercy's *Vida* does not exactly screw nuclear energy, but she does, echoing the old Rolling Stones's song, "paint it black," making black humor out of terrorist action. In her more violent exploits and in her contempt for women's groups who protest rape, she weaves scenarios that express her myth of herself as an action "hero" who will always fly high, remain on top, and never behave "like a woman."

Destructive egotism may sever the connection between conquest and material gain and project terrorist violence as a form of theater in which the heroine plays a starring role. Protests designed for the six o'clock news and scripted for display make it difficult to distinguish between entertainment, self-promotion, or celebrity-building through protest and provide a real-world context for fictional exploits.

Fiction is not alone in focusing on destructive egotism as a style of self-promoting politics. More disturbing than fictional representations are episodes in the real world that are described as theatrical fabrications. Representations of actual protests may further blur the distinctions between street theater and substance, particularly in describing the activities of a group in which women played a major activist role as recruiters and inspirational speakers, as did Kathy Soliah (Sara Jane Olson) for the Symbionese Liberation Army. Jena Howlett and Rod Mengham describe Cheryl Bernstein's claims that the SLA, even in the kidnapping of Patty Hearst, were "in fact, a group of postmodern performance artists," noting "the surrealistic character of the SLA's politics, its carefully timed releases of information and instructions geared to the most skillful manipulation of the mass media, its nice sense of irony in kidnapping the daughter of a media mogul, and the sophisticated ambiguities of its baffling communiqués" (2–3).

Bernstein proposes that the SLA was "a highly self-conscious group of experimentalists who had chosen as their medium prime-time national network TV news. Intentionally or not, the SLA . . . disclosed . . . the moral and political bankruptcy of all the available institutions of representation, which became virtually dominated by its own creation of its own story, its own spectacle, its occupation of 'all the available space' with a performance of revolutionary and avant-garde gratuitousness" (Howlett and Mengham 3–4).

Such an analysis of real world terrorism as performance art underscores how completely literary models and styles of destructive egotism can swallow substantive politics and turn actual violence into a takeover of the media during prime time. The fact that a woman was killed during one of the SLA's bank robberies is rarely mentioned by those committed to extremism in viewing actual events as merely evidence of media unreality. As described in chapter 4, exceptions occur in works by émigrés or descendents of those concerned with actual tyrannical governments in other countries such as Castro's Cuba or the Dominican Republic under Trujillo. In Julia Alvarez's treatment of the latter, radical women who accumulate arms for the struggle consider themselves devotees of the Blessed Virgin, invoking faith in the militant Holy Virgin as fighters for a Christian reign of compassion. In treatments of Cuba, the appeal of Castro to some and repudiation of his rule by others animates cultural portraits of women responding to the limitations on their lives in different ways—an older generation idealizes and sexualizes Castro's revolution as if it were a glorious exposure to male power. Their daughters may seek escape from Castro's brutality or politicize their subversion of male power through murdering their lovers. Joining, or escaping from the revolution, or retreating into personal acts of retribution express a fictional spectrum of engagements with actual tyranny.

The fiction of women terrorists makes meanings, not actual murders. Fictional realism is relieved of the burden of actual bloodshed and free to pursue the darker meanings of human action. The fiction discussed reaches beyond ideology to deal with the existential condition of women and the construction of self-concepts. It adds to the literary procession of iconic figures who have dramatized cultural ideals new figures who represent changes in self-definition. From Henry Adams's Virgin as a traditional ideal of compassion, to a female vision of the militant Virgin, that procession passes on to the *femme fatale*, to the IBMized Virago in *V.*, the Pixel renegade Frenesi in *Vineland* who wants to transcend carbon-based life for a deathless cyberreality, and on to the fun-loving, materialistic and affluent "Floozy with an Uzi" in her Mercedes-Benz, or bomb-planting Vida in her coordinated makeup and dress. All of these figurations of violent resistance exploit expectations of female beauty and vulnerability as weapons against those very stereotypes.

Hurling misogyny against itself figures powerfully in political and entertainment violence. Activist Susan Stern's account of painting herself as "an eight-foot-tall nude woman with flowing green blond hair, and a burning American flag coming out of her cunt," suggests a kind of terrorist's Barbie doll. It reveals the use of misogynistic female images as complex structures that reflect an appropriation of the sex-object as both an ideal and a weapon. Stern claimed, "I had painted what I wanted to be somewhere deep in my mind; tall and blond, nude and armed, consuming—or discharging— a burning America" (see chapter 1). The political activist as a sex-object, like the law student wearing a glitter "HO" sign and others described in chapter 5, combines beauty and misogyny into an explosive rage against the status quo. Literary representations have forged icons out of the dream of a revolution against constricting norms. The fiction of women terrorists incorporates a range of mythic figures who escape ideological traps but focus attention on the condition of women as citizens, mothers, lovers, and wives, and a rebellion in which destructive egotism emerges as a political style. Destructive egotism as a revolutionary style can go even further.

WOMEN AGAINST MISOGYNY AS IDEOLOGY

Revolutions against the status quo in contemporary literature may call into question the meaning and role of political ideology and the devaluation of movements for empowerment that have marked much theoretical academic discourse. Violent women constitute a revolt against patriarchal French theories of the feminine. Alice A. Jardine's and Julia Kristeva's attack on feminism, described in chapter 1, as the product of a despised or outmoded humanism, as a form of advocacy of capitalist dominance, or as a refusal to accept the irremediable abjection of women can be cast in a harsh light when its very premises are rejected. Jardine became a devotee of French theory because it confronts modernity as the collapse or rejection of past "conceptual apparatuses" including feminism which are "based in movements of liberation" she sees as part of a "vicious circle of intellectual imperialism and of liberal and humanist ideology" (*Gynesis* 24). Jardine affirms the *feminine* other as a chaotic space of the unrepresentable, of "nonknowledge . . . coded as *feminine, as woman*" (*Gynesis* 25). In this politics, the argument against the West, rationalism, humanism, and the Anglo-American belief in "the self" is supported by advocacy of female abjection, lack of agency, and insistence on the *feminine* as outside individualism and the speaking subject (*Gynesis* 58). Although the *feminine* is embraced as the opposite of imperialism, it reveals those tyrannical effects and misogyny its supporters claim to reject in the name of modernity.

The literature of violent women overthrows the intellectual constructions that have sought to deny individualism altogether and to devalue individual creativity as inherently suspect. For example, Jardine cites Nietzsche's declaration that God is dead as a milestone in the collapse of foundational master narratives that included the eclipse of all forms of authority. Presumably, even the "author" as the epitome of literary authority quickly followed Him into oblivion, the individual died soon after, and the decentered self and the *feminine* were born along what seems to her to constitute a march toward modernity. Left behind are the American feminists, among others in America, who remain afflicted by the continuing survival of the "notion of the Self" Jardine acknowledges as "intrinsic to Anglo-American thought" (*Gynesis* 58).

Such sweeping dismissal of American intellectual traditions of relativism, subjectivity and individualism is a somewhat authoritarian "master narrative" in its own right. It suggests the wider belief that what followed the collapse of foundational narratives and even reality is a Baudrillardian storm of symbols and "hyper-reality" in which individuals are theoretically replaced by simulated beings manufactured by capitalism to be only consumers. Yet that viewpoint merely advances its own master narrative of a post-Marxist world, dominated by the totalitarian power of late capitalism operating through the media it controls. In doing so, it substitutes paranoias of dominance through linguistic structures for political solutions. It posits the permanent marginalization of women as women as a function of language. It has a preference for itself and its own theoretical forms as the ultimate in art. Like the claim that all past master narratives have been destroyed, it is invented by theoreticians like Baudrillard and Žižek (see chapters 1, 4 and 5) who lay claim to every "male" mechanism of control—access to the Phallus as "speaking subjects" and to colonization of the well of circulating images within the *"feminine"* position. Such reified definitions of gender only promote what some might call a commodity fetishism fabricated out of sexual stereotypes.

Such theoreticians of the feminine follow a long line of radical philosophers of the new who were anything but new in their vision of women. The sorry history of the misogyny of otherwise innovative thinkers is beyond the scope of this project, but the formulations of Rousseau and Nietzsche are both succinct and typical of the problem. The otherwise iconoclastic Jean-Jacques Rousseau who idealized the noble savage excluded from his romantic conceptions of freedom and sentiment the sex he considered most adept at feeling. In *Émile,* his revolutionary vision of the ideal education for young people, he sharply differentiated the ideal education for male and female students. He declared that the nature of women suited them "to please and to be subjected to man" (qtd. in Canovan 86). The education of women should always be for one purpose: "To please, to be useful to us, to make us love and esteem them, to educate us when young, to take care of us when grown up; to advise, to console us, to render our lives easy and agreeable. These are the duties of women at all times, and what they should be taught in their infancy." He felt that "woman is made to give way to man and to put up even with injustice from him. You will never reduce young boys to the same condition, their inner feelings rise in revolt against injustice; nature has not fitted them to put up with it" (qtd. in Canovan 87).

Nietzsche's willingness to announce the death of God, the Great Author, was not accompanied by a comparable willingness to dethrone Eve or Woman as the source of a fallen world of misfortune. Lodging his argument against the oppressions of church and state, Nietzsche praised a "human nature" he idealized as heroically male. Christianity and the social institutions it fostered had subverted the primacy held by nature in the ancient world, largely with the aid of weak men (especially priests) and women whose nature is unalterably opposed to what is good for "natural man." For Nietzsche, men could only regain the freedom they had lost by recognizing woman as an eternal enemy endowed by nature with an unremitting resentment of male authority: "To go wrong on the fundamental problem of 'man and woman,' to deny the most abysmal antagonism between them and the necessity of an eternally hostile tension, to dream perhaps of equal rights, equal education, equal claims and obligations, that is a *typical* sign of shallowness" (qtd. in Kennedy 179). He opposed the emancipation of women because he saw the sex as the enemy of heroic greatness, as the very soul of *ressentiment,* more dangerous, it would seem, than a truckload of priests: "Woman is indescribably more evil than man; also cleverer; good nature is in a woman a form of degeneration . . . The fight for equal rights is actually a symptom of a disease; every physician knows that. Woman, the more she is a woman, resists rights in general hand and foot; after all, in the state of nature, the eternal war between the sexes gives her by far first rank . . . Love—in it means, war; at bottom, the deadly hatred of the sexes. Has my answer been heard to the question of how one *cures* a woman—'redeems' her? One gives her a child" (qtd. in Kennedy 187).

Jacques Derrida, usually a measured and subtle commentator, approaches the problem of reconciling radicalism with retrogressive views of women by restating it in terms of the difficulty of reconciling experience and theoretical abstraction. His ambivalence is evident in "Spurs" when he writes: "Although there is no truth in itself of the sexual difference in itself, of either man or woman in itself, all of ontology, appropriation, identification and verification, has resulted in concealing, even as it presupposes it, this undecidability" (qtd. in Gilbert and Gubar, vol. III, 65). Yet "undecidability" as an attribute of the relationship between reality and theory gives way to ideological certainty when Derrida comments, "feminism is nothing but the operation of a woman who aspires to be like a man. And in order to resemble the masculine dogmatic philosopher this woman lays claim—just as much claim as he—to truth, science, and objectivity in all their castrated delusions of virility. Feminism too seeks to castrate. It wants a castrated woman" (qtd. in Gilbert and Gubar, vol. III, 372).

American feminist critics have asserted the practical and political need to "insist on the validity of female experience as it has been socially shaped and on the urgent need to defend the woman-centered ideology known as feminism from definitions like Derrida's which see it as castrated or castrating" (Gilbert and Gubar, vol. III, 372). Gilbert and Gubar effectively endorse the importance of that fluidity. They raise a crucial question: "how can feminist criticism even begin to discern those systems of representation which have historically collaborated with oppressive social institutions to limit possibilities for women?"(xiii). Their response addresses the political problem by invoking the importance of experience or reality as tools for breaking the rigid, defining categories of the "feminine" and "phallic." This may answer the political question: if women are never addressed as women, how can their specific situation be understood, much less improved? But that is not all that is involved.

What is also at stake for representation is the theoretical problem of the reified definition of the "feminine" and the consequences of agreeing with Lacan that "nothing can be said about woman" or that "woman does not exist." When Jardine questions the applicability of feminism to "modernity," as she defines it, she is pitting a linguistic category that effectively reifies gender by definition, denies biological reality, and defines women as merely "the feminine position" against realistic conceptions of the social construction of sexual roles. The result is often an impasse between theoretical extremism and more balanced views of social experience.

Those who have tried to retain their ideological commitments to Lacanian formulations of the feminine position while acknowledging the limitations of those formulations have fallen into a torturous logic. Gilbert and Gubar note: "At the very least, what Gayatri Spivak has called 'strategic essentialism'—a provisional assumption that there *are* men, women, and meanings in history—may be politically necessary." As Diana Fuss adds: "to insist that essentialism is always and everywhere reactionary is, for the constructionist, to buy into essentialism in the very act of making the charge: *it is to act as if essentialism has an essence*" (Gilbert and Gubar, vol. III, xiii).

Contemporary theoreticians who see woman as a linguistic category or claim the permanent social irrelevance, abjection, and irremediable otherness of women, or who see them as only tools used by a capitalist-dominated media to sell products have failed to deal with the agency of women in American fiction and the recent emergence of violent women on center stage in the media or imaginative literature. For Rousseau or Nietzsche, the closed logic that defines the "nature" of women is used to reinforce and perpetuate the social position of women whose tolerance of the abjection of their position only proves their "nature." For representation theorists the definition of the linguistic category of the feminine creates a similar circular logic, ruling out alternatives by definition. All of the patterns of violence discussed, including the analysis of political violence, make clear that representations of the violence of women are not merely snapshots of the will to power of capitalist-dominated media spewing images designed to enforce loyalty to consumption. Nor are they only evidence of the Lacanian "presymbolic" and impure feminine position, or of a modernity composed of sexual differences so wild as to amount to Jardine's description of disconnected body parts that form neither man nor woman (see chapter 1). The prevalence of extremism in such formulations suggests a triumph of ideology over experience.

Violence by women in American fiction constitutes a revolt against ideological entrapment and the revenge of experience on abstraction. It reflects an effort to restore the fluid interaction between reality, representation, and change at the heart of modernity. The hard encounter with reality and the bursting of felt life through abstraction are often projected in images of violence that position crucial dramas as issues of life or death.

The fiction and poetry discussed in this book constitute a refutation of the dehumanizing force leveled by representation theory against women in particular and humankind in general. The female voice in its sheer mastery of language weaves out of a woman's violent act a narrative that cuts to the heart—the affective core—of public and private life. "Modernity" emerges as more than Jardine's "crisis in master narratives by men," precipitated by the loss of clear sources of traditional authority. Modernity appears as narratives of turbulent change that are developed in a process that appropriates past narratives of perception and self-affirmation and revises them. The dark use to which those past narratives have been put in the violence narratives described in this book should not obscure their importance as a return to American styles of thought in contemporary writing.

AMERICAN CHANGE: NEWNESS AS A TRADITIONAL STYLE

American intellectual history is rich in traditions that have recognized the fluidity of meaning and perception, the oscillation between sexual roles, and conceptions of consciousness other than those of the "binary logic" targeted as "tyrannical" or "imperialistic" in French representation theory. If the Anglo-American vision of the self remains important, it is because it is a vision that accommodates responsiveness, change and individual differences.

As a concept, the self remains important in fiction and poetry because it enables the construction of those dramatic characterizations and crises that animate art. William Faulkner's *The Sound and the Fury* and *Absalom! Absalom!* are obvious examples in which fiction provides experiences of the perspectival nature of truth as the same events are related by different characters. Such works constitute the role of multiple perspectives as structural devices for organizing the wealth of meanings life holds for individuals. Such vitality and fluidity have been conceptualized in American intellectual history through pragmatism as a philosophy of knowledge and action that locates its energies in subjectivity and in the importance of individual perception. Pragmatism stresses the processes of knowing, choosing, and willing, locating in the individual a dynamic and reflexive interaction with social codes.

My construction of modernity as change, relativism, oscillation, and subjectivity includes theories of voluntarism and consciousness derived from William James and others. That concept facilitates an expansion into a cosmopolitanism that encompasses not only the narratives of women but social multiplicity derived from ethnic, racial, class, and gender differences. It incorporates these into a pluralistic vision of both meaning and social interaction. These constitute core origins of the American construction of modernity along lines that stress variable perspectives, place importance on the psychology of knowledge and expression, and emphasize the role of affect. The imaginative play evident in fiction of violent women is heir to these practices.

How we experience, see, or define change and its gains and losses is crucial to any conception of modernity and the past. The narratives of violent women exploit the provisional nature of the truths encoded in past narratives. Additionally, the individual voice serves as an instrument for revising and retelling old tales. Walter Benjamin commented that "each epoch dreams the next, but in doing so it revises the one before it." The violence narratives of women achieve newness partly by revising past perceptions and formulations. Violent women in fiction emerge through narratives that take the stereotypical gentleness or subordination of women as a starting point. Breaking the bonds of definition that imprison them in metaphors of silence and abjection, American portrayals of violence by women return us to the intense, personal motivations for violence and the variety of narratives surrounding it. In French representation theory the perpetrator of violence is always the same—the dominant super-phallic force of capitalism operating through media to control language, a force that has already swept individualism away. In the American fiction of violent women, the perpetrator is always pursuing distinctive ends that are scripted individualistically to reflect particular goals.

Individual experience returns in the literature of violent women and constitutes an assault on the displacement of personal experience. The prospect of the return of the actual, or reality, or "presence" arouses a strong response in those who remain committed to seeing representation as an alternative to individualism, or "presence" rather than something coextensive with narrative reality or even literary realism. Žižek, for example, tries to deal with violence by employing the otherwise eclipsed Freud to account for the resurgence of violence in art while also relegating it back to a Lacanian presymbolic status (within the feminine Real) through an appeal to "repression." In that arena, violence and trauma cannot really be expressed in language and may, in fact, be escapes from all symbolic structures. Žižek writes, somewhat opaquely, "a human subject can acquire and maintain a distance towards symbolically mediated reality only through the process of 'primordial repression.' What we experience as 'reality' constitutes itself through the foreclosure of some traumatic X which remains the impossible-real kernel around which symbolization turns. . . . What sets the dynamism that pertains to the human condition is the very fact that some traumatic X eludes every symbolization. 'Trauma' is that kernal of the Same, which returns again and again, disrupting any symbolic identity" (*Plague of Fantasies* 95).

Žižek's fantasy of Trauma as the disruption of symbols, a condition of being in the presymbolic or perpetual repetition of the "Same," which effectively returns one to the feminine position is disproved by the American postwar literature of the violent woman. Her feeling, speaking "presence," and her communicative violence are registered in a powerful, individual voice determined to express, articulate, and even vary "trauma" and self-image by scripting violence in expansive and subjective ways. Far from providing an escape from "symbolization," trauma provides an escape into language through narrative.

Psychiatrist Judith Lewis Herrman's *Trauma and Recovery* describes how women who have been raped or battered experience healing effects from writing their own stories. This suggests that trauma is not an escape from symbolization, but a catalyst for writing one's own story, for restructuring one's future through narrating one's past from the different perspective of present hope. In fiction, trauma is often expressed not as a recapitulation but as reinvention or reinterpretation of what happened. Like Maso's heroine in *Defiance* whose use of the memoir form reveals an inventive, methodical organization of verbal forms ranging from lyrical poetry to mathematical formulas to describe her seductions, teachings and murders, the violent woman conveys mastery of action and speech. Moreover, inventive reinterpretation, perspectives ranging from the perpetrator to victim to distant narrator of events multiply perspectives on sexuality as the model for dramatic interaction. The revealed complexity of her motives for killing and the rituals surrounding her murders also demonstrate how mastery of the symbolic structures of language, science, and sexuality can defeat repression and silence. Such women provide dark versions of those

American discourses of individualism articulated in William James's theory of will or choice and Ralph Waldo Emerson's faith in individual power. Violent women appropriate the narratives and affirmations of individual will and power for use on the dark side, adapting them for a time shadowed by cynicism and skepticism.

WOMEN AND AMERICAN INTELLECTUAL NARRATIVES: GETTING PERSONAL

American individualism, as found in the writings of Ralph Waldo Emerson and William James, drives the animating, positive energies that have sustained historical American tales of multiplicity, subjectivity, and the power of individual narratives to shape and transform understanding. The literature of violent women revives and extends those traditions into violent action in private as well as public life. Its exploitation of the personal can be seen in the context of an American history of outbreaks of violence that Richard Hofstadter, as previously noted, has shown are unprogammatic and have resisted explanation by unifying, ideological goals or a clear political dialectic, or sustained class hatred. The violence of women, long ruled out as a historical phenomenon, has, I believe, enormous importance in bringing an individualistic American form to that unruliness. It insists on a radical personalization of social and historical events and experiences.

The condensation of sexuality and aggression that inspires representations of violent women in forms ranging from Indian myth, films, and newscasts to fiction and popular culture moves to center stage the overlooked relation of violence by women to the paradigms of American thought that structure individualism through subjective truth, an emphasis on will, and a conception that belief is fulfilled only through action. Violence by women brings master narratives associated with cognition, individualism, and violent action together. Unprogrammatic, it demonstrates a logic of radical personalization. It writes the narrative of politics or culture as confession. It affirms even in its perversity those narratives of individualism and power that speak to the intellectual and spiritual traditions articulated in William James's theory of will and choice and Ralph Waldo Emerson's faith in individual power.

The radical personalization found in literary representations of violent women exploits positive and idealistic American formulations of the centrality of the self, the subjective nature of thought, and the importance of pluralistic perspectives. These are enshrined in *The American Scholar* in Emerson's remarkable ability to call "the world . . . this *other me*" (55). Such convictions were refined and expanded in William James's vision of the centrality of individual choice in defining social reality. As James wrote in *The Dilemma of Determinism,* "the indeterminism I defend, the free-will theory of popular sense . . . [is] devoid either of transparency or of stability. It gives us a pluralistic, restless universe, in which no single point of view can ever take in the whole scene" (114). What determines meaning and order are the choices of the observer who selects what she will acknowledge as meaningful and real from diverse experiences. In *Reflex Action and Theism,* James defined the individual's task as forging coherence through selection from the multiplicity of prospects. He wrote: "by picking out . . . the items which concern us, and connecting them with others," it will be possible "to make out definite threads of sequence and tendency" (*Reflex* 95). To know is to chose and select and give meaning to those selections by acting on them.

Contemporary narratives of violent women disrupt James's song of pluralism by denying the power of "the whole scene" to counteract individual acts of violence and produce, out of many voices, a harmonious chorale. For example, William James was able to choreograph a dance of variables—individual perception, social agreement, and joy in action—to achieve moral poise. James counts on the human tendency to seek approval to maintain social harmony, offering what amounts to an idealized definition of action as social rather than strictly personal. James optimistically believed that gratification depended on winning approval from society for one's actions.

Popular culture once also stressed the role of the community, often dramatized by the extended family, as a corrective to the excesses of malign self-interest. The intrusion of violence often served to prove the accuracy of James's optimism. For example, *Shadow of a Doubt* (1943), a Hitchcock thriller starring Joseph Cotten as a killer who married wealthy widows and murdered them to inherit their fortunes, showed the criminal as all the more reprehensible for his immense charm, which he works on the relatives he visits to evade a manhunt. However, the amiably villainous Cotten is undone by his virtuous niece who adores him until she discovers his identity as the Merry Widow killer and his ruthlessness in exploiting her and her family. She turns him in to the honorable detective who becomes her suitor. The good people of his family, among whom he had hoped to hide, represent a shrewdness, stability, and decency that thwart the evil in their midst. The film depends on clear distinctions between the killer's specious charm and the genuine virtue of his family and the detective.

Destructive egotism has replaced that moral clarity. It has virtually swallowed moral difference and concern for consequences, as well as the possibility that there is a corrective in the family and in law enforcement. Current entertainment violence conveys the destructive egotist as an ideal when no one around is alien to evil and all succumb to a vision of universal fascination with the processes of violence. Like the detective and suspect in *Basic Instinct* who are equally in love with violence and at home in an L.A. world of cocaine clubs and celebrity killers, the cop and the crook are frequently shown as equally compromised. William James's "restless will," endlessly multiplying its perspectives, can find expression in science fiction images of mutable life forms. By condensing rational structures that separate realism and fantasy into slick visual images in which everything feels real, film and television undermine processes of cognition that insist on clear distinctions between pathology and culture. Culture is made to appear as if it were pathological because it is seen only from pathological perspectives; the perceiving eye determines what is real.

Destructive egotism is evident in the voyeuristic appreciation of violence. The suitability of sensational acts by beautiful women for visual media increases concentration on every graphic detail of the women's actions and the processes of crime. An obsession with the stages of choice and change from vulnerability to violence is evident in more subtle ways in the serious literature of violent women that reveals what happens through the eyes of the aggressor. Some examples displace responsibility for violence onto the victim. These can be as simple as Diane Di Prima's one line poem, "Nightmare No. 6," which insists: "Get your cut throat off my knife." They can be as complex as Carole Maso's *Defiance* (see chapter 2) or as ironic and witty as Mary Gaitskill's comedies in which seductive, apparently masochistic women (see chapter 5) lure and outmaneuver men who ultimately become their victims.

Violent women achieve mythic proportions by so reversing expectations that they come to embody destructive egotism on the grand scale. The Native American legend of Sister and Brother (see chapter 1) locates consuming self-interest in the entire human family but grants Sister the power to destroy all human life by cursing humanity with disease. In effect, woman as destructive egotist is used to symbolize fears that the optimistic American individualist, imbued with a desire for retributive justice or social betterment, has changed into a malevolent, potent figure. A variety of literary forms seem perverse satires of William James's articulation of an actual process and sequence by which the individual could be the arbiter of his own truth. In *Reflex Action and Theism,* James would *identify* will with action, believing that the will, thought, and action of an individual were inseparable. For James in *The Feeling of Effort,* individual decisiveness was the mother of reality (187). The choice of what to believe constituted a "psychic and moral fact, a dramatic "knife-edged moment" in which the individual arrived at his truth and tested it in action (196).

Portrayals of violent women often travesty formulations of cognition stressing subjectivity, relativism, and pluralism. For example, in the literature of violent women, the drama of will and uncertainty is played out like a symphony of volition theory complicated by the new cacophony of violence. Joyce Carol Oates's girl gang in *Foxfire* consists of poor teenagers abused by boys, male teachers, and storekeepers who see them as easy marks. The girls find strength only when their leader, Legs, provides the will to see that their victimization can be altered by their own action and justifies their resistance by criminal aggression against men usually enacted through scenarios of seduction. The processes of self-making and story-making both depend on this "knife-edged moment" in which crisis and climax are often marked by literally violent action as well as language. The violent woman, seeing the world as hostile, must act. There is a focus on the moment of choice, passage and change from old to new, or from one experience to another. Most frequently, this involves the experience of change epitomized by the passage from times of innocence and vulnerability toward violence.

Destructive egotism affects self-concepts. Flowing from a woman's will to brutal action is an identity violence I see as a documentation of a radical personalization in which objective realities as well as personal fantasies are made interchangeable. Subjective experience and visions of the social world are described according to will and choice, often linking inner and outer realities in unexpected ways. These are underscored ironically in "the knife-edged moment" in which literal "cutting" is invoked as a means of carving out identity. "Cutting" as a "knife-edged moment" of putting will in action can be a tragicomedy of the literal, of willing the metaphoric into actuality.

Identity violence, destructive egotism, and radical personalization intertwine when the ethos of self-invention and self-improvement enter the beauty culture of botox and collagen shots, tattooing, and plastic surgery. A pain-ridden cosmetic procedure and the pathological self-mutilation of the cutter can be presented as analogous processes directed toward achieving control over outward appearance and inner suffering. In popular spectacles, films, and Mary Gaitskill's sophisticated literary satires, discussed in detail in chapter 5, cutting and identity formation are conflated. In a pop culture universe of fashion and beauty slaves and female victims, the cosmetic and the aberrant both emerge as ways to seize control of image, self-image, and pain in order to restructure one's self. Both cutting and cosmetic "cutting" serve as metaphors for determining how and where pain strikes, for taking control of suffering in a world of hurt.

The voice and perspective of the cutter underscore the radical personalization of female victimization as a general condition. Both can be exploited to expose the ugly, pathological side of the popular obsession with beauty and self-improvement culture by highlighting the subjective psychological truths that drive its appeal. The subjective, psychological goals implicit in descriptions of this behavior are described from the perspective of the cutter who sees them as ways to master and control the scarring effects of the human condition itself. The dysfunctional cutter who creates her own flaws and the woman addicted to cosmetic chipping, injecting, and cutting to recreate her face can be presented as sisters under the skin. Self-destructive behavior and destructive egotism can be satirized as flip sides of the will to control.

Such identity violence has deeper dimensions that combine those alternating mysteries of abjection and power evident in the structures of American thought that use emotionally powerful language to describe change and possibility. Those mysteries of self-inflation and self-castigation are captured in Emerson's "Circles" in his declaration, "I am God in nature; I am a weed by the wall" (286). They are evident in his assertion in "History" that he can appropriate all other selves and experiences and announce "I am one with Confucius," or elsewhere claim the world for himself as the "*other me*." Identity violence also parodies a Jamesean focus on will. Both the appropriative self and the insistent will can be echoed and travestied in the development of entertainment violence by women.

Popular culture has forged ironic, witty statements of women who can subordinate times, places, and environments to their own will. *The Avengers* introduced Emma Peel, played by Diana Rigg, as the beautiful, clever female equivalent of the impossibly cool James Bond. This television series in the late sixties presented a violent woman as a new mock-heroic, ironic comedienne, one whose quick moves were expressed in jujitsu and tai chi and whose dialogue was the smart repartee of an ironic survivor in the war *against* evil. The credits for *The Avengers* were visually sophisticated, as if specifically aiming to compete with the sexy, violent, and imaginative images of the credits in James Bond films. Opening with shadow images of Emma Peel in a sleek bodysuit shooting the top off a champagne bottle and closing with credits featuring her graceful jujitsu attacks, the series exploited Diana Rigg's striking looks, and sixties style, particularly the geometric tailoring popularized by André Courrèges's designs and Mary Quant's A-line chic. Emma Peel's partner, John Steed, played by Patrick Macnee, was her stuffy foil who dressed in standard British bowler and immaculately tailored suits. A nonsexual, gentlemanly version of the supporting role supplied by the procession of beautiful women in the Bond films, his nonchalant rescues set off the unorthodoxy of the Emma Peel role.

The spiraling sophistication that marked the series reached its zenith in an episode that first aired on April 1, 1967 and introduced the concept of the snuff film to the American mass audience. Called "The Destruction of Emma Peel," the show dealt with two men and woman who want Emma Peel as the star-victim in a snuff film they are making. They succeed in gassing and kidnapping Emma and taking her unconscious to Schnerk Studios. There she wanders into a series of surrealistic scenes: she finds invitations to her wedding and to her funeral; she wanders into a graveyard in which all the tombstones say "Emma Peel." On a series of crude stage sets, Emma encounters world conquerors who try to kill her and makes her way thorough dangerous historical moments in which she is slated for death: she defeats Alexander of Macedon, and an American Indian warrior, survives a Wild West gunfight, the Civil War, as well as modern battles. Witty through time, she is literally a performer on the stage of history.

A mock-serious sorcerer's apprentice, Emma performs in a magic act with a villain in a black cloak who is about to saw her in half. She remarks, "I think I'm in danger of becoming a split personality!" In this snuff theater of ironic identity violence, Emma remains stylish, laughing, the eternal woman who overcomes history, the fate of women in snuff porn films, and all else by being completely unimpressed by the power of men or limiting notions of female destiny. The high ironic cool of Emma Peel stresses the need for the violent heroine to master emotion and to prevail through potentially lethal encounters by a mixture of violence and cool intelligence.

Self-mastery as the key to controlling others is evident in the creation of that newest star, the action heroine who provides a sendup of James's philosophic emphasis on will. Traveling the universe in a spaceship, achieving eternal youth through suspended animation, cloning, and sci-fi science, and reconciling differences in gender, species, and origin, the first action heroine literally triumphed over space and time, becoming a new kind of eternal woman. The *Alien* series starring Sigourney Weaver as Lt. Ellen Ripley began with the 1979 release of *Alien* and culminated in 1997 with *Alien Resurrection* (see chapter 5). Hundreds of years separate the events dramatized in the films, permitting Ripley to emerge as a different kind of "eternal woman"—violent, decreasingly emotional, and eventually only partly human. Her transition uses science fiction metaphors of mutation to convey the takeover of old-style female compassion by a destructive egotism that defines and enables her future survival.

Emerson celebrated power as occurring in the "moment of transition" from savage to civilized. Metaphors of transition abound in the film but in reverse visions of transition presented as the passage from human to alien, civilized to savage. And it is that idea of transformation to an unapologetic violence that survives as entertainment. In *Dark Angel,* a television series that aired in fall 2000, a beautiful eighteen-year-old actress, Jessica Alba, stars as a genetically altered mutant with superhuman powers and plenty of attitude.

The violence of women invokes core myths associated with the origins of life and death. To impose violence as a female style requires additions to those myths that open the possibility of breaking the genetic determinism that ensures the survival of the human. In the futurism of science fiction the emphasis on transforming genetic sequences is a metaphor for rapid change. Just as Rip Van Winkle's awakening after a long sleep expressed the early nineteenth century's metaphoric vision of the shock of the new as waking up one morning and finding that everything is as different as if twenty years had passed, so contemporary references to mutations that enable transformations from docility to aggression provide contemporary images for modernity.

Grandiosity achieved and sustained by amoral violence eerily appropriates Emerson's notion that power can itself bespeak an identity violence that resides in the moment of change and is amoral. In "Self-Reliance," Emerson wrote: "Power ceases in the instant of repose; it resides in the moment of transition from a past to a new state, in the shooting of the gulf, in the darting to an aim. This one fact the world hates; that the soul *becomes;* for that forever degrades the past, turns all riches to poverty, all reputation to a shame, confounds the saint with the rogue, shoves Jesus and Judas equally aside. . . . Power is in nature the essential measure of right" (179–80).

By reversing the passage from "savage to civilized" to one from traditionally "civilized" to inhumanly "savage," science fiction images of violent women travesty the spiritual idealism that sweetened Emerson's celebration of the self and nature. Such travesty follows a process of radical personalization that exploits American structures of thought that emphasize subjectivity and multiplicity and enacts an identity violence that serves as a marker of change. The women found in a new literature of violence show moral life and moral agony through their violation.

SHAPES OF UNREST

The violence of women—performance, identity, retaliatory or fueled by destructive egotism—holds a magnifying mirror up to behavioral chaos and dilemmas. In the exaggerations of scale and frequency found in narratives of violent women, impulses at work in the culture can be seen more clearly. All illuminate a two way street between social upheaval and private disorder, the imaginative ground that has made personal relations and family courts arenas for social revolution. Representations of violent women make such upheavals immediate and intelligible by dramatizing them in vivid but recognizable contexts. Portrayals of intimacy, family life, and relations with children illustrate the close connection between public and private spheres. The equation of civil society with forms of public speech mediated by the infotainment and entertainment needs of visual media underscores the effects of deceptive speech, narrative ingenuity, and skill in weaving justifications for violence into a competition between meanings, values, and truths. William James believed in an individualism relieved from destructive egotism by higher goals of citizenship and social betterment supported by a broad consensus of people. Narratives of violent women underscore the breakdown of consensus and raise doubts about the capacity for it.

Destructive egotism—what wins for oneself—replaces ideals of substantive consensus. Our public sphere is providing condensations of entertainment, news, and personal behavior around violence and treachery. By making the index of value what wins instead of what works for social value, media culture may convert moral violation into both instruction and entertainment. The violent women in fiction both exemplify and unmask that process. The force and frequent brilliance of violence narratives illustrate the erosion of moral certainty in virtually every area in which consensus might exist. Television brings that process to a mass audience. The commercial hopes and success surrounding reality television shows are based on the assumption that people will betray each other for money or celebrity and sex, want to be filmed doing so on *Survivor* and *Temptation Island,* and will attract a large audience of other young people who will admire any winning tactics. On *The Bachelor,* the competitive aggression involved in romance provides the interest.

In *The Origins of Totalitarianism,* Hannah Arendt described the growing fascination with underworlds in Paris during the *decadence* at the end of the nineteenth century, and found reason to see the seeds of the future in a culture "constantly on the lookout for the strange, the exotic, the dangerous" (82). Now the dangerous is democratized as mass art, given its own TV show in *Fear Factor,* and violent women are icons of seductive danger. No longer exceptional, no longer just a joke, they are entrenched in the daily news, in media representations of ordinary life, in accounts of the high school or college class, in fantasies of mutants and cyberimages, and in sitcoms and news stories that make the domestic tragicomedy that dysfunctional place where the hostile is the true.

The fiction of violent women performs an important function by doing far more than entertaining. It is an avant garde of truth-telling and unmasking that gives full weight to the destructive egotism in which any concern for others collapses. In its portraits of troubled intimacy and the disillusioned public world, and in its use of ingenious narratives to spin violence, it remains inventive, original, and revelatory. It exposes moral hypocrisy at a time when cynicism is high and the use of conventional moral speech is often tainted by ideology. It acknowledges that we are comfortable approaching and examining moral issues through their violation. Even as the wall comes down between the actual and the stylized, the taboo and the acceptable, serious fiction continues to give full weight to the dangers posed by the destructive egotism this fiction portrays. The haunting power of much of the fiction of violence by women provides a corrective all its own. It shows the dynamics of the passage to violence, the effort to withstand the destabilizing power of negation, and the complexity of living with and through deformations of feeling.

Violence as a communicative device in fiction exposes cultural hypocrisy. It indicts as deformations of ideology portrayals of women as either all-compassionate or all-predatory. Its communications unmask the misogyny that infects even those who use it to resist male contempt. It discloses the odds against defeating violence by embracing it. It underscores the failure of traditional explanations to fit the way things are. It charts the discovery of impasse as inevitable for contemporary women who strive to meet untenable goals. It suggests the increasing rage and aggression endemic in popular culture. The writer's frequent choice of confessional and memoir forms implicates the teller in the tale, the audience in the events. The price of understanding is the willingness to accept that violence by women is an important indicator of unrest. The emergence of violent women as iconic figures of modernity rivets a larger anxiety over change.

Women in the real world remain the mainstays of family life; there is no widespread danger that hordes of women will suddenly turn murderous. But in serious literature, portrayals of violence underscore change, mark a discontinuity with the past, and reveal an identity violence that nourishes destructive egotism and spawns unrest. Images of that instability fill civil society and coarsen our public discourse. The emergence of remorseless, violent women in pop culture serves to deny the actual vulnerability of women, justify male violence, and project a world without sensibility that sanctions aggression. But it is the serious exploration of violence in contemporary literature that, through its major expressions, bears witness to the social and personal costs paid by women for the dream of empowerment.

WORKS CITED

CHAPTER 1: THE HEARTBREAKER EFFECT

Adler, Freda. *Sisters in Crime: The Rise of the New Female Criminal.* New York: Mc-Graw-Hill, 1975.

Apter, David E. "Political Violence in Analytical Perspective." *The Legitimization of Violence.* Ed. David E. Apter. New York: New York University Press, 1997. 1–32.

Basic Instinct. Dir. Paul Verhoeven. Perf. Michael Douglas, Sharon Stone. TriStar Pictures, 1992.

Baudrillard, Jean. *Cool Memories 1980–1985.* Trans. Chris Turner. 1987. London; New York: Verso, 1990.

———. *For a Critique of the Political Economy of the Sign.* Trans. Charles Levin. St. Louis, MO: Telos Press, 1981.

———. *Forget Foucault.* New York: Semiotext(e), 1987.

———. *In the Shadow of Silent Majorities or, the End of the Social and Other Essays.* Trans. Paul Foss, John Johnston, and Paul Patton. New York: Semiotext(e), 1978, 1983.

———. *Simulacra and Simulation.* Trans. Sheila Faria Glaser. Ann Arbor, MI: University of Michigan Press, 1994.

Bonnie and Clyde. Dir. Arthur Penn. Screenplay by Robert Benton and David Newman III. Perf. Warren Beatty, Faye Dunaway. Warner Brothers, 1967.

Brownstein, Henry. H. *The Social Reality of Violence and Violent Crime.* Needham Heights: Allyn and Bacon, 2000.

Derber, Charles. *The Wilding of America: How Greed and Violence Are Eroding Our Nation's Character.* New York: St. Martin's Press, 1996.

Ehrenreich, Barbara. "Feminism Confronts Bobbittry." *Time,* 24 January 1994. 74.

Eisler, Riane "Human Rights and Violence: Integrating the Private and Public Spheres." *The Web of Violence: From Interpersonal to Global.* Eds. J. Turpin and L. R. Kurtz. Urbana: University of Illinois Press, 1997. 161–186.

Elias, Robert. "A Culture of Violent Solutions." *The Web of Violence: From Interpersonal to Global.* Eds. J. Turpin and L. R. Kurtz. Urbana: University of Illinois Press, 1997. 117–148.

Emerson, Ralph Waldo. "Circles." *The Works of Ralph Waldo Emerson: Essays First and Second Series.* Boston: The Jefferson Press and Houghton Mifflin, 1883. 279–301.

Euripides. *Medea.* Trans. E. P. Coleridge. *The Complete Greek Drama,* Vol. I. Eds. Whitney J. Oates and Eugene O'Neill, Jr. New York: Random House: 1938. 723–763.

Ewen, Stuart, and Elizabeth Ewen. *Channels of Desire: Mass Images and the Shaping of American Consciousness.* Minneapolis: University of Minnesota Press, 1992.

Gilligan, Carol. *In a Different Voice: Psychological Theory and Women's Development.* Cambridge: Harvard University Press, 1982.

Gilligan, James. *Violence: Reflections on a National Epidemic.* New York: Vintage Books, 1996.

Gitlin, Todd. *The Sixties: Years of Hope, Days of Rage.* New York: Bantam, 1993.

Girl Fight. Dir. Karyn Kusama. Perf. Michelle Rodriguez.

Goodstein, Laurie, and William Glaberson. "The Well-Marked Roads to Homicidal Rage." *New York Times.* 10 April 2000. A1+.

Hass, Nancy. "When Women Step into the Ring, Myths Take a Pounding." *New York Times.* 1 October 2000. Sec. 9: 1+.

Hawthorne, Nathaniel. "The Golden Fleece." *Tanglewood Tales* (1851). *The Complete Works of Nathaniel Hawthorne,* Vol. IV. Riverside Edition. Ed. George Parsons Lathrop. Boston: Houghton Mifflin & Co., 1883. 379–425.

Hoberman, J. "A Test for the Individual Viewer: "Bonnie and Clyde's" Violent Reception." *Why We Watch: The Attractions of Violent Entertainment.* Ed. Jeffrey H. Goldstein. New York: Oxford University Press, 1998. 116–144.

Hofstadter, Richard. "Reflections on Violence in the United States." *American Violence: A Documentary History.* Eds. Richard Hofstadter and Michael Wallace. New York: Knopf, 1970. 3–43.

Howe, Irving. "What's the Trouble? Social Crisis, Crisis of Civilization, or Both." *The Critical Point: On Literature and Culture.* New York: Delta, 1973. 13–39.

Jardine, Alice. *Gynesis: Configurations of Woman and Modernity.* Ithaca: Cornell University Press, 1985.

Jones, Ann. *Women Who Kill.* 1980. Boston: Beacon Press, 1996.

Kernberg, Otto F. *Severe Personality Disorders: Psychotherapeutic Strategies.* New Haven: Yale University Press, 1984.

Kristeva, Julia. *Powers of Horror: An Essay on Abjection.* Trans. Leon S. Roudiez. New York: Columbia University Press, 1982.

———. "Women's Time." Trans. Alice Jardine and Harry Blake. 1981 [*Signs: Journal of Women in Culture and Society* 7: 13–35]. *Critical Theory Since 1965.* Eds. Hazard Adams and Leroy Searle. Tallahassee: Florida State University Press, 1986. 471–486.

Menand, Louis. "Paris, Texas: How Bonnie and Clyde Stole the Movies." *The New Yorker,* 17 and 24 February 2003. 168–177.

Miller, Arthur. *The Crucible.* New York: Viking Press, 1953.

Mourning Dove. (Hum-Ishu-Ma) *Coyote Stories.* [1984. New York: AMS Press] Quotations from "The Origin of Diseases." *The Norton Anthology of Literature by Women.* Eds. Sandra M. Gilbert and Susan Gubar. New York: W. W. Norton, 1985. 1538–1539.

Moynihan, Daniel Patrick. "Defining Deviancy Down." *The American Scholar.* Winter 1993. 17–30.

Murray, Gilbert. *The Classical Tradition.* London: Oxford University Press, 1927.

On the Ropes. Dir. Nanette Burstein, Brett Morgan. Highway Films, 1999.

Owens, Craig. "The Discourse of Others: Feminism and Postmodernism." *The Anti-Aesthetic: Essays on Postmodern Culture.* Ed. Hal Foster. New York: The New Press, 1998. 57–83.

Pearson, Patricia. *When She Was Bad: Violence, Women, and the Myth of Innocence.* New York: Viking, 1997.

Rowbotham, Sheila. *Women, Resistance and Revolution: A History of Women and Revolution in the Modern World.* New York: Pantheon Press, 1972.

Segal, Naomi. "Who whom? Violence, politics and the aesthetic." *The Violent Muse: Violence and the Artistic Imagination in Europe, 1910–1939.* Eds. Jana Howlett and Rod Mengham. Manchester: Manchester University Press, 1994. 141–150.

Sekules, Kate. *The Boxer's Heart: How I Learned to Love the Ring.* New York: Villard, 2000.

Shadow Boxers. Dir. Katya Bankowsky. No distributor, 1999.

Shakespeare, William. *Macbeth . Shakespeare: The Complete Works.* Ed. G. B. H. Harrison. New York: Harcourt, Brace and World, 1952. 1184–1219.

Simon, Rita James. *Women and Crime.* Lexington: Lexington Books, 1975.

Slotkin, Richard. *Regeneration Through Violence: The Mythology of the American Frontier 1600–1860.* Middletown: Wesleyan University Press, 1973.

———. *Fatal Environment: The Myth of the Frontier in the Age of Industrialization 1800–1890.* New York: Atheneum, 1985.

———. *Gunfighter Nation: The Myth of the Frontier in Twentieth Century America.* New York: Atheneum, 1992.

Smith, Adam. *The Theory of Moral Sentiments.* (1790). Eds. D. D. Raphael and A. L. Macfie, Oxford: Oxford University Press, 1976.

Smith, Philip. "Civil Society and Violence: Narrative Forms and the Regulation of Social Conflict." *The Web of Violence: From Interpersonal to Global.* Eds. J. Turpin and L. R. Kurtz. Urbana: University of Illinois Press, 1997. 91–117.

Stern, Susan. *With the Weathermen: The Personal Journal of a Revolutionary Woman.* New York: Doubleday, 1975.

Turpin, Jennifer, and Lester R. Kurtz, Eds. *The Web of Violence: From Interpersonal to Global.* Urbana: University of Illinois Press, 1997. Introduction and Conclusion.

Uniform Crime Reports. Federal Bureau of Investigation: Crime in the United States, 1996. Washington, DC US Government Printing Office. 1997.

Wolfe, Tom. "Pornoviolence." *Mauve Gloves & Madmen, Clutter & Vine.* New York: Farrar, Straus and Giroux, 1976.178–188.

———. *Radical Chic & Mau Mauing the Flak Catchers.* New York: Farrar, Straus and Giroux, 1970. 47–49.

Žižek, Slavoj. *The Plague of Fantasies.* London: Verso, 1997.

CHAPTER 2:
LOVE ON THE KNIFE EDGE AND LETHAL FAMILIES

Acker, Kathy. *Blood and Guts in High School.* New York: Grove Press, 1978.

Adler, Jerry. "Hanging by a Thread." *Newsweek,* 22 November 1993. Jerry Adler with Ellen Ladowsky in Manassas, VA and Melinda Liu in Washington. 50–51.

Alexander, Shana. *Nutcracker: Money, Madness, Murder; a Family Album.* Garden City, New York: Doubleday, 1985.

Baudrillard, Jean. *Cool Memories 1980–1985.* Trans. Chris Turner. London: 1987; New York: Verso 1990.

Brownmiller, Susan. *Against Our Will: Men, Women and Rape.* New York: Simon & Schuster, 1975.

Coburn, Judith. "Solanas Lost and Found: Valerie shot Andy when he couldn't find her play, rediscovered, "Up Your Ass" opens at last." *Village Voice, VLS* 18 January 2000. 47.

Coleman, Jonathan. *At Mother's Request: A True Story of Money, Murder and Betrayal.* New York: Atheneum, 1985.

Di Prima, Diane. "Nightmare #6," "Prayer to the Mothers," and "Brass Furnace Going Out: Song After an Abortion." *Selected Poems 1956–1976.* Plainfield: North Atlantic, 1977.

Ellis, Bret Easton. *American Psycho.* New York: Simon & Schuster 1985, Reprint. Vintage Books, 1991.

Freud, Sigmund. "The Uncanny." *The Collected Papers of Sigmund Freud.* Vol IV. Trans. Joan Riviere. Ed. Ernest Jones. London: Hogarth Press and The Institute of Psycho-Analysis Press, 1949. 368–408.

Gardner, John. *October Light.* New York: Knopf, 1976.

———. *Nickel Mountain.* New York: Knopf, 1973.

Genêt, Jean. *Our Lady of the Flowers.* New York: Grove, 1963.

Gioseffi, Daniela. "My Venus Fly Trap is Dying." *The Dream Book: An Anthology of Writings by Italian American Women.* Ed. Helen Barolini. Schocken, 1985. Reprinted Syracuse University Press, 2000.

Goldstein, Jeffrey H. *Aggression and Crimes of Violence.* New York: Oxford University Press, 1986.

Greenhouse, Linda. "Family Law: Battleground in Social Revolution." *The New York Times,* 2 September 1988, B6.

Harrison, Kathryn. *The Kiss.* New York: Random House, 1997.

Heimel, Cynthia. "Sure, Women are Angry: But more than female rage, the case taps male anxiety and self-doubt." Cynthia Heimel. *Newsweek,* 24 January 1994. 56–57.

Homes, A. M. *The End of Alice.* New York: Scribner, 1996.

"Irreconcilable Differences Revealed: Women's Groups Hail a Verdict that Makes Some Grown Men Wail." Maria Odum, *Washington Post,* 22 January 1994, A1, A9.

Kaplan, David A. "Bobbitt Fever: Why America Can't Seem to Get Enough." *Newsweek,* 24 January 1994. 52–55.

Limbaugh, Rush. "No Tears for Lorena: Shame on Feminists for backing her, and damn us all for watching." *Newsweek,* 24 January 1994, 56.

Mailer, Norman. *An American Dream.* New York: Dell, 1965.

Maso, Carole. *Defiance.* New York: Dutton, 1998.

Oates, Joyce Carol. *Marya: A Life.* New York: Dutton, 1986.

Pynchon, Thomas. *Gravity's Rainbow.* New York: Viking Press, 1973.

Selby, Hubert, Jr. *Last Exit to Brooklyn.* New York: Grove Press, 1964.

Sex: The Annabel Chong Story. Dir. Gough Lewis. Perf. Annabel Chong. Coffee House Films, 1999.

Shakespeare, William. *Macbeth. Shakespeare: The Complete Works.* Ed. G. B. H. Harrison. New York: Harcourt Brace and World, 1952. 1184–1219.

Smolowe, Jill. "The Swift Sword of Justice: The tawdry case of the Bobbitts of Manassas heads for round 2." With reporting by Jay Peterzell. *Time,* 22 November 1992.

Solanas, Valerie. *SCUM Manifesto.* (1971) San Francisco: AK Press, 1996.

Stone, Robert. *A Flag for Sunrise.* New York: Knopf, 1981. Reprinted New York: Ballantine, 1981.

Thornhill, Randy, and Craig T. Palmer. *A Natural History of Rape: Biological Bases of Sexual Coercion.* Cambridge: MIT Press, 1999.

Trilling, Diana. *Mrs. Harris: The Death of the Scarsdale Diet Doctor.* New York: Harcourt Brace Jovanovich, 1981.

———. *The Beginning of the Journey: The Marriage of Diana and Lionel Trilling.* New York: Harcourt Brace & Co., 1993.

Yeats, William Butler. "Crazy Jane Grown Old Looks at the Dancers" and "Who Goes with Fergus?" *Collected Poems of W. B. Yeats.* London: Macmillan & Co., 1958. 295, 48.

CHAPTER 3: MOTHER LOVE ON THE ROCKS

Belkin, Lisa. "The Backlash Against Children" Cover. "Your Kids Are Their Problem." *The New York Times Magazine,* 23 July 2000, sec. 6. 30–35, 42, 56, 60, 62, 63.

Emerson, Ralph Waldo. "The American Scholar." *Ralph Waldo Emerson: Selected Prose and Poetry.* Intro. Reginald L. Cook. New York: Holt, Rinehart and Winston, 1962. 47–69.

Euripides. *Medea.* Trans. E. P. Coleridge. *The Complete Greek Drama.* Volume I. Eds. Whitney J. Oates and Eugene O'Neill, Jr. New York: Random House.1938. 723–763.

Fitch, Janet. *White Oleander.* Boston: Little, Brown & Co., 1999.

Freeman, Mary E. Wilkins. "Old Woman Magoun." *The Norton Anthology of Literature by Women.* Eds. Sandra M. Gilbert and Susan Gubar. New York: W.W. Norton & Co., 1985. 1104–1119.

Freud, Sigmund. "An Analysis of Anxiety." Trans. Henry Alden Bunker. *The Problem of Anxiety,* New York: The Psychoanalytic Quarterly Press and W.W. Norton & Co., 1936. 69–85.

Hanley, Robert. "In a Plea Deal, Youth to Testify in Baby's Death" *New York Times.* 10 March 1998 A1, B5.

Jones, Ann. *Women Who Kill.* New York: Holt Rinehart Winston, 1980. Reprinted Boston: Beacon Press, 1996. Quotations from 1996 edition.

Kerouac, Jack. *On the Road.* New York: Viking Press, 1957.

Meyer, Cheryl L., and Michelle Oberman, with Kelly White, Michelle Rone, Priya Batra, and Tara C. Proanao. *Mothers Who Kill their Children.* New York: New York University Press, 2001.

Morrison, Toni. *Beloved.* New York: Knopf, 1987.

Pearson, Patricia. *When She Was Bad: Violence, Women, and the Myth of Innocence.* New York: Viking, 1997.

Plath, Sylvia. "Edge" *Ariel: Poems by Sylvia Plath.* Ed. Robert Lowell. (1965) New York: Harper Perennial Classics, 1999. 93.

Price, Richard. *Freedomland.* New York: Broadway Books, 1998.

Puryear, Lucy J. "Bridging Two Worlds: Consulting in the Yates Trial." *The American Psychoanalysis Quarterly Newsletter of the American Psychoanalytic Association.* 36:3. 2002, 1,4,8.

Rendall, Jane. "Virtue and Commerce: Women in the Making of Adam Smith's Political Economy." *Women in Western Political Philosophy: Kant to Nietzsche.* Eds. Ellen Kennedy and Susan Mendus. New York: St. Martin's Press, 1987. 44–77.

Sexton, Anne. "Mother and Daughter." *The Book of Folly.* Boston: Houghton Mifflin, 1972. 11–12.

Sexton, Linda Gray. *Searching for Mercy Street: My Journey Back to My Mother, Anne Sexton.* Boston: Little, Brown & Co., 144–145.

Smith, Adam. *The Theory of Moral Sentiments.* Eds. D. D. Raphael and A. L. Macfie. Oxford: Oxford University Press, 1976.

Thernstrom, Melanie. "Child's Play." *New York Magazine,* 31:26. 13 July 1998, 18–23,54.

Updike, John. *Rabbit, Run.* 1980. Reprint. New York: Fawcett Crest, 1983.

———. *Rabbit Redux.* New York: Knopf, 1971.

CHAPTER FOUR: THE LADY IS A TERRORIST

Apter, David E. "Political Violence in Analytical Perspective." *The Legitimization of Violence.* Ed. David Apter. New York: New York University Press, 1997. 1–33.

Alvarez, Julia. *In the Time of the Butterflies.* Chapel Hill, NC: Algonquin Books of Chapel Hill, 1994. Reprinted New York: Plume, 1994. Quotations are from Plume edition.

Arendt, Hannah. *On Violence.* New York: Harcourt, Brace and World, 1970.

Barthes, Roland. "Lecture in Inauguration of the Chair of Literary Semiology, College de France." *October* 89 (Spring 1979): 39, 15.

Baudrillard, Jean. "Consumer Society." Trans. Paul Foss. *Jean Baudrillard: Selected Writings.* Ed. Mark Poster. Stanford: Stanford University Press. 1988. 29–57.

———. *Cool Memories 1980–1985.* Trans. Chris Turner. London and New York: Verso 1990.

———. *Cool Memories II 1987–1990.* Trans. Chris Turner. Durham: Duke University Press, 1996.

———. *For a Critique of the Political Economy of the Sign.* Trans. Charles Levin. St. Louis, MO: Telos Press, 1981.

———. *Forget Foucault.* New York: Semiotext(e), 1987.

———. *In the Shadow of Silent Majorities or, the End of the Social and Other Essays.* Trans. Paul Foss, John Johnston, and Paul Patton. New York: Semiotext(e), 1978, 1983.

———. *Simulacra and Simulation.* Trans. Sheila Faria Glaser. Ann Arbor: University of Michigan Press, 1994.

Billington, James. *Fire in the Minds of Men: Origins of the Revolutionary Faith.* New York: Basic Books, 1980.

Clarke, James W. *American Assassins: The Darker Side of Politics.* Princeton: Princeton University Press, 1982.

Doctorow, E. L. *The Book of Daniel.* Toronto: Bantam Books, 1981.

Emerson, Ralph Waldo. "Self-Reliance." *Ralph Waldo Emerson: Selected Prose and Poetry.* Intro. Reginald L. Cook. New York: Holt, Rinehart and Winston, 1962. 169–193.

———. "Power." *The Conduct of Life. The Complete Works of Ralph Waldo Emerson,* Vol. vi(1860). Boston: Houghton Mifflin, 1922.

Fanon, Frantz. *The Wretched of the Earth.* (1961) New York: Grove Press, 1968.

Fuller, Margaret. *Woman in the Nineteenth Century and Kindred papers relating to the sphere, condition and interests of women.* (1874) Ed. Arthur B. Fuller. New York: Greenwood Press, 1968.

Garcia, Cristina. *Dreaming in Cuban.* New York: Ballantine Books, 1993.

Hofstadter, Richard. "Reflections on Violence in the United States." *American Violence: A Documentary History.* Eds. Richard Hofstadter and Michael Wallace. New York: Knopf, 1970.

Lasswell, Harold. *Power and Personality.* (1948). New York: The Viking Press, 1962. 39–58.

Oates, Joyce Carol. *Angel of Light.* New York: Dutton, 1981.

———. *Foxfire: Confessions of a Girl Gang.* New York: Dutton, 1993.

Piercy. Marge. *Vida*. New York: Summit Books, 1979.

Pynchon, Thomas. *Vineland*. New York: Penguin Books, 1991.

———. *V.* New York: Perennial Library, 1986.

Rowbotham, Sheila. *Women, Resistance and Revolution: A History of Women and Revolution in the Modern World*. New York: Pantheon Press, 1972.

Roth, Philip. *American Pastoral*. Boston: Houghton Mifflin, 1997.

Silko, Leslie Marmon. *The Almanac of the Dead*. New York: Simon & Schuster, 1991. New York: Penguin, 1991. Citations from Penguin edition.

Sorel, Georges. *Reflections on Violence*. Trans. T. E. Hulme. New York: Peter Smith, 1941.

CHAPTER 5:
VIOLENCE LITE: ENTERTAINING AGGRESSION

Ai. "Salome." *The Before Columbus Foundation Poetry Anthology: Selections from the American Book Awards 1980–1990*. Eds. J. J. Phillips, Ishmael Reed, Gundars Strads, and Shawn Wong. New York: W. W. Norton & Co., 1992.

Alien. Dir. Ridley Scott. Perf. Sigourney Weaver. Twentieth Century–Fox, 1979.

Alien 3. Dir. David Fincher. Perf. Sigourney Weaver. Twentieth Century–Fox, 1992.

Alien Resurrection. Dir. Jean-Pierre Jeunet. Perf. Sigourney Weaver. Twentieth Century–Fox, 1997.

Aliens. Dir. James Cameron. Perf. Sigourney Weaver. Twentieth Century–Fox, 1986.

Atwood, Margaret. "Rape Fantasies." *The Norton Anthology of Literature by Women*. Eds. Sandra M. Gilbert and Susan Gubar. New York: W. W. Norton & Company, 1985. 2299–2307.

Auster, Paul. *Leviathan*. New York: Viking, 1992.

Basic Instinct. Dir. Paul Verhoeven. Perf. Michael Douglas, Sharon Stone. TriStar Pictures, 1992.

Beach, Daytona. "The Kid." *Love is Strange*. Eds. Joel Rose and Catherine Texier. New York: W.W. Norton 1993. 211–224.

Blaushild, Lisa. "Love Letter to My Rapist." *Love is Strange*. Eds. Joel Rose and Catherine Texier. New York: W. W. Norton 1993. 169–177.

Brownworth, Victoria, and Judith Redding. "Introduction," *Night Bites: Tales of Blood and Lust*, Ed. Victoria A. Brownworth. Seattle, WA: Seal Press, 1996. vii–xv.

Cather, Willa. *Song of the Lark*. Boston and New York: Houghton Mifflin Co., 1915.

Cecil B. Demented. Dir. John Waters. Perf. Melanie Griffith, Patricia Hearst. Artisan Entertainment, 2000.

Cortez, Jayne. "Rape." qtd. by Barbara Christian in the introduction to Jayne Cortez, *The Before Columbus Foundation Poetry Anthology: Selections from the*

American Book Awards 1980–1990. Eds. J. J. Phillips, Ishmael Reed, Gundars Strads, and Shawn Wong. New York: W. W. Norton & Co., 1992. 56–59.

Crane, Hart. *The Bridge. The Collected Poems of Hart Crane.* Ed. Waldo Frank, New York: Liveright.1933. "The River." 13–19.

Dr. No. Dir. Terence Young. Perf. Sean Connery, Ursula Andress. United Artists, 1962.

Entrapment. Dir. Jon Amiel. Perf. Catherine Zeta-Jones. Twentieth Century–Fox, 1999.

Foster, Hal. *The Return of the Real.* Cambridge: MIT Press, 1996.

Gaitskill, Mary. "Trying to Be." "Something Nice." "A Romantic Weekend." *Bad Behavior.* New York: Poseidon Press, 1988. 105–131, 53–73, 31–52.

———. "The Dentist." "The Blanket." "Processing." *Because They Wanted To.* New York: Scribner, 1998. 137–190, 89–102, 209–226.

Janowitz, Tama. *Slaves of New York.* New York: Washington Square Press, 1986.

———. *A Cannibal in Manhattan.* New York: Crown, 1987.

Marinetti, F. T. *Futurist Manifesto.* Ed. Umbro Apollonio. London: Thames and Hudson, 1973.

The Matrix. Dir. Andy and Larry Wachowski. Perf. Carrie-Anne Moss, Keanu Reeves. Warner Bros., 1999.

Miller, Mark. "Two Birds of a Feather: John Waters and Patricia Hearst conspire in the kidnapping caper 'Cecil B. Demented.'" Interview with Waters and Hearst in *Newsweek,* 14 August 2000. 62.

Politically Incorrect with Bill Maher. ABC, 7 August 2000. Guest John Waters.

Rice, Anne. *Interview with the Vampire.* New York: Knopf, 1976.

Robson, Ruthann. "Women's Music." *Night Bites: Tales of Blood and Lust.* Ed. Victoria Brownworth. Seattle, WA: Seal Press, 1996. 179–195.

Sarris, Andrew. "SPANKORAMA." *New York Observer.* 7 October 2002, 23.

Sea of Love. Dir. Harold Becker. Perf. Al Pacino, Ellen Barkin. Universal Pictures, 1989.

Seven Beauties. Dir. Lina Wertmuller. Cinema 5 Distributing, 1976.

Sex: The Annabel Chong Story. Dir. Gough Lewis. Perf. Annabel Chong. [Grace Quek]. Coffee House Films, 1999. See also *New York Magazine.* 14 February 2000. 145

Smith, R. J. "Among the Mooks: As entertainment entrepreneurs align the fantasy lands of rap, rock wrestling and pornography, a generation of fans grows ever more brutish." *New York Times Magazine.* 6 August 2000. Section 6, 36–41.

The Sopranos. TV Series. HBO, 2000. Producer and Writer, David Chase.

Strauss, Neil. "New Spirit of Woodstock: Music, TV, More TV and Trashing." *New York Times,* 26 July 1999. B8.

———. "On the Night Music Died, Many to Blame for Mayhem." *New York Times,* 27 July 1999. B8.

Urbanska, Wanda. "Debutante in a Seamy Subculture." Rev. of *Bad Behavior. Los Angeles Times,* 28 November 1989. E5.

Walsh, Susan. "Notes on Trick: Mary Gaitskill Talks with Susan Walsh about Money, Fisting, and Nabokov." Interview. *Village Voice,* 5 September 1995: *VLS*15+

Zielbauer, Paul. "Fans Rampage in Last Hours of Music Show: Upstate Festival Ends with Fires and Chaos." *New York Times,* 26 July 1999, B1, B8

———. "Woodstock Festival Faces a Bad Hangover: What Began With Peace, Love and Music Ends in Fire, Rampage and Loot." *New York Times,* 27 July 1999. B1,B5.

Žižek, Slavoj. "Otto Weininger, or 'Woman doesn't Exist.'" *The Žižek Reader.* Eds. Elizabeth Wright and Edmund Wright. Oxford: Blackwell Publishers, 1999. 127–148.

———. "There is No Sexual Relationship." *The Žižek Reader.* Eds. Elizabeth Wright and Edmund Wright. Oxford: Blackwell Publishers, 1999. 174–206.

———. *The Plague of Fantasies.* London: Verso, 1997.

CHAPTER 6: HEARTBREAKING PATTERNS

Adams, Henry. *The Education of Henry Adams: An Autobiography.* Boston: Houghton Mifflin, 1927.

Arendt, Hannah. *The Origins of Totalitarianism.* New York: Harcourt, Brace and World, 1966.

The Avengers. Television Series. "The Destruction of Emma Peel." First aired April 1, 1967. 67: vol. 6, cat#AAE 171432.

Billington, James H. *Fire in the Minds of Men: Origins of the Revolutionary Faith.* New York: Basic Books, 1980.

"Black Scorpion." Television Performance. "TV Notes." *New York Magazine,* 8 January 2001. 57.

Brownstein, Henry. H. *The Social Reality of Violence and Violent Crime.* Needham Heights: Allyn and Bacon, 2000.

Canovan, Margaret. "Rousseau's Two Concepts of Citizenship." *Women in Western Political Philosophy: Kant to Nietzsche.* Eds. Ellen Kennedy and Susan Mendus, New York: St. Martin's Press, 1987. 78–106.

Cook, T. D., D. A. Kendzierski, and S. V. Thomas. "The implicit assumptions of television research: An analysis of the 1982 NIMH report on television and behavior." *Public Opinion Quarterly,* 1983. 47: 161–201.

Di Prima, Diane. "Nightmare #6." *Selected Poems 1956–1976.* Plainfield: North Atlantic Press, 1977.

Emerson, Ralph Waldo. "History." *The Works of Ralph Waldo Emerson: Essays First and Second Series.* Boston: The Jefferson Press and Houghton Mifflin, 1883. 1–43.

———. "Circles." *The Works of Ralph Waldo Emerson: Essays First and Second Series.* Boston: The Jefferson Press and Houghton Mifflin, 1883. 279–301.

————. "The American Scholar." *Ralph Waldo Emerson: Selected Prose and Poetry.* Intro. Reginald L. Cook. New York: Holt, Rinehart and Winston, 1962. 47–69.

————. "Self-Reliance." *Ralph Waldo Emerson: Selected Prose and Poetry.* Intro. Reginald L. Cook. New York: Holt, Rinehart and Winston, 1962. 169–193.

Freud, Sigmund. "Mourning and Melancholia." Trans. Joan Riviere. *Sigmund Freud: The Collected Papers,* Vol. IV. Ed. Ernest Jones. London: Hogarth Press, 1949. 152–173.

Foster, Hal. *The Return of the Real.* Cambridge: The MIT Press, 1996.

Fuss, Diana. *Essentially Speaking: Feminism, Nature and Difference.* New York: Routledge, 1989.

Gilbert, Sandra M. and Gubar, Susan. *No Man's Land: The Place of the Woman Writer in the Twentieth Century.* 3 vols. New Haven: Yale University Press, 1988–1994.

Hanley, Robert. "New Jersey Charges Woman, 18, With Killing Baby Born at Prom." *New York Times,* 25 June 1997, A1, B4.

Harris, Frank. *The Bomb.* (1920) Intro. John Dos Passos. Chicago: University of Chicago Press, 1963.

Hofstadter, Richard. "Reflections on Violence in the United States." *American Violence: A Documentary History.* Eds. Richard Hofstadter and Michael Wallace. New York: Knopf, 1970. 3–43.

Howlett, Jana and Rod Mengham. "Introduction," *The Violent Muse: Violence and the Artistic Imagination in Europe, 1910–1939.* Manchester: Manchester University Press, 1994.1–5. Summary of Bernstein, Cheryl. "Performance as News" in *Performance in Postmodern Culture.* Milwaukee: Center for Twentieth Century Studies, University of Wisconsin at Milwaukee Press, 1977.

James, Henry. *The Princess Casamassima.* (1886). Introduced by Lionel Trilling. New York: MacMillan, 1948.

James, William. "The Dilemma of Determinism." *The Will to Believe and Other Essays in Popular Philosophy* (1897). *The Works of William James.* Ed. Frederick H. Burckhardt et al. Cambridge: Harvard University Press, 1979. 114–140.

————."The Feeling of Effort." *Collected Essays and Reviews.* Ed. Ralph Barton Perry. New York: Longmans, Green & Co., 1920. 151–219.

————."The Moral Equivalent of War" *The Works of William James: Essays in Religion and Morality.* Ed. Frederick H. Burckhardt et al. Cambridge: Harvard University Press, 1982. 162–175.

————. "Reflex Action and Theism." *The Will to Believe and Other Essays in Popular Philosophy* (1897). *The Works of William James.* Ed. Frederick H. Burckhardt et al. Cambridge: Harvard University Press, 1979. 90–95.

Jardine, Alice. *Gynesis: Configurations of Woman and Modernity.* Ithaca: Cornell University Press, 1985.

Kennedy, Ellen. "Nietzsche: Women as Üntermench." *Women in Western Political Philosophy: Kant to Nietzsche.* Eds. Ellen Kennedy and Susan Mendus. New York: St. Martin's Press, 1987. 179–202.

Koehl, Carla. "Tragedy at the Prom: Why did a teenager hide her pregnancy and then deliver and dump the baby between dances?" *Newsweek,* 23 June 1997, 64.

Luckenbill, D.F. "Domestic Violence as a Situated Transaction." [*Social Problems.* 1977:25. 176–186] cited in *Violence in America: A Public Health Approach.* Ed. Mark A. Rosenberg and Mary Ann Fenley. New York: Oxford University Press, 1991. 25, 48.

Natural Born Killers. Dir. Oliver Stone. Perf. Juliette Lewis, Woody Harrelson, 1994. Pynchon, Thomas. *Vineland.* Boston: Little, Brown & Co., 1990.

———. *V.* Philadelphia: J. D. Lippincott Co., 1961. New York: Harper Perennial, 1990.

Rosenberg, Mark A., and James A. Mercy. "Assaultive Violence." *Violence in America: A Public Health Approach.* Eds. Mark A. Rosenberg and Mary Ann Fenley. New York: Oxford University Press, 1991. 14–50.

Rossner, Judith. *Perfidia.* New York: Doubleday. 1997.

Shadow of a Doubt. Dir. Alfred Hitchcock, Perf. Joseph Cotten. 1943.

Staiger, Janet. *Blockbuster TV: Must-See Sitcoms in the Network Era.* New York: New York University Press, 2000.

Žižek, Slavoj. *The Plague of Fantasies.* London: Verso, 1997.

INDEX